EASTERN COLLEGE
LIBRARY
ST. DAVIDS, PA. 19087

SHAKESPEARE
AND THE
ROMANCE TRADITION

EASTERN COLLEGE
LIBRARY
ST. DAVIDS, PA. 19087

SHAKESPEARE
AND THE
ROMANCE TRADITION

By E. C. PETTET, M.A., B.Litt.
Lecturer in English, Goldsmiths' College, University of London

With an Introduction by
H. S. BENNETT

STAPLES PRESS
STAPLES PRESS LIMITED   STAPLES PRESS INCORPORATED
Mandeville Place, London   70 East 45th Street, New York

FIRST EDITION 1949

SET IN 'MONOTYPE' BASKERVILLE SERIES

Made and printed in England by
STAPLES PRESS LIMITED
at their St. Albans, Herts, establishment

To
Reginald Lye
Liveliest of Teachers

4332

'ROMANCE. A species of tale, originally in metre, in the Romanic dialects, afterwards diffused in verse or prose, such as the tales of the court of Arthur, and of Amadis of Gaule; hence, any fictitious or wonderful tale; now, especially, a sort of novel, whose interest lies not so much in the depiction or analysis of real life or character as in adventure, surprising incident, or the like.'

Webster's New International Dictionary.

'Romance ... reverence for women ... the idealising imagination exercised about sex.'   C. S. LEWIS, *The Allegory of Love.*

'The poetry and romance of the Renaissance follow naturally upon the literature of the Middle Ages.... There is no such line of division between Ariosto and Chrestien of Troyes as there is between Chrestien and the primitive epic.'   W. P. KER, *Epic and Romance.*

'That tradition [of medieval love-poetry] continued to be the inspiration of all the love-poetry composed in sonnet or song or pastoral or romance or romantic comedy.'   H. J. C. GRIERSON,
Cross Currents in English Literature of the XVIIth Century.

'Truly, I have known men, that even with reading *Amadis de Gaule* (which God knoweth wanteth much of a perfect Poesy) have found their hearts moved to the exercise of courtesy, liberality, and especially courage.'   SIR PHILIP SIDNEY, *Apologie for Poetrie.*

'Now is he for the numbers that Petrarch flowed in.'
SHAKESPEARE, *Romeo and Juliet*, II. iv. 39-40.

'In its first intention, Elizabethan romantic comedy was an attempt to adapt the world of romance and all its implications to the service of comedy.'   H. B. CHARLTON, *Shakespearian Comedy.*

'What we have lost is a world of fine fabling.'
HURD, *Letters on Chivalry and Romance* (1762).

'It is difficult for a younger generation to realize how closely woven with thought and imagination was the romantic ideal of love. Novels, and painting and poetry, all fed the imagination on romance.'
M. C. D'ARCY, *The Mind and Heart of Love.*

CONTENTS

	Introduction	PAGE 9
CHAPTER ONE	*The Romance Tradition*	11
TWO	*The Comedies of Lyly*	36
THREE	*The Comedies of Greene*	54
FOUR	*Shakespeare's 'Romantic' Comedies*	67
FIVE	*Shakespeare's Detachment from Romance*	101
SIX	*The 'Dark' Comedies*	136
SEVEN	*The 'Romances'*	161
	Additional Notes to Chapter Two	200
	Bibliography for Main References	204
	Index	205

INTRODUCTION

It is strange indeed that among the many thousands of volumes devoted to Shakespearean criticism so few works on his comedies seem worth remembering. A sentence of Johnson ('His tragedy seems to be skill, his comedy to be instinct'), or some words of Hazlitt ('The spectators rather receive pleasure from humoring the inclinations of the persons they laugh at than wish to give them pain by exposing their absurdity') come to the mind, but not the extended treatises we should expect. In our own day, Professor H. B. Charlton has made a gallant attempt to provide us with what we need, but while we rejoice in much that he tells us, much is still to do. Investigations of parts of Shakespearean comedy, such as Professor W. W. Lawrence's *Shakespeare's Problem Plays* (or the 'Dark' Comedies, as Mr. Pettet prefers to call them), throw light on part of the field, and innumerable studies of characterisation, of imagery, or of stage technique enable us to see certain aspects of the comedies more clearly. A satisfying guide through the whole body of the plays, however, is still to seek. Mr. Pettet would be the last to claim that his is such a guide, but the book he has given us will constantly be in the hands of anyone in future who essays the task, for he will find Mr. Pettet's study to be a clear and convincing discussion of one of the most important factors of Shakespearean comedy – romance and romantic love.

When Shakespeare came to London in the eighties of the sixteenth century he found a flourishing theatrical world about him, practising many forms of drama, among which was romantic comedy. What could have been more acceptable to a youthful dramatist – but what in time could have become more unsatisfying as a dramatic form? A careful scrutiny of Shakespeare's plays shows how this feeling of dissatisfaction crept in, and how it modified his drama as it moved inevitably from the confident ebullience of *The Two Gentlemen of Verona* to the uneasy comedy world of *Much Ado about Nothing* and *The Merchant of Venice*. Once Shakespeare had arrived at the anti-romantic stage so perfectly expressed by Rosalind:

> The poor world is almost six thousand years old, and in all this time there was not any man died in his own person, *videlicet*, in a love-cause. Troilus had his brains dashed out with a Grecian club; yet

Introduction

he did what he could to die before, and he is one of the patterns of love. Leander, he would have lived many a fair year, though Hero had turned nun, if it had not been for a hot midsummer night: for, good youth, he went but forth to wash him in the Hellespont and being taken with the cramp was drowned; and the foolish chroniclers of that age found it was 'Hero of Sestos'. But these are all lies: men have died from time to time, and worms have eaten them, but not for love.

– once at this point, Shakespeare wore his romance 'with a difference'. There followed the period of the 'Dark' Comedies from which the only escape was by way of *Hamlet*, *Othello* and the rest of the tragedies.

This, fortunately, was not the end. In his latest plays Shakespeare returned to his old love – the romantic drama, yet

> not as in the hour
> Of thoughtless youth, but hearing oftentimes
> The still, sad music of humanity
> Nor harsh, nor grating, though of ample power
> To chasten and subdue.

Mr. Pettet traces this side of Shakespeare's art with sensitive skill as he follows play by play the treatment of the romance convention. As we go with him he not only helps us to realise this, but also to see how far-reaching was Shakespeare's conception of comedy. Where Lyly or Jonson were content to dwell on a single theme, Shakespeare ranges over many, and among the most important of them all was the romance tradition so admirably surveyed in the pages which follow.

H. S. BENNETT.

CHAPTER ONE

THE ROMANCE TRADITION

ELIZABETHAN DRAMA, youthful-lusty, lawless and original as it was, a reflex of the turbulent, creative age in which it was written, nevertheless owed much to two ancient dramatic traditions – to the classical plays of Seneca, Plautus, and Terence, and to the native tradition, still far from dead, of Miracle Play, Morality and Interlude. Yet neither of these traditions left such a deep impress on it as that of romance,[1] for while only a small and later part of romantic[2] literature was dramatic in form, this literature had been dominant in England and Europe for many centuries past. No Elizabethan writer could help absorbing it into his consciousness; and even if, in more mature years, he confined his reading to the classics and theology, as a child he would certainly have heard many times some such popular romance tale as *Sir Bevis* and *Guy of Warwick*, or, unsuspecting, have imbibed the raw, though potent spirit of romance in such poems as *Earl Mar's Daughter*:

> When day was gone, and night was come,
>   About the evening-tide,
> This lady spied a gallant youth
>   Stand straight up by her side. . . .
>
> 'What country come ye frae?' she said,
>   'An' what's your pedigree?' –
> 'O it was but this verra day
>   That I cam' ower the sea.
>
> 'My mither lives in foreign isles,
>   A queen o' high degree;
> And by her spells I am a doo
>   With you to live an' dee.'[3]

The writer might, of course, like Marlowe or Donne or Jonson, react violently against the romance tradition; might even purge

---

[1] Another distinct literary influence on Elizabethan drama was Italian renaissance drama. But much of this was an imitation of Latin models or an adaptation of romantic material. See p. 35.

[2] In this book I have tried to keep the word 'romantic' purely as an adjective to 'romance'.

[3] *Oxford Book of Ballads*, p. 111.

himself of it. But the direction and nature of his recoil would still be determined in some measure by what he was reacting from.

Not only was the influence of romance deep; it was wide and intricate too, for romance literature was a diverse and complex stream of verse and prose, the product of five changing centuries and of half a dozen European countries of varying culture and civilisation. We can trace at least four courses along which it flowed into Elizabethan drama and poetry. First in time, there was the medieval romance, either of the native variety like *The Tale of Gamelyn, Sir Bevis, Guy of Warwick*, and the *Morte d'Arthur*, or of the foreign type like the popular Spanish *Palmerin* and *Amadis de Gaule*. Distinct from these, there were the Italian romantic epics of Boiardo, Ariosto and Tasso, which C. S. Lewis has described as 'the noble viaduct on which the love of chivalry and "fine fabling" travelled straight across from the Middle Ages to the nineteenth century'.[1] There was also Petrarchian poetry, which came to England partly through such English poets as Wyatt, but more through Du Bellay, Ronsard and Desportes;[2] and, finally, there were certain of the early Spanish and Italian novels and short stories of writers like Montemayor, Boccaccio, Cinthio and Bandello.

In order to appreciate this romance tradition as it must have presented itself to the imagination of the Elizabethan dramatist and to recreate in ourselves a sense, however dim, of its spirit, conventions, surviving forms and unfaded colours, there is no need to explore these four courses in detail. It so happens that we have in English two outstanding epitomes of all that was most vital at the time in the romance tradition – Spenser's poetry and Sidney's *Arcadia*. Moreover, both of these works themselves exercised a powerful influence on Elizabethan poetry and drama.

§

> But never wist I till this present day,
> Albe of love I always humbly deemed,
> That he was such an one as thou dost say,
> And so religiously to be esteemed.[3]

Above all else romance literature was a literature of love and

[1] *The Allegory of Love*, p. 298.
[2] Lee, in his *Elizabethan Sonnets*, has demonstrated the debt that such sonneteers as Lodge, Daniel, and Spenser owed to these French poets, whose work was frequently made available through direct (though not always acknowledged) translation.
[3] Spenser, *Colin Clout's Come Home Again*, 828-31 (Globe edition).

love-making;[1] and its most revolutionary element, which has survived recognisably into the twentieth century, was its original attitude to love. This attitude in its characteristic late sixteenth-century manifestation is recorded with singular subtlety and beauty in the poetry of Spenser.[2]

To the classical writer, who was faithfully reflecting the actual life of Graeco-Roman civilisation, love was little more than natural sexual appetite, a minor activity of life that was not to be regarded too seriously.[3] To the romance writer, on the other hand, love was a sublime and momentous experience, perhaps the most important of all human experiences. By it a man was transfigured; to its cult he might, without absurdity, dedicate his whole being.

In the earliest, chivalric stage of romance the supreme value of love had been considered to be its stimulus to a life of the highest moral excellence. Such is the doctrine boldly stated by Andreas Capellanus in his *De Arte Honeste Amandi*: 'It is agreed among all men that there is no good thing in the world, and no courtesy, which is not derived from love as from its fountain'.[4] In particular, since early romantic love was saturated with the ethos of chivalry,[5]

---

[1] It is necessary to make this refinement since modern literature, in its fiction at least, might be described as a 'literature of love'. In romantic literature the chief interest was of love-*making*, which often meant the courtship of young lovers.

[2] Most of my illustrative quotations are drawn from Spenser's minor poems, since these provide the most concentrated expressions of the romantic attitude to love. But this attitude, in a more diffused form, runs through the whole of the *Faerie Queene*. As H. J. C. Grierson says: 'Spenser could not reconcile the pagan spirit of the *Romance of the Rose* with the Christian Puritan spirit in which he began to compose his poem and to sing of the Red Cross knight and Una. Justify it as he might by the high allegoric teaching of which his poem is the vehicle, it is love, romantic, human love, that becomes more and more his subject as he goes on to tell of Florimell and Amoret, of Britomart and Calidore, and Pastorella and Serena.' (*Cross Currents in English Literature of the XVIIth Century*, p. 133.)

[3] 'In ancient literature love seldom rises above the level of merry sensuality and domestic comfort, except to be treated as a tragic madness.' (*The Allegory of Love*, p. 4.)

[4] Quoted by C. S. Lewis, *The Allegory of Love*, p. 34.

[5] C. S. Lewis, op. cit., p. 2, quotes a pithy summary of Wechssler's to the effect that romantic love was a 'feudalisation of love', and H. B. Charlton (*Shakespearian Comedy*, p. 24) expresses the same conclusion: 'the romances reflect the ideal of knighthood by their imaginative idealisation of the experience of knights. What chivalry is in morals and feudalism in politics, so are the romances in literature. They are the artistic counterpart of the moral and political society which produced them.' M. C. D'Arcy in *The Mind and Heart of Love* not only denies this impress of chivalry and feudalism on romantic love, but emphasises what he considers to be its anti-feudal aspect. He also accepts, with qualifications, a large part of De Rougemont's thesis in *Passion and Society* that romantic love was inspired by revived Manichaeanism and Gnosticism, with their contempt for the world and human life as irremediably evil, their cult of ecstasy, and their ultimate desire for death and annihilation.

this moral transformation was towards service, a dedicated life of active good. What Chaucer said of his Troilus was true, ideally, of all the knightly heroes of medieval romance:

> And most of love and vertu was his speche,
> And in despit hadde alle wrecchednesse;
> And douteles, no nede was him biseche
> T'honouren hem that hadden worthinesse,
> And esen hem that weren in distresse.[1]

Two centuries later we find poets like Spenser still writing poetical paraphrases of the doctrine of Andreas Capellanus on love:

> For it of honour and all virtue is
> The root, and brings forth glorious flowers of fame,
> That crown true lovers with immortal bliss,
> The meed of them that love, and do not live amiss.
>
> Which who so list look back to former ages,
> And call to count the things that then were done,
> Shall find that all the works of those wise sages,
> And brave exploits which great Heroës won,
> In love were either ended or begun.[2]

It is to be noted in these lines that, like Chaucer, Spenser prefers to believe that this virtue arising from love is an essentially active one; and every book of the *Faerie Queene* is filled with knightly lovers riding forth on a dedicated life of service, 'defending Ladies' cause and Orphan's right'.[3]

However, the two centuries that stretch between Chaucer and Spenser had inevitably brought forth important changes in the romantic attitude to love. In particular, it had been reshaped by the poetry of Guinicelli, Cavalcanti, Dante and Petrarch, and by the neo-platonic[4] writers like Bembo and Ficino, whose teachings were easily available to the Elizabethans through Castiglione's *Courtier* (first translated in 1561). This remoulding of the tradition is first clearly discernible in England with the revival of courtly

---

[1] *Troilus and Criseyde*, III. 1786-1790 (Globe edition).
[2] *Faerie Queene*. Introduction to Book IV, 15-23. In his own person Spenser bears witness to the morally transforming power of love: see *Amoretti*, iii, and *An Hymn in Honour of Love*, 190-196.
[3] *Faerie Queene*, III. ii. xiv.
[4] C. S. Lewis, op. cit., p. 5, points out that this is really an inaccurate label for these writers, or at least for their attitude to love.

literature in the middle of the sixteenth century, especially in Tottel's *Miscellany* (1557).[1]

Probably the most momentous change effected by the poetry of Dante and Petrarch was the bringing of sexual love into a more harmonious and explicit relation with religion. In early romantic literature love, with its believed power of moral regeneration, its elevating cause to which a man might devote his life, and – if we follow De Rougement[2] – its dark undercurrent of Gnosticism, was commonly regarded as a substitute for religion; and the early romances propagate what C. S. Lewis has truly described as the 'Religion of Love', which led, at least on the side of the writers of romance, to conflict between love and religion.[3] But by the time of Spenser we have the firmly established and later romantic conception of a harmony between love and religion. Love is a 'sacred' fire, kindled not by Venus or Cupid, but by God in heaven:

> Most sacred fire, that burnest mightily
> In living breasts, ykindled first above
> Emongst th' eternal spheres and lamping sky,
> And thence poured into men, which men call Love!
> Not that same, which doth base affections move
> In brutish minds, and filthy lust inflame,
> But that sweet fit, that doth true beauty love,
> And chooseth virtue for its dearest Dame,
> Whence spring all noble deeds and never-dying fame.[4]

Occasionally, even in Spenser, the identity between amatory and religious experience is somewhat forced and crude;[5] but in the main it is subtilised by mystical and platonic notions. The

---

[1] Of Wyatt, one of the two chief contributors to this volume, E. M. W. Tillyard writes: 'From Petrarch he derived the sonnet and certain conventional sentiments, which, once introduced into English love poetry, formed its staple subject-matter, with certain interruptions and revolts, for about a century and a half.' (*The Poetry of Sir Thomas Wyatt*, Introduction, p. 23.)

[2] *Passion and Society*.

[3] Cf. C. S. Lewis, op. cit., p. 18: 'this erotic religion arises as a rival or a parody of the real religion and emphasises the antagonism of the two ideals'. Lewis explains this conflict along two lines: first, that the medieval Catholic Church taught that sexual love in a passionate form was wrong, if not wicked; and secondly, that the romance writers in their turn were aware that their values were essentially of the flesh and this world. Father D'Arcy, the Catholic apologist, maintains that it was not the Church but the romance writers, influenced by Gnosticism, who ultimately regarded the world and the flesh (and therefore sexual love) as eternally unsatisfying and an evil to be transcended (See *The Mind and Heart of Love*).

[4] *Faerie Queene*, III. iii. 1.

[5] E.g. *Amoretti*, LXVIII. 13-14.

Creation is celebrated as a manifestation of love,[1] sexual love as an earthly type of Divine Love, and physical beauty as an image of that Heavenly Beauty to the contemplation of which love leads us:

> For sure of all that in this mortal frame
> Contained is, nought more divine doth seem,
> Or that resembleth more th' immortal flame
> Of heavenly light, than Beauty's glorious beam.
> What wonder then, if with such rage extreme
> Frail men, whose eyes seek heavenly things to see,
> At sight thereof so much enravished be?[2]

Of course this transformation does not mean that after Dante and Petrarch all writers, or even the majority of them, attempted, like Spenser, to integrate sexual love with religious experience. But it does mean that this tendency, however fugitive, was present in most late romantic writing, while even when they were not aspiring to the loftiest heights, poets were prone to use a religious vocabulary in their love-verses. Spenser himself furnishes several bold examples of this religious style, notably in Sonnet XXII of *Amoretti*.[3]

Another important consequence of this attempt in late romantic writing to reconcile love and religion was that a heavy, even an excessive, emphasis was thrown on the spiritual aspect of love. Admittedly, early romance sets a high price on chastity and often makes a virtue of abstinence.[4] The lady is frequently married, so that her lover is forced to content himself with the slightest marks of her favour, enraptured if he may but now and then behold her countenance:

> And though he do not win his wish to end,
> Yet thus far happy he himself doth ween,
> That heavens such happy grace did to him lend,
> As thing on earth so heavenly to have seen,
> His heart's enshrined saint, his heaven's queen,
> Fairer than fairest, in his feigning eye,
> Whose sole aspect he counts felicity.[5]

---

[1] See *An Hymn in Honour of Love*.
[2] *An Hymn in Honour of Love*, 113-119; see also *Amoretti*, LXI.
[3] There is also a passage in *Colin Clout's Come Home Again*, 473 ff., that provides another good example of this style.
[4] Another element of romantic love that De Rougemont traces to Gnosticism.
[5] *An Hymn in Honour of Love*, 211-217.

But the sentiment expressed by Spenser in these lines, particularly in the last, belongs to the older and milder doctrine of romance. What, deriving from Petrarchianism and neo-platonism, is new in Spenser is the sharp severance of love from man's physical and sexual nature, the professed desire of deliverance from 'flesh's frail infection';[1] and sometimes this later spiritualisation of love runs to the extreme of condemning the physical as a hindrance to the richest sort of amatory experience and fulfilment. This, of course, was one of the extravagances of Petrarchianism that provoked the passionate and sensual counter-assertion of Donne's poetry:

> Love's not so pure, and abstract, as they use
> To say, which have no Mistress but their Muse.[2]

This new stress thrown by Spenser and others on the spiritual aspect of love was accompanied by a changed attitude to marriage. One of the main, and to modern readers, most curious features of early romantic love was the convention of Adultery,[3] which meant simply that love and courtship were represented as something outside marriage, usually with the Lady as already married. Sidney's *Astrophel and Stella*, which is the record of his moods as he attempts to win the love of a married woman, is a late example of this convention; but the general tendency in the poetry of the time was to invert the convention and transform marriage from a merely mundane and convenient social institution into a spiritual union of souls, the natural consummation of love.[4] This conception, visible as early as the *Kingis Quair*, is ever present in Spenser's poetry, notably in *Amoretti*, *Epithalamion*, *Prothalamion* and Books III and IV of the *Faerie Queene*, which mark 'the

---

[1] *An Hymn in Honour of Beauty*, l. 217; see also ibid. 211-217, *Amoretti* LXXXIII, and the attack on court licentiousness in *Colin Clout's Come Home Again*.

[2] *Love's Growth*.

[3] This convention probably arose from a complex of causes – the Gnostic objection to marriage, the inferior social status of the early romance-makers, the frequent absence of lords on Crusades and military expeditions, and the medieval conception of marriage in which considerations of property were paramount. See C. S. Lewis, op. cit., p. 13: 'any idealisation of sexual love, in a society where marriage is purely utilitarian, must begin by being an idealisation of adultery'.

[4] This changed attitude towards marriage was probably connected with the intense spiritualisation of love in later romantic writing. Certainly we cannot account for it by any obvious change in society, where a love marriage was still extremely rare: 'Marriage was not otherwise regarded at the Court of Elizabeth or James than in the fourteenth century'. (Grierson, op. cit., p. 152.)

final defeat of courtly love by the romantic conception of marriage'.[1]

A similar blend of continuity and change is to be observed in the code of behaviour that the ideal romantic lover was expected to follow. From Chaucer to Spenser, Humility[2] remained one of the cardinal virtues: having chosen his Lady, the lover had to dedicate himself to her without reservation, submitting with slave-like abasement to her will, and prompt in the spirit of 'meek humblesse'[3] to obey her every command. However hard or unfavourable to his suit these commands might be, there was no honourable escape, for the romantic lover was sworn to a lifelong, unswerving loyalty, even though his cause were a hopeless one:

> For knight to leave his Lady were great shame
> That faithful is, and better were to die.
> All loss is less, and less the infamy,
> Than loss of love to him that loves but one.[4]

Another enduring element in the romantic lover's code was Courtesy, which implied not merely refined manners and gentlemanly conduct,[5] but a form of courtship in which the lover manifested his love and proved himself worthy of his Lady's regard by undertaking all sorts of hazardous quests and missions on behalf of distressed ladies, the weak and oppressed.[6] But though this active form of Courtesy remains the chief motive force behind the narrative of the *Faerie Queene*, it was by the sixteenth century losing its power and significance, since it no longer corresponded with social reality. The typical medieval knight was now being transformed into a leisured aristocrat, and 'derring-do' and 'puissant conquests' were becoming something of an anachronism. Hence, in late romantic writing, including Spenser's own poetry, we find that these brave exploits, quests and trials are replaced

---

[1] *The Allegory of Love*, p. 298. But long after Adultery had disappeared its corollary, Secrecy, survived. This convention Andreas Capellanus had set down as the second of the thirty-one rules of courtly love: 'Qui non celat, amare non potest'.

[2] Following C. S. Lewis' quadruple formula of Humility, Courtesy, Adultery, and the Religion of Love. (Op. cit., Ch. I, passim.)

[3] *Amoretti*, II. l. 11.

[4] *Faerie Queene*, III. i. xxv.

[5] Chaucer admirably describes this aspect of Courtesy in his portrait of the Knight, *Canterbury Tales*, Prologue, 68-72.

[6] See *An Hymn in Honour of Love*, 218-224.

more and more by another pattern of behaviour and devotion, which at the same time manages to include certain features of the old form.

This new type of love affirmation (by no means unknown in earlier romance) may perhaps be best described as the Cult of Dejection, for it included fasting, the haunting of such solitary places as woods and wildernesses, the keeping of sleepless vigils, and a fantastically lachrymose ceremonial of tears, groans and sighs.[1] Spenser's most typical and elaborate expression of this sort of sentiment is Cuddie's song in the *August Eclogue* of *The Shepheard's Calendar*, which is too long to quote. But the same note is repeated again and again in *Amoretti*, in lines like –

> Unquiet thought! whom at the first I bred
> Of th' inward bale of my love-pined heart;
> And sithens have with sighs and sorrows fed,
> Till greater than my womb thou woxen art –[2]

or –

> Bring therefore all the forces that ye may,
> And lay incessant battery to her heart;
> Plaints, prayers, vows, ruth, sorrow, and dismay,
> Those engines can the proudest heart convert.[3]

In this late romantic Cult of Dejection there are two or three other features that call for separate mention. First, there is the sense of devastating misery and prostration produced by separation, even of a temporary kind, from the beloved:

> So oft as homeward I from her depart,
> I go like one that, having lost the field,
> Is prisoner led away with heavy heart,
> Despoiled of warlike arms and knowen shield.

---

[1] E. M. W. Tillyard (*The Poetry of Sir Thomas Wyatt*, Introduction, p. 23) has a succinct definition of this aspect of romantic poetry: 'Despair, not fruition is the lot of the Petrarchian lover'. This is the cult Cervantes burlesques when, in the desert region of Sierra Morena, Don Quixote decides, in the manner of Orlando and Amadis, to rave in solitude over his absent Dulcinea: ' "Behold, O Heavens!" cried he, "the place which an unhappy lover has chosen to bemoan the deplorable state to which you have reduced him: here shall my flowing tears swell the liquid veins of this crystal rill, and my deep sighs perpetually move the leaves of these shady trees, in testimony of the anguish and pain that harrows up my soul!" ' (*Don Quixote*, Everyman's Library, Vol. I, p. 185.)

[2] *Amoretti*, II. 1-4.

[3] Ibid., XIV. 9-12. (See also, for further examples of this style, the *January Eclogue* of *The Shepheard's Calendar*, and *An Hymn in Honour of Love*, 127-133.)

> So do I now myself a prisoner yield
> To sorrow and to solitary pain;
> From presence of my dearest dear exiled,
> Long-while alone in languor to remain.[1]

Such strains as these were not, of course, unknown in earlier romantic writing. What is new in the later work is their intensification and exaggeration; and this also holds for the emphasis that is thrown on the excruciating tortures of jealousy, which make the lover's life a hell:

> Yet is there one more cursed than they all,
> That canker-worm, that monster, Jealousy,
> Which eats the heart and feeds upon the gall,
> Turning all love's delight to misery,
> Through fear of losing his felicity.
> Ah, gods! that ever ye that monster placed
> In gentle love, that all his joy's defaced.[2]

There is much less stress on jealousy in the sentiments of the early romantic lover, just as jealousy is a much less frequent motive in the plots of early romance tales. Nor is this surprising, for the chivalric lover was usually absorbed in his deeds of prowess. It was his less active, languishing and often bored successor who had the leisure to cultivate the bitter-sweets of jealousy.

While this Cult of Dejection provided a substitute love-affirmation for the previous mode of Courtesy, it was more likely to pass unnoticed by the beloved. Moreover, according to late romantic ideas, love not only moulded a man to the highest moral excellence, but was also the most exhilarating and intense of all emotional experiences, the 'intelligenza nuova' of Dante's phrase, a revelation and a rebirth that quickened the lover to a heightened poetic awareness and sensibility. Indeed, love *was* the soul of poetry and imagination. Hence, faced with the problem of preserving his precious tears and sighs, which might otherwise have been vainly squandered in some desert place, and blessed with the power of poetic utterance, the lover of late romance turns frequently to verse-making as part of his courtship. This was how Spenser himself wooed his wife-to-be:

---

[1] *Amoretti*, LII; see also LXXXVII.
[2] *An Hymn in Honour of Love*, 266-272.

> Happy, ye leaves! whenas those lily hands,
> Which hold my life in their dead-doing might,
> Shall handle you, and hold in love's soft bands,
> Like captives trembling at the victor's sight.
> And happy lines! on which, with starry light,
> Those lamping eyes will deign sometimes to look,
> And read the sorrows of my dying sprite,
> Written with tears in heart's close-bleeding book;[1]

and there were innumerable imaginary lovers in sixteenth-century romance who followed Spenser's example (and hope) as they worked off their dejection into a sheaf of well-turned sonnets. In fact sonneteering became as indispensable in the late romantic manner of courtship as prowess in arms had been in the earlier; and it is interesting to note Sidney's curse, at the end of his *Apologie for Poetrie*, on those who despise verse, 'that while you live, you live in love, and never get favour for lacking skill of a sonnet'.

Finally among these conventions of romantic love there was the image of the Lady herself. From the first she had always been a heavenly creature, incomparably beautiful and radiant with virtue; and so she remained in the late romantic love-poetry of writers like Spenser and Sidney. The sense of her virtue was enhanced by Petrarchian and neo-platonic ideas; and though in one mood the poets affected to despise 'flesh's frail infection', platonic notions of beauty, combined with the aesthetic exhilaration of the Renaissance in the human body, encouraged them to exaggerate the Lady's physical beauty. Spenser's poetry, notably the luscious sixty-fourth sonnet in *Amoretti* and the tenth stanza of *Epithalamion*, contains many richly sensuous descriptions of feminine loveliness. But there were certain features in the image of the Lady as she appeared in post-Petrarchian poetry that, while not entirely new in themselves, were harped upon with a new and characteristic emphasis. In particular, the Cult of Dejection demanded that the Lady should be – at first anyhow – scornful of love and hard as adamant to be wooed. *Amoretti* is tedious with this complaint; and the lover's chief solace seems to be the belief that love so hardly won will be the more enduring, coupled

---

[1] *Amoretti*, 1. Sidney opens *Astrophel and Stella* in much the same manner:
> Loving in truth, and fain my love in verse to show,
> That the dear She might take some pleasure of my pain:
> Pleasure might cause her read, reading might make her know,
> Knowledge might pity win, and pity grace obtain,
> I sought fit words to paint the blackest face of woe, &c.

with the hope of heightened felicity in his ultimate conquest of his Mistress's proud and scornful heart.[1] There is also a wearisome insistence on the fair one's pitiless cruelty. In the twentieth *Amoretti* sonnet Spenser's mistress is declared to be crueller than a lion:

> But she, more cruel, and savage wild,
> Than either lion or the lioness;
> Shames not to be with guiltless blood defiled,
> But taketh glory in her cruelness;[2]

in the fifty-sixth sonnet she is a ravening tiger:

> Fair ye be sure, but cruel and unkind,
> As is a tiger, that with greediness
> Hunts after blood;[3]

and somehow we have to harmonise these images with more reverential ones like:

> More than most fair, full of the living fire,
> Kindled above unto the Maker near.[4]

The truth is that, when we have allowed for artificialities of sentiment and the convention of this image of the cruel, proud, disdainful lady, there is something curiously ambivalent[5] in the romantic attitude to love. The logic of this ambivalence is clear enough, for idealisation of love does not necessarily imply idealisation of women; the explanation is more obscure. The conclusions of modern psychology on the proximity and inter-penetration of love and hate certainly have an important bearing here; while common observation would lead us to expect that a highly exaggerated and artificial attitude towards love would produce its own reaction. But probably the chief explanation of this contradiction is that romantic poems and stories, even in their late forms, were produced in an intensely religious age, and that from first to last, in spite of compromise and reconciliation, there was always a sense of fundamental conflict between divine and sexual love, with inevitable moments when sexual love was felt to be a sin and a snare. H. C. Grierson sums up this conflict well when he

---

[1] *Amoretti*, VI and LI.
[2] 9-12.
[3] 1-3.
[4] *Amoretti*, VIII. 1-2.
[5] See for this ambivalence in Spenser the *December Eclogue* of *The Shepheard's Calendar*.

writes: 'the spirit of romance is secular, humanist, not Christian – as devout medieval Catholic or seventeenth-century protestant understood "Christian". Their splendid joy in life and love, their cult of personal prowess and the service of a mistress, the medieval dream of love and heroism, are at the opposite pole from Christian humility, distrust of passion and contempt for temporal wealth or glory'.[1]

§

Besides this complex and singular attitude to love, the term 'romance' denotes a peculiar type of narrative. This too, though modified from time to time, was highly traditional and can therefore be defined with some precision; and just as Spenser's poetry epitomises the romantic attitude to love in the period when Elizabethan drama was written, so Sidney's *Arcadia*, written between 1580 and 1585, concentrates all that was most vital at that time in the romance tradition of story-telling. 'If any book then combined in the highest degree delight with instruction', writes E. M. W. Tillyard,[2] 'it was *Arcadia*. This vast prose romance was immensely popular, probably on account of its rich and vital style and of its wealth of romantic incident'. Further, it is as certain as such matters can be that Shakespeare was well acquainted with *Arcadia*: there are several reminiscences of it in *The Two Gentlemen of Verona*, a few of the character-names in *The Winter's Tale* are taken from it, and it provides the sub-plot of *King Lear*.

While *Arcadia* is an elaborate work with several distinct and important facets, it is a typical romance in that it consists primarily of love-stories. Its main narrative deals with the love affairs of the two princes, Pyrocles and Musidorus, who fall in love at first sight[3] with Philoclea and Pamela, the daughters of King Basilius

[1] *Cross Currents in English Literature of the XVIIth Century*, p. 8. For further discussion of this point, see Additional Note (*b*), p. 202.

[2] *Shakespeare's Last Plays*, p. 11. In this book Tillyard strongly emphasises the influence of *Arcadia*, which is not, he maintains, to be measured simply by the borrowings from it but by its elevation and re-creation of the whole romantic tradition. An opinion particularly apposite to the present theme is the following: '... we shall not understand what Shakespeare's contemporaries expected from the romantic material and what types of feeling they thought it capable of treating, unless we remember what they thought of *Arcadia*'. (pp. 10-11.)

[3] A stock convention of romance. With Pyrocles it is the portrait of Philoclea that does the trick. An even more startling use of this convention is made when the blunt and braggart Anaxius, having sworn to slay Philoclea for her treatment of Amphialus, falls hypnotised with love at his first sight of her. (Feuillerat's edition of Sidney's *Works*, Vol. I, *Arcadia*, Bk. III. Ch. 26.)

of Arcadia; and this principal love tale is itself crossed with several prominent love interests, such as Basilius and his wife Gynecia falling in love with Pyrocles when he disguises himself as the Amazon Zelmane. Also it is love that furnishes the chief substance of those stories – of Argalus and Parthenia, Amphialus and Queen Helen of Corinth, Antiphilus and Erona – that Sidney expanded or added to the early books in his later revisions.

All these love stories are typically romantic in that they are to a large extent concerned with love-making, or at least attempted love-making. They also reveal another salient feature of the romantic tale: time and again we are presented with the theme of faithful love subjected to some grievous and abnormal strain. So, when Pyrocles realises that Gynecia has penetrated his disguise as Zelmane, he pretends, as a protective stratagem, to fall in love with her and desert Philoclea; and though this trick succeeds, the price of it is the anguish of knowing that Philoclea really believes him to be unfaithful. Again, later in the story, when he is discovered in a lodge with Philoclea by the shepherd Damoetas, who locks the lovers in and goes off to raise the alarm, he is torn by the cruel possibility that his suicide may be the means of preserving Philoclea's honour. And there are several such dilemmas in the subordinate stories, as when Erona is forced to choose between the execution of her lover Antiphilus and, as the payment for his reprieve, marriage with his captor Tiridates.[1]

A common variant of this dramatic formula was the situation that brought love into conflict with the claims of friendship. There are several instances of this in *Arcadia*, the most notable being the plight of Amphialus when he discovers that Queen Helen, whom he is courting for his friend Philoxenes, is in love with himself. But in spite of such conflicts as this one and the prominent treatment and idealisation of male-friendship,[2] which was common in late romantic literature, the chief emphasis of *Arcadia* is on sexual love.

As might be expected, this love is characteristically coloured

[1] *Works*, Vol. I, pp. 232-236, Bk. II, Ch. 13.
[2] This idealisation of male-friendship could be illustrated abundantly from Spenser's poetry, especially from Books III and IV of the *Faerie Queene*. One of Spenser's best modern critics, Miss Spens, has no doubt at all that he valued friendship above sexual love, and maintains that it was touch and go whether friendship rather than love became the emotional mainspring of modern European literature. (*Spenser's Faerie Queene*, Ch. 5, passim). Lyly's *Euphues*, too, makes much of the friendship theme, and Edwards' *Damon and Pithias* (1564) and *Palamon and Arcite* (1566) furnish early examples of plays on the subject.

with romantic doctrine and sentiment.[1] For instance, in the first few pages of the book, we hear the two pastoral shepherds, Strephon and Claius, uttering the familiar romantic tribute to the spiritual elevation of love:

> Hath not the only love of her made us (being silly ignorant shepherds) raise up our thoughts above the ordinary level of the world, so as great clerks do not disdain our conference? hath not the desire to seem worthy in her eyes made us when others were sleeping, to sit viewing the course of heavens? when others were running at base, to run over learned writings? when others mark their sheep, we to mark ourselves? hath she not thrown reason upon our desires, and, as it were given eyes unto Cupid? hath in any, but in her, love-fellowship maintained friendship between rivals, and beauty taught the beholders chastity?[2]

Pyrocles, when he first falls in love, shows that he has been thoroughly schooled in the vein of solitariness and moping melancholy:

> But such a change was grown in Daiphantus [Pyrocles], that (as if cheerfulness had been tediousness, and good entertainment were turned to discourtesy) he would ever get himself alone, though almost when he was in company he was alone, so little attention he gave to any that spake unto him: even the colour and figure of his face began to receive some alteration; which he showed little to heed: but every morning early going abroad, either to the garden, or to some woods towards the desert, it seemed his only comfort was to be without a comforter.[3]

There is another excellent specimen of the high romantic love-code in the description of Pamela's behaviour after Musidorus has taken her into his arms for the first time and attempted to kiss her: in spite of his previous addresses, which have thawed her considerably, she properly reasserts herself in the style of the proud, scornful lady:

> So did she put him away from her: looking first unto heaven, as amazed to find herself so beguiled in him; then laying the cruel punishment upon him of angry Love, and louring beauty, shewing disdain, and a despising disdain, Away (said she) unworthy man to

[1] See also *Astrophel and Stella* and my article in *English*, Vol. VI, No. 35.
[2] Sidney's *Works*, Vol. I, pp. 7-8, Bk. I, Ch. I.
[3] *Works*, Vol. I, p. 54, Bk. I, Ch. 9.

love, or to be loved. Assure thyself, I hate myself for being so deceived; judge then what I do thee, for deceiving me. Let me see thee no more, the only fall of my judgement, and stain of my conscience.[1]

Musidorus responds with the conventional abashment and runs away to the appropriate place and penance:

> It was not an amazement, it was not a sorrow, but it was even a death, which then laid hold of Dorus: which certainly at that instant would have killed him, but that the fear to tarry longer in her presence (contrary to her commandment) gave him life to carry himself away from her sight, and to run into the woods, where, throwing himself down at the foot of a tree, he did not fall to lamentation (for that proceeded of pitying) or grieving for himself (which he did no way) but to curses of his life, as one that detested himself.[2]

However, while a considerable part of *Arcadia* is given up to the courtship of young lovers, conducted according to the romantic code and concluding in marriage, most of these stories are crammed with a complexity of incident.[3] Often this incident is the outcome of scheming and intrigue; but what makes the narrative of *Arcadia* characteristic of the romance tradition of 'fine fabling'[4] is that it is primarily one of adventure, of happenings (often unforeseen) in which the heroes and heroines are involved, rather than of intrigue. By chance (a shipwreck) Pyrocles and Musidorus arrive in Arcadia to fall in love with two princesses who live under most strange conditions; Pyrocles' position is complicated, through no fault of his own, by the amorous attentions of Basilius and Gynecia; the two princesses and Pyrocles are kidnapped by the wicked Cecropia; the lovers are foiled in

---

[1] *Works*, Vol. I, p. 355, Bk. III, Ch. 1.

[2] Ibid., Vol. I, p. 355.

[3] Some of this incident, notably the chapters in Bk. III describing the fights between Amphialus and the various knights who come to rescue the princesses from captivity, is drawn from the oldest layer of romance – those tales of knightly prowess that go back to the *chansons de geste*. It should also be remembered that this narrative element is of particular importance in the English romantic tradition. Most of the first English romances were popularisations of French models and skipped the sentimental parts to concentrate on the plots and adventures. These cruder versions were a hardy species and survived down to the sixteenth century and beyond.

[4] Hurd's famous phrase, *Letters on Chivalry and Romance*.

their elopements and implicated in the murder of Basilius. Plainly the narrative-pleasure that Sidney intended for his readers was not the following, and to some extent the anticipating, of an intrigue. Like a traditional romance-writer, he preferred to harrow his readers with suspense, to play on the childish curiosity of 'What is going to happen next?' Will Pyrocles, disguised as Zelmane, be able to evade the attentions of Gynecia? Will something happen in time to save the young princes after they have been sentenced to death for rape and complicity in the murder of Basilius? And with this suspense we find frequent use of the other principal device of romantic narrative – the shock of surprise. So Pamela is not really dead after all, though Philoclea believes she has seen her executed on the instructions of Cecropia? And Basilius is not actually dead either, though the princes have been sentenced for his murder?

Nor is it merely the recurrence of suspense and surprise that gives *Arcadia* its romantic, fairy-tale quality. Broadly speaking, we may divide stories of adventure into two types: there are the adventures of real life that, however highly coloured they may be, could possibly happen, and there are the adventures of the extraordinary and marvellous kind that never conceivably could. Most of the adventures related in *Arcadia* belong, like those of the fairy-tale and traditional romance story, to the second type, so that *Arcadia* presupposes not only readers with the curiosities and easily aroused anxieties of children, but readers capable of indulging in a large and sustained suspension of disbelief.

Though there is only an occasional touch of the marvellous that we find in many of the older romances – dreams, fabulous beasts,[1] a magical, ever-available pharmacopœia of drugs and ointments[2] – there is plenty of preposterous stuff of another kind. Nothing, for instance, could be more far-fetched than the machinations of Cecropia – her fantastic release of a bear and lion to kill the two princes, the insurrection she instigates among the admirable Arcadians (as unbelievable in its inception as in its suppression by the strong arm and oratory of Zelmane), her illusionist's trick to present the execution of Pamela and the head of Philoclea,

[1] E.g. Pyrocles' account of how he slew 'a monstrous beast, of most ugly shape, armed like a Rhinoceros, as strong as an Elephant, as fierce as a Lion, as nimble as a Leopard, and as cruel as a Tiger'. (Vol. I, p. 300, Bk. II, Ch. 23.)

[2] Parthenia is hideously disfigured by some mysterious ointment and then magically healed of all taint.

and finally her death when she falls off the roof thinking her son Amphialus has come to kill her.[1]

All this inherent extravagance of the narrative is heightened by Sidney's employment of certain stock conventions of romantic story-telling. Time and again, either to stir a sense of wonder in his reader or to unravel some complication in his story, he resorts to coincidence. When Musidorus leads a small force against the Helots who are holding Kalander's son captive, their new Captain, of course, turns out to be his friend Pyrocles,[2] from whom he had been separated in the shipwreck. Queen Helen, after long search for Amphialus, arrives just when he has mortally wounded himself. Euarchus reaches Arcadia at a critical moment to act as judge and arbiter in the situation arising from Basilius' death, and Kalodulus comes on the scene in the nick of time to reveal the true identity of the princes and so save them from execution.

This last coincidence, which enables Sidney to effect his final *dénouement*, also illustrates another important convention of romantic story-telling – that of disguises, mistaken identities, and lack of recognition. In order that the concluding part of the main story should have the full dramatic or sensational impact that Sidney no doubt intended, we are supposed to swallow the fiction that both father and son are incapable of recognising each other. And if this is completely incredible, it is no more preposterous[3] than Pyrocles' masquerading throughout the story as the Amazon Zelmane, whose real sex only Gynecia appears to suspect.

Further, Sidney's narrative keeps faithfully to the romantic convention of poetic justice, for in the main story and most of the digressions events are so manipulated that, while they may produce misery and suffering in their main course, the conclusion is on the whole a happy one, with the good and virtuous triumphant and the bad discomfited. Cecropia, the villain of the piece, is persistently foiled, and it is really her own plotting that brings about her abrupt end. Amphialus, who had at least connived with her in many of her schemes, is punished, first, by being the accidental cause of her death, and then by a remorse that leads him to kill himself. Gynecia does penance for her love for Zelmane by being forced for a while to believe that she is the murderess of her

---

[1] For further examples, see the incredible prowess of Amphialus against the champions of the princesses, followed by his remarkable bungling when he tries to kill himself, and also Pyrocles' rescue of Musidorus. (Bk. II, Ch. 8.)

[2] *Works*, Vol. I, pp. 38-45, Bk. I, Ch. 6.

[3] And no more preposterous than Parthenia's long concealment of her identity.

husband; but she is not, like Cecropia, evil or irredeemably bad, and in the end she and Basilius are reconciled. The lovers – it goes without saying – emerge from all their trials with deepened love and tested fidelity to the reward of happy marriage.

A narrative of this sort, crammed with extravagant, far-fetched adventures and shaped by such conventions as coincidence, mistaken identity, and poetic justice, could only be achieved at the cost of strained sentiments and slight or impossible motivation. A particularly glaring, though by no means isolated, example of this occurs when Basilius and Gynecia discover each other in the cave of Zelmane. Here, to straighten out a complicated situation and initiate the last phase of the plot, Basilius is supposed to be quite taken in by his wife's moderate and controlled complaint at his unfaithfulness, never to ask what she has been doing in the cave or why she is wearing Zelmane's upper garment, and, without any questioning, to snatch and drain off the love-potion. Just as incredible is the behaviour of Gynecia who, when Basilius falls apparently dead, is determined to proclaim herself to all the world as her husband's murderer.

Romantic love, no less than the necessities of a sensational narrative, also leads to some absurdly strained psychology. When Philoclea believes Pyrocles has deserted her and fallen in love with Gynecia, one of her chief reactions to the situation is to persuade herself that she was not worthy of the love of Pyrocles anyway! –

> There was no fault but in me, that could ever think so high eyes would look so low, or so great perfections would stain themselves with my unworthiness. Alas! why could I not see? I was too weak a band to tie so heavenly a heart: I was not fit to limit the infinite course of his wonderful destinies. Was it ever like that upon only Philoclea his thoughts should rest? Ah silly soul that couldst please thyself with so impossible an imagination![1]

Was there ever such folly in a woman scorned?

But it would be pointless to instance further examples of crude psychology and motivation in *Arcadia*: the simple fact is that all the characters are pasteboard, and never intended as anything more. In this respect, too, *Arcadia* is a typical romance, for, with a few rare exceptions, the great majority of romantic heroes, heroines, and villains are puppets, actuated by impossible motives, roughly simplified, and grouped in rigid categories of good and

[1] *Works*, Vol. II, pp. 34-35.

bad. The men are seldom more vital than personifications of abstract human qualities, while the women have two main functions – to look beautiful, of course, and to inspire love and devotion.[1] What little psychological subtlety and complexity there is in the typical romance story is primarily that of a single sentiment – love; and even that one sentiment is often highly artificial.

To account fully for this psychological crudity and immaturity of romance, particularly so far as individual characterisation is concerned, would take us deep into the fundamental attitudes and beliefs of the Middle Ages and into the sharply contrasted humanist outlook that was an essential part of the Renaissance. But at least it can be immediately perceived that, given the two primary objectives of romance-writers – highly coloured adventure and the delineation of rarified, artificial sentiments of love – anything in the nature of the psychological realism and depth of modern literature was well-nigh impossible. Sometimes a genius, by his magic, might successfully combine polar opposites: Chaucer in his *Troilus and Criseyde*[2] managed somehow to blend acute psychology and vivid characterisation, to say nothing of drama with typical romantic adventure and amatory sentiment. Shakespeare, some two centuries later, possessed the same powers of alchemy. But had there been at any time, and by merely talented writers, a sustained attempt to create characters of flesh and blood, the whole romantic tradition must, of necessity, have been shattered.

Two slighter features of *Arcadia* remain to be briefly noted since they are, in their way, characteristic of the romantic tradition. First, all the principal characters are high-born – kings, queens, princes and princesses. The only time the common people are allowed to obtrude into the story is to furnish a contemptible mob – the revolting Helots from whom Musidorus rescues Kalander's son Clitophon, the rioters who, stirred on by Cecropia's agent, rise against Basilius,[3] and the bandits, a remnant of the

---

[1] H. B. Charlton (*Shakespearian Comedy*, p. 40) does not exaggerate very much when he dismisses the general run of romance heroines as 'charming nonentities'.

[2] 'Chaucer's *Troilus and Criseyde* is the poem in which medieval romance passes out of itself into the form of the modern novel.' (W. P. Ker, *Epic and Romance*, p. 367.)

[3] It is not surprising that an aristocrat like Sidney is plainly contemptuous of the mob. But there is a less expected callousness and brutality in the relish and would-be grotesque humour with which he describes the suppression of the rioters. (Vol. I, p. 312, Bk. II, Ch. 25.)

defeated rioters, who capture Musidorus and Pamela when they are eloping. Certainly the blending of romance with pastoralism in the sixteenth century gave a new prominence to shepherds and shepherdesses. But either these Arcadian figures are really, like Musidorus, lords or ladies in disguise,[1] or else, like Strephon and Claius, they are courtly, refined figures, speaking the sentiments and conventions that the aristocracy professed or aspired to.

The chief exception to this aristocratic setting is furnished by the shepherd Damoetas, his wife Miso, and his daughter Mopsa, who, as the guardians of Pamela, enter prominently into the story. This group of 'low-life' characters is interesting because it indicated, in advance of Elizabethan drama, one of the possible ways in which romance might be infused with comedy. Some of the comic relief provided by Damoetas and his family is good, notably the opening of Book IV where Damoetas, tricked by Musidorus, digs vainly for gold, Mopsa sits up in a tree and, after jumping down and nearly breaking her neck, takes her father for Apollo, and Miso, thinking she has caught her husband with a mistress, cudgels him stoutly when he has his arms round Mopsa. Such an episode would have gone easily into any Elizabethan romantic comedy.

The setting and scenic background of *Arcadia* is eclectic and highly artificial. Most of the action takes place in a wood, a 'desert' as it is frequently called, to which Basilius has retired from court with his family. This wood and its environs is inhabited by shepherds who live an idyllic and primitive life. The country is supposed to be Arcadia in Greece and the time the distant classical past. But much of the action is in and around the castle of Cecropia and her son, which is plainly of the medieval type, while the warfare and fighting that takes up a considerable part of the story is conducted by knights in armour. We might, for simplicity, say that the background is medieval Europe superimposed on a vaguely classical Greece; or we might say that it is a fantastic, operatic one unknown to geography or history book. Description hardly matters one way or the other.

A classical Greek background was not common in romance; but otherwise the setting of *Arcadia* is typical of the romantic

---

[1] Another humbler wit to shepherds' pipes retires,
Yet hiding royal blood full oft in rural vein.
— *Astrophel and Stella*, VI.

tradition. When the romantic backcloth did not represent some strange and remote country undreamt of even by the imaginative cartographers of the time, it was often conservatively medieval, not to say stylised. Castles obviously, with their walled rose-gardens and tilt-yards, monasteries and abbeys, mountains, forests, streams and fountains, all the wild and untamed medieval hinterland fascinating for its age-old accretions of legend and mystery – these are the recurrent scenes in the romantic back-cloth, so that when, in *The Knight of the Burning Pestle*, Beaumont made 'deserts' and 'wildernesses' such a prominent symbol of Ralph's day-dreams, he was but fastening on an obvious point for satire. It is true that the emergence of the early Italian novel, reflecting something of a new bourgeois and urban society, did to a certain extent transform the traditional background of romance. But this transformation was not so much in the direction of actuality as might be supposed, for quite early the Italian novel, like Italian Renaissance drama, became a course for that great flood of pastoralism that swept through Europe in the sixteenth century. One extremely artificial setting was simply substituted for another – shepherds and shepherdesses for knights and their ladies, a pastoral pseudo-Sicilian landscape for the unreclaimed Gothic landscape of forest and mountain; or else, as in *Arcadia*, an attempt was made to combine the two types of setting.

§

Why did Sidney and Spenser, and later a number of the dramatists, respond so readily to the influence of the romantic tradition in its various literary forms?

We have already suggested one simple answer to this question at the beginning of this chapter: apart from the classics, romantic literature was almost the only non-didactic reading matter available, and it was bound, therefore, to exercise a strong and continuous pressure on creative writing. Moreover, the flood-tide of the Renaissance into England in the last half of the sixteenth century helped to stimulate an immense interest in all things Italian; and while one fundamental feature of the Renaissance was the revival of classical learning and literature, in which the Italians had been energetic and leading pioneers, the later forms of romance – the romantic epic, Petrarchian poetry, the pastoral and the romantic novel – were all primarily Italian in inspiration.[1]

There was also a strong social reason why, so far from any reaction against romance, that tradition should enjoy a fresh lease of life. The landed (and what we may perhaps still call feudal) aristocracy of Elizabethan England was in a weakened and challenged position: many of its members enjoyed newly created honours, and, with the gilt and colours of their coats of arms barely dry, must have felt some of the parvenu's sense of inferiority; many again, as R. H. Tawney has demonstrated,[2] were in hazardous financial straits; and as a class their political and economic power was increasingly menaced by the growing strength of the bourgeoisie. What more natural in such circumstances than that Elizabethan courtiers and aristocrats should cherish a tradition that was largely a repository of its own values, attitudes and beliefs?

Nor was the situation merely one in which the Elizabethan aristocracy had to content itself with passively cherishing an admired literary tradition. Apart from the fact that a number of writers like Spenser and Sidney came from its own circle, it still exercised considerable power and influence through its patronage of the arts. In particular, it was, with the Court, the most influential patron of drama.

But there is another reason why the dramatists especially were sympathetic to romantic influences. This is indicated in a passage, well worth quoting at length, in Sidney's *Apologie for Poetrie*, where he is discussing the state of contemporary comedy:

> So falleth it out, that having indeed no right Comedy, in that comical part of our Tragedy we have nothing but scurrility unworthy of any chaste ears, or some extreme show of doltishness, indeed fit to lift up loud laughter, and nothing else: where the whole tract of a Comedy should be full of delight, as the Tragedy should be still maintained in a well-raised admiration. But our Comedians think there is no delight without laughter; which is very wrong, for though laughter may come with delight, yet cometh it not of delight, as

[1] 'The Italianate Englishman, bitterly reproached by his contemporaries, brought back from Italy, with his fantastic costume and new-fangled manners, a love of Italian literature and of romance.' (C. Whibly, *Cambridge History of Literature*, Vol. IV, p. 6.)
[2] Introduction to Wilson's *Discourse Upon Usury*, pp. 32-33. According to Tawney, among those heavily in debt were the Earls of Essex and Leicester, Sir Philip Sidney, and Shakespeare's patron, the Earl of Southampton.

though delight should be the cause of laughter; but well may one thing breed both together: nay, rather in themselves they have, as it were, a kind of contrariety: for delight we scarcely do but in things that have a conveniency to ourselves or to the general nature: laughter almost ever cometh of things disproportioned to ourselves and nature. Delight hath a joy in it, either permanent or present. Laughter hath only a scornful tickling. For example, we are ravished with delight to see a fair woman, and yet are far from being moved to laughter. We laugh at deformed creatures, wherein certainly we cannot delight. We delight in good chances, we laugh at mischances; we delight to hear the happiness of our friends, or Country, at which he were worthy to be laughed at that would laugh; we shall, contrarily, laugh sometimes to find a matter quite mistaken and go down the hill against the bias, in the mouth of some such men, as for respect of them one shall be heartily sorry, yet he cannot choose but laugh; and so is rather pained than delighted with laughter. Yet deny I not but that they may go well together; for as in Alexander's picture well set out we delight without laughter, and in twenty mad antics we laugh without delight, so in Hercules, painted with his great beard and furious countenance, in woman's attire, spinning at Omphales' commandment, it breedeth both delight and laughter. For the representing of so strange a power in love procureth delight: and the scornfulness of the action stirreth laughter.[1]

One or two small details apart, the gist of Sidney's argument is quite clear. Making a clean-cut division between delight and laughter, he condemns such contemporary comedy as there is as crude and debased on the ground that it stirs nothing but laughter with its coarseness and knock-about foolery. Mature and polished comedy, he maintains, should be infused with 'delight', and at several points he attempts to explain what he means by that word: it is the presentation of fair women, 'good chances', the spirit of joy and happiness: it is inoffensive to chaste ears. Assuming, as we may, that this attitude of Sidney had the sympathy and approval of other cultured aristocrats and of some of the dramatists they patronised and commissioned, what better source was there from which the stage could import the required ingredient of 'delight' than romantic literature and tradition? Nor would this question have been merely hypothetical to Sidney's contemporaries and immediate successors, for he himself in his *Arcadia*, which enjoyed enormous popularity, had both

[1] *Elizabethan Critical Essays*, ed. Gregory Smith, Vol. I, pp. 199-200.

elevated the status of romance and, as Tillyard says,[1] 'combined in the highest degree delight with instruction'.

Further, there was the example of Italian comedy, which had long been under the influence of the romantic tradition. Croce[2] has pointed out that for some fifty years before Shakespeare the *Commedia dell' Arte* had been fashioning and adapting romance material for the theatre. H. B. Charlton, who is also familiar with sixteenth-century Italian comedy, states a similar conclusion: though the aim of the early Italian dramatists, he writes, had been to imitate classical comedy, 'without intention, and as yet, without much change in outward form, classical comedy is moving gradually to romantic comedy, and is taking to itself a situation and a temper which in due course will transform the type to the sort which characterises romantic comedy'.[3] What is less certain is the extent to which Elizabethan writers were acquainted with this early Italian comedy. But the probability is that they knew it in its literary form and may have seen something of it on the stage. We are not entirely without evidence on the point, for apart from the plays mentioned by Bond[4] as owing 'a considerable and definite debt . . . to the Italian novellieri or poets' – *Tancred and Gismunda*, Whetstone's *Promos and Cassandra*, and Gascoigne's *Supposes* – there is a record of Italian players performing twice before the Court in 1574, while Gosson's *Plays Confuted in Five Actions* (1582) bears witness to the influence of Italian comedy, along with medieval romance and the Italian romantic novel, on English drama: 'I may boldly say it because I have seen it, that the *Palace of Pleasure*, the *Golden Ass*, the *Aethiopian History*, *Amadis of France*, the *Round Table*, bawdy Comedies in Latin, French, Italian, and Spanish, have been thoroughly ransacked to furnish the Playhouses in London'.[5]

Even Gosson himself, as he candidly admits, had in his time been depraved enough to try his hand at a play in the Italian manner.[6]

---
[1] *Shakespeare's Last Plays*, p. 11.
[2] *Ariosto, Shakespeare, and Corneille* (translated Douglas Ainslie, 1921), p. 189.
[3] *Shakespearian Comedy*, p. 23.
[4] *Works of John Lyly*, Vol. II, p. 473.
[5] *Roxburghe Library*, ed. W. C. Hazlitt, pp. 188-189.
[6] A play 'of Italian devices, called *The Comedy of Captain Mario*'. See Gosson's letter, ibid., p. 165.

CHAPTER TWO

THE COMEDIES OF LYLY

THE FIRST notable response to Sidney's plea for a comedy of 'delight' came from John Lyly, whose *Blackfriars Prologue* to *Sapho and Phao* might almost be taken as a deliberate reply to the passage already quoted from the *Apologie for Poetrie*: 'Our intent was at this time to move inward delight, not outward lightness, and to breed (if it might be) soft smiling, not loud laughing: knowing it to the wise to be as great pleasure to hear counsel mixed with wit, as to the foolish to have sport mingled with rudeness.'[1]

Coming to dramatic work straight from the university, and writing directly for a queen and courtiers who prided themselves on their classical taste, Lyly had every incentive to draw heavily on the classical tradition in creating his own distinctive comedy of delight. Hence, out of his eight undoubted plays, no less than seven contain elements of plot that can be traced to classical (mainly Latin) sources. Ovid provided material for *Endymion*, *Midas*, *Love's Metamorphosis* and *Sapho and Phao*; Pliny and Plutarch furnished suggestions for *Campaspe*, Hesiod for *The Woman in the Moon*, Aelian's *Varia Historia* for *Sapho and Phao*, Lucian for *Endymion*, while *Gallathea* bears traces of several classical sources.

However, it would be a mistake to exaggerate Lyly's debt to Greek and Latin literature for the material of his plots. Frequently his reading served as nothing more than a stimulus or suggestion to a story that he invented and elaborated entirely out of his own head; and in an age whose playwrights are characterised by their habit of adapting existent stories Lyly stands out conspicuously as an original plot-maker. Thus in *Gallathea* all that can be attributed to classical sources is the incident of the virgin exacted by Neptune as a tribute; the main substance of the plot – Cupid's attack on Diana's nymphs, his capture and punishment by Diana and his subsequent rescue, the love story of Gallathea and Phillida, and the miller's shipwrecked sailor sons – is Lyly's own invention. The same is true of *Endymion*, *Midas*, *Mother*

[1] *Works of John Lyly*, ed. R. W. Bond, Vol. II, p. 371. (All the quotations in this chapter are taken from Bond's edition.)

Bombie and *Love's Metamorphosis*. Further, even where Lyly does draw freely on classical material it would be wrong to say that his interest or treatment is always, or primarily, classical. None of his plays owes more to classical sources than *Campaspe*, probably his first dramatic work; but to concentrate, as he does, on an obscure incident in Alexander's life, to transform this great warrior into a lover in what is essentially a love story, is hardly a classical method of treatment.[1]

In one important respect, however, Lyly's handling of his material was influenced by classical precept and – incidentally – followed the doctrines of Sidney. There can be no doubt that he was familiar with the dogma of the Three Unities. Admittedly, he does not observe the unities of time and place with the closeness of such early comedies as *Ralph Roister-Doister* or *Gammer Gurton's Needle*; all his plays require a considerable lapse of time, and in *Gallathea* there are two inconsistent time-sequences. But though all his comedies contain diversity of scene, he never, except in *Midas* and *Endymion*, shifts his action far from the neighbourhood of the opening scene, and indeed in *Gallathea*, *Mother Bombie* and *The Woman in the Moon* there is virtually one setting for the entire play. In sum, it may be said that while Lyly often claimed considerable licence from the Unities, in practice he showed more respect for them than did many of his obscure predecessors and most of his more celebrated successors.

The third and most important unity, that of action, involves us in more general features of Lyly's dramatic technique. Apart from the lively and polished prose dialogue that he developed, a stimulating and richly suggestive model for Shakespeare in his comedies, Lyly's chief contribution to English drama was the 'fundamental brainwork'[2] with which he informed his technique. His alert consciousness of design is manifest in numerous directions – in his balancing of characters, his general sense of proportion, his avoidance of undue digressive material, his careful linking of scene with scene and often act with act, his clean and dexterous weaving of plot, and in his increasingly successful attempts to co-ordinate a sub- with a main plot. All these features of Lyly's plays were, at the time when he was writing, technical

[1] This point is developed later in the chapter.
[2] This is a phrase of R. W. Bond's (Vol. II, p. 279). Lyly, he writes, was the 'first in the long roll of Englishmen who have brought to the difficult task of the Playwright the service of a powerful brain, quickened, illuminated, and conducted to a successful issue by a sense of art'. (Vol. II, p. 299.)

achievements of considerable value; and it cannot be doubted that Lyly's sense of artistry was fostered by his knowledge of classical literature in general and of classical drama in particular, whether the latter was familiar to him in its original Latin form or in the sixteenth-century Italian imitations of such writers as Ariosto.

Finally, no reader can fail to notice how his dialogue abounds with Latin tags and with references and allusions to classical writers, stories and legends. It would be difficult to find a page of his text that does not contain some phrase or expression with a classical reminiscence. Even the chatter of his ubiquitous pages is pedantically patched with scraps of Latin and various odds and ends of classical learning.

All these forms of direct classical influence are so palpable that there is no danger of their being underrated. Indeed, the prevailing tendency has been to exaggerate these influences and to represent Lyly's work as a compound of the classics and his own original invention. But this is a distorted and unsatisfactory interpretation, for no less prominent than the classics in his comedies is a deep and sustained impress of the romance tradition.

There is, to begin at the most superficial level, his fondness for a courtly setting and high-born characters – gods, goddesses, kings, queens, princes, and courtiers. Apart from *Mother Bombie*, a marked exception, this is a universal characteristic of his work; and even his more broadly comic sub-plots are, in four[1] out of his eight plays, largely given over to the intrigues and gossip of pages, to characters, that is to say, directly in contact with aristocratic life. His shepherds and foresters too, following the pastoral convention, are more shepherds and foresters in name than in their conversation, behaviour, sentiments and refined breeding. Admittedly, there are characters drawn from other social strata; and he clearly gave a cue to Shakespeare in his comic use of 'low-life' characters, like the Witch in *Endymion*, the barber and huntsman in *Midas*, and the hackneyman and musicians in *Mother Bombie*. But, provided we do not overlook these important exceptions, 'courtly' is the inevitable epithet to apply to the settings and dramatis personæ of his work; and even if this characteristic must be explained by the fact that he was writing for the court, at least it is in harmony with the romance tradition that inspired so much else in his comedy.

Moreover, if most of Lyly's illustrious and refined characters

[1] *Campaspe, Sapho and Phao, Endymion, Midas.*

appear in his plays primarily because he was writing for Elizabeth and her courtiers, some of them might have stepped straight out of the pages of romance. There are the fairies who flit in and out of *Gallathea* and *Endymion*, though they never, as in *A Midsummer Night's Dream*, exercise an important influence on the plot; there are the wise old women – Sybilla in *Sapho and Phao* and Mother Bombie; there is the witch, Dipsas, in *Endymion* and, perhaps most directly from the world of romance, there is Geron, the old hermit of *Endymion*, who lives in a desert place, the guardian of an enchanted fountain.[1] It is also interesting to observe how two of Lyly's characters, Endymion and Alexander, are moulded to an early romantic pattern. All through the play in which he is the main figure, Endymion is manifestly a hero of chivalry, whole-heartedly devoted to the adoration and service of a lady he can never hope to win; and, before the spell is laid upon him, he has retired to the conventional solitary and melancholy life – 'that Endymion, who divorcing himself from the amiableness of all Ladies, the bravery of all Courts, the company of all men, hath chosen in a solitary Cell to live, only by feeding on thy favour, accounting in the world (but thyself) nothing excellent, nothing immortal; thus mayest thou see every vein, sinew, muscle, and artery of my love, in which there is no flattery, nor deceit, error, nor art'.[2] And once at least before the end of the play he flashes before our eyes as the romantic knightly lover not only in sentiment but in very shape and substance: 'Am I that Endymion who was wont in Court to lead my life, and in jousts, tourneys, and arms to exercise my youth?'[3]

An even more striking example of the romance type is the figure of Alexander in *Campaspe*. This classical hero is completely metamorphosed into a chivalric knight, who 'thirsteth after honour', is scrupulously respectful of the honour of ladies and treats them generously when they fall into his hands as captives through the fortunes of war, and who, like Valentine in *The Two Gentlemen of Verona*, is willing without jealousy to surrender his lady to a rival. The chiming of romantic key-words, at least in the opening scene of *Campaspe*, is quite remarkable: in the very

---

[1] Sir Tophas, though his name has a reminiscent ring, and though, as Bond demonstrates, he is modelled to some extent on Chaucer's Sir Thopas, does not come into this category. He is much nearer to the classical *miles gloriosus* than to any medieval knight, and, as will be shown, Lyly uses him for a burlesque of romantic love.
[2] *Endymion*, II. i. 39-44.
[3] Ibid., v. i. 60-61.

first words of the play Alexander is presented to us not merely as a great conqueror, but as a lord of 'courtesie',[1] while there is much play with the word 'honour'.

Usually the plots of Lyly's comedies are slight and attenuated. But what there is of them is strongly infused with romantic ingredients. Though there is no trace of the 'derring-do' element, which anyhow did not lend itself happily to dramatic presentation, there is an abundance of other types of romantic material – love stories (frequently love at first sight), sorcery, disguises, transformations, magic spells, dreams, monsters, witches and fairies. The briefest summary of the plays will indicate the markedly romantic nature of Lyly's narrative. *Campaspe* is a love-tale of a painter and one of Alexander's captives, with Alexander first a rival, then a match-maker in the affair. *Sapho and Phao* depicts the havoc wrought in the love-sick hearts of a queen and a goddess by a young ferryman, magically transformed by Venus into a figure of irresistible male beauty. In *Gallathea* two maidens, disguised as youths to avoid becoming tributes to a sea-monster, fall in love, and the dilemma is solved by Venus, who promises to turn one of them into a man. *Endymion* tells of a young man who, having been cast into a forty-year spell of life-in-death sleep, is rescued by the loyalty of a friend who discovers the way to save him through the oracle of an enchanted fountain. *Midas* is the story of that king's gold-transforming touch and ass's ears; and in *Mother Bombie* we have two instances of true love emerging triumphant from a tangle in which four mercenary-minded old men are foiled in their match-making schemes for their children. In *The Woman in the Moon* the story (mainly a love one) tells of a woman created by Nature and falling in turn under the influence of the seven planets. In *Love's Metamorphosis* three nymphs are changed into a rock, a rose and a bird by Cupid for their scornful attitude to love; a farmer is punished for wantonly hewing down a tree in which a nymph was imprisoned; and his daughter, a faithful lover, saves her sweetheart from the wiles of a Siren. Six out of the eight plays have happy endings, while the majority of those that have an important love-interest conclude with marriage, though Lyly never idealises marriage in the loftiest, late romantic manner.

---

[1] 'Parmenio, I cannot tell whether I should more commend in Alexander's victories, courage, or courtesy, in the one being a resolution without fear, in the other a liberality above custom.' (*Campaspe*, I. i. 1-4.)

There is also a prominent pastoral element in the setting and story of several of these plays. In *Gallathea* and *Love's Metamorphosis* (both of which may be correctly described as pastoral dramas), and to a lesser extent in *Midas* and *The Woman in the Moon*, we find several or most of the pastoral conventions – the open-air setting of woods and fields, the figures of nymphs, shepherds and foresters (usually speaking the refined language of courtiers and romantic lovers)[1], references to the business of hunting and sheep-tending, the singing contests, set debates and discussions, especially on love, and stories of unrequited love.

Beyond these simple and easily definable romantic elements in his comedy, there is an obvious kinship between its spirit and the spirit of romance. Though this resemblance is certainly not the least in importance, it is a vague and elusive quality that does not admit of brief or precise definition. To a large extent (and possibly because the spirit we are dealing with is a superficial one) we must express the similitudes in negatives; like so much romantic literature Lyly's plays are never penetrating in their psychology or moral implications, never preoccupied with human suffering, never bitter, sharply satirical, socially reformative, brutal, or realistic. Yet some of the affinities that we can point to are positive enough: there is the pure entertainment, the allegory, the frequency of the happy ending, and the reflection of a courtly, sophisticated, highly civilised mode of life. And, above all, there is the illusion of an artificial world dominated by love, the love of youth and courtship.

§

It is precisely because the main ingredient of his comedy of delight was love that Lyly played such an outstanding part in assimilating romance to Elizabethan drama. In his prologue to *Midas* he wrote, 'Comedies, their subject is love', and that definition fairly covers the bulk of his own plays. However, this simple description requires at least two important qualifications. In the first place, the strength of the ingredient varies considerably from play to play: in *Campaspe* the love story of Apelles and Campaspe, with Alexander making the third, if ineffectual, point of the triangle, provides the main substance of the plot: 'We

---

[1] I cannot accept Bond's conclusion that 'the pastoral talk of Lyly's nymphs, shepherds and foresters is fairly distinguished from that of his courtiers'. (Vol. II, p. 250.)

calling Alexander from his grave, seek only who was his love',
explains Lyly simply in the *Court Prologue*. So too, in *Endymion*,
Tellus' love for Endymion and Endymion's for Cynthia are the
two main pivots of the story. In *Midas*, on the other hand, apart
from a very brief passage between Eristus and Caelia (Act II,
Scene 1) the love-interest is non-existent. The importance of
love in the rest of the plays varies between these extremes. In the
second place, while there are several scenes of direct love-making
in Lyly, love as he presents it is in the main an engrossing sentiment for discussion and dissection rather than an intense passion
flowering in scenes of lyrical courtship. Conversation about love,
not wooing, is Lyly's natural bent.

This amatory discussion and conversation is richly and indelibly
coloured with romantic sentiments and conventions,[1] particularly
with those of the post-Petrarchian period. In *Campaspe*, for example,
the cult of dejection – eternal vows, heart-consuming sighs, bouts
of melancholy – is notably prominent:

Campaspe: How is she [Venus] hired: by prayer, by sacrifice, or bribes?
Apelles: By prayer, sacrifice, and bribes.
Campaspe: What prayer?
Apelles: Vows irrevocable.
Campaspe: What sacrifice?
Apelles: Hearts ever sighing, never dissembling.[2]

What Apelles preaches he practises:

Now must I paint things impossible for mine art, but agreeable
with my affections: deep and hollow sighs, sad and melancholy
thoughts, wounds and slaughters of conceits, a life posting to death;[3]

and again:

Thy pale looks when he blushed, thy sad countenance when he
smiled, thy sighs when he questioned, may breed in him a jealousy,
perchance a frenzy.[4]

[1] There is also a similar colouring in the two parts of *Euphues*. Thus Philautus'
letters to Camilla abound in the stock phraseology – 'fayre lady', 'service', 'curtesie',
'duty', 'devotion', and so on.
[2] *Campaspe*, III. iii. 34-39.
[3] Ibid., III. v. 44-47.
[4] Ibid., v. ii. 5-8.

The Comedies of Lyly

Even the stout Alexander, if we are to believe the report of Clitus, falls at times into the conventional dumps:

> I cannot tell how it cometh to pass, that in Alexander nowadays there groweth an impatient kind of life: in the morning he is melancholy, at noon solemn, at all times either more sour or severe, than he was accustomed.[1]

From *Sapho and Phao*, setting aside the moping melancholy of love, which, along with the knowledge of Phao's low birth, brings Sapho to her sick bed, we may isolate another familiar, inflated note – the divinity of love – as rhapsodised by Phao:

> O divine love! and therefore divine, because love, whose duty no conceit can compass, and therefore no authority can constrain; as miraculous in working as mighty, and no more to be supressed than comprehended. How now Phao, whither art thou carried, committing idolatory with that God, whom thou hast cause to blaspheme? O Sapho! fair Sapho![2]

Gallathea contains another excellent specimen of the sighing and lugubrious vein, of oaths and prayers:

> *Phillida:* Suppose I were a virgin (I blush in supposing myself one) and that under the habit of a boy were the person of a maid, if I should utter my affections with sighs, manifest my sweet love by my salt tears, and prove my loyalty unspotted, and my griefs intolerable, would not then that fair face pity this true heart?
>
> *Gallathea:* Admit that I were as you would have me suppose that you are, and that I should with entreaties, prayers, oaths, bribes, and whatever can be invented in love, desire your favour, would you not yield?[3]

Even when we allow for the alleged flattery of Elizabeth, *Endymion*, in its whole design, with Endymion utterly devoted to the service and adoration of his lady, is so palpably an expression of romantic sentiment that illustration is almost superfluous. One sample will suffice for a tightly-woven harmony of those notes we have already indicated in the other plays and for an expression

---

[1] *Campaspe*, III. iv. 1-4.
[2] *Sapho and Phao*, II. iv. 14-20.
[3] *Gallathea*, III. ii. 17-25.

of two other points of the romantic love-code – the tasks and trials the genuine lover must essay to show his prowess, and the cultivation of solitude. Endymion is soliloquising:

> There is no Mountain so steep that I will not climb, no monster so cruel that I will not tame, no action so desperate that I will not attempt. Desirest thou the passions of love, the sad and melancholy moods of perplexed minds, the not-to-be expressed torments of racked thoughts? Behold my sad tears, my deep sighs, my hollow eyes, my broken sleeps, my heavy countenance. Wouldst thou have me vowed only to thy beauty? and consume every minute of time in thy service? Remember my solitary life, almost these seven years: whom have I entertained but my own thoughts, and thy virtues? What company have I used but contemplation? . . . I am that Endymion . . . whose eyes never esteemed anything fair but thy face, whose tongue termed nothing rare but thy virtues, and whose heart imagined nothing miraculous but thy government. Yea, that Endymion, who divorcing himself from the amiableness of all ladies, the bravery of all Courts, the company of all men, hath chosen in a solitary Cell to live, only by feeding on thy favour, accounting in the world (but thyself) nothing excellent, nothing immortal.[1]

And there is another important item in the romantic code clearly expressed in this play – that of secrecy.[2] Eumenides has not only remained faithful to Semele through the years of empty waiting; he has kept his passion to himself:

> How secret hast thou been these seven years, that hast not, nor once darest not, to name her, for discontenting her.[3]

This resolution he firmly keeps till Endymion reveals the name of the mistress for him.

In *Midas*, *Mother Bombie* and *The Woman in the Moon*, since the straightforward love-interest is so slight, there is not so much of the romantic love liturgy, though there are some echoes in a snatch of dialogue between Eristus and Caelia, as for instance in:

> My tears which have made furrows in my cheeks, and in mine eyes fountains; my sighs, which have made of my heart a furnace,

[1] *Endymion*, II. i. 6-42.
[2] Cf. *Euphues and his England*, Vol. II, p. 176: 'For what is there in the world that more delighteth a lover than secrecy, which is void of fear, without suspicion, free from envy: the only hope a woman hath to build both her honour and honesty upon.'
[3] *Endymion*, III. iv. 53-55.

and kindled in my head flames: my body that melteth by piecemeal, and my mind that pineth at an instant, may witness that my love is both unspotted and unspeakable.[1]

In *Mother Bombie* it is interesting to note how freely Candius paraphrases Ovid into romantic parlance:

Livia: Is there art in love?
Candius: A short art and a certain, three rules in three lines.
Livia: I pray thee repeat them.
Candius: Principio quod amare velis repirire labora,
Proximus huic labor est placidam exorare puellam,
Tertius ut longo tempore duret amor.
Livia: I am no Latinist, Candius, you must conster it.
Candius: So I will, and pace it too: ... First, one must find out a mistress whom before all others he voweth to serve. Secondly, that he use all means that he may to obtain her. And the last, with deserts, faith, and secrecy, to study to keep her.[2]

Also *The Woman in the Moon* contains a good example of the romantic trial of prowess: certainly the quest is only a wild boar's head, and the episode is treated in a comic spirit; but Pandora is keeping up the convention when she promises that the successful one of her shepherd lovers shall wear her glove in his hat.

Finally, we may notice two brief passages in *Love's Metamorphosis*:

Ceres: What is the substance of love?
Cupid: Constancy and secrecy.
Ceres: What the signs?
Cupid: Sighs and tears.[3]
Cupid: What have you used in love?
Ramis: All things that may procure love – gifts, words, oaths, sighs, and swoonings.
Cupid: What said they of gifts?
Montanus: That affection could not be bought with gold.
Cupid: What of words?
Ramis: That they were golden blasts, out of leaden bellows.
Cupid: What of oaths?
Silvestris: That Jupiter never sware true to Juno.

[1] *Midas*, II. i. 29-34.
[2] *Mother Bombie*, I. iii. 133-144.
[3] *Love's Metamorphosis*, II. i. 104-107.

Cupid: What of sighs?
Silvestris: That deceit kept a forge in the heart of fools.
Cupid: What of swoonings?
Montanus: Nothing, but that they wished them deaths.[1]

Assembling these passages, we have a full and revealing anatomy of romantic love, particularly of love as it had been refined and sentimentalised by Petrarch and his successors – of courtship as a serious, perhaps the most serious, part of human experience, of utter devotion and unswerving loyalty ('vows irrevocable'), though the lover's suit may be vain, of love as a sweet torment, where the true lover can hardly hope to escape profound fits of melancholy ('tears' and 'sighs'), of solitariness, secrecy and testing. All that is notably absent, though there are some formal and superficial traces of the attitude, is the conception of human love as a type of divine love and an induction to it. Beyond any doubt, the amatory dialogue of his comedies proves Lyly to have been deeply and continuously influenced by the romance tradition.

But there is more to Lyly's treatment of love than this. A careful reading of the plays will reveal another attitude to love, not only different from the romantic conception, but at many points sharply antithetical to it.[2]

This contradiction in Lyly's sentiments is exposed most plainly in *The Woman in the Moon*, the chief substance of which is a revelation of woman in her most unattractive moods. In turn Pandora is moody and melancholy, imperious and proud, an irascible termagant, wanton and deceitful, restless, fickle and inconstant – such an impossible character indeed that in the end all the Utopian shepherds, her own husband included, renounce her. It might, of course, be argued that Pandora is a puppet tied to the strings of the various planets who successfully transform her to their whims and wishes. But no one was responsible for that necessity but Lyly himself, and certainly the conclusion of the play seems to point to a satirical intention on the author's part and to Pandora as a typical representative of her sex:

> Now rule, Pandora, in fair Cynthia's stead,
> And make the moon inconstant like thyself;
> Reign thou at women's nuptials, and their birth;

[1] *Love's Metamorphosis*, IV. i. 64-76.
[2] See additional note (*b*), p. 202.

> Let them be mutable in all their loves,
> Fantastical, childish, and foolish, in their desires,
> Demanding toys:
> And stark mad when they cannot have their wills.

However we interpret this passage, it is certainly not the work of a whole-hearted Petrarchian.

This strongly censorious attitude to women, more pronounced than anything usually found in romance writers, though these often represent women as proud, cruel and disdainful, often approaches flat misogyny and can be observed frequently in Lyly's writing. It is strongly concentrated in his earliest work, the first part of *Euphues*, and is present, in disguised undertones, in the second part,[1] in spite of the ostentatious apologies and protests to the women of England that the author was concerned with Italian ladies. It is also a recurrent note in the comedies. In *Campaspe*, for instance, Hephestion is allowed a lengthy diatribe against women when he is endeavouring to persuade Alexander from his love-fancies; and the source of his contempt is not merely that Campaspe is a captive and of low birth, but that she is a woman:

> Ermines have fair skins but foul livers; Sepulchres fresh colours, but rotten bones; women fair faces, but false hearts;[2]

– a platitude perhaps, but freshly and violently coloured by the imagery of euphuistic parallelism. Nor will Hephestion have any truck with the romantic deification of women; his catalogue of Campaspe's undoubted perfections is brought crudely and deliberately to earth:

> Though she have heavenly gifts, virtue and beauty, is she not of earthly metal, flesh and blood?[3]

Similar sentiments might be instanced from other plays, especially from *Love's Metamorphosis*, while the odious Pandora of *The Woman in the Moon* may be paired with the venomous figure of Tellus in *Endymion*.

---

[1] As Bond points out (Vol. I, pp. 161-2), the Euphues of the second part is a figure 'bitterly cynical at first, taking a somewhat melancholy pleasure in observing the workings of a passion in which he has no further share'. Euphues is, as Bond suggestively demonstrates, a prototype of Shakespeare's Jaques.

[2] *Campaspe*, II. ii. 55-57.

[3] Ibid., II. ii. 68-70.

Nor is it merely in his unflattering picture of feminine temperament that Lyly breaks from the romantic tradition. Whereas in the romantic writers woman's physical beauty was a major postulate, in Lyly feminine charms evoke few lyrical passages – certainly fewer than in Shakespeare. More striking still, there is both in *Euphues* and the plays a frequent emphasis on the swift transformation of physical beauty into ugliness and loathsomeness:[1]

> Beauty is a slippery good, which decreaseth whilst it is increasing, resembling the medlar, which in the moment of his full ripeness is known to be in a rottenness. Whiles you look in the glass, it waxeth old with time; if on the Sun, parched with heat; if on the wind, blasted with cold. A great care to keep it, a short space to enjoy it, a sudden time to lose it.[2]

Of course the note of beauty's transience was a monotonous one in the French sonneteers and their Elizabethan imitators. We find it in Spenser:

> For that same goodly hue of white and red,
> With which the cheeks are sprinkled, shall decay,
> And those sweet rosy leaves, so fairly spread
> Upon the lips, shall fade and fall away
> To that they were, even to corrupted clay.
> That golden wire, those sparkling stars so bright,
> Shall turn to dust, and lose their goodly light.[3]

But where with such writers as Spenser the stress was chiefly on the transience of beauty, with Lyly the emphasis fell rather on the final images of decay – the crow's foot in the eyes and the black oxen on the foot.[4] It is this obsession with beauty's corruption that flaws for a modern sensibility, less robust or crude than the Elizabethan, the farce of Sir Tophas' infatuation. Sir Tophas'

---

[1] Further, there is in *Euphues and his England* at least one explicit rejection of the neo-platonic conception of beauty: 'Believe me the qualities of the mind, the beauty of the body, either in man or woman, are but the sauce to whet our stomachs, not the meat to fill them. For they that live by the view of beauty still look very lean, and they that feed only upon virtue at board, will go with a hungry belly to bed.' (Vol. II, p. 160.)

[2] *Sapho and Phao*, II. i. 100-106.

[3] *Hymn in Honour of Beauty*, 92-98.

[4] Two common and combined images in Lyly; e.g. *Love's Metamorphosis* (IV, i, 134-138): 'Let all ladies beware to offend those in spite, that love them in honour; for when the Crow shall set his foot in their eye, and the black ox tread on their foot, they shall find their misfortunes to be equal with their deformities, and men both to loathe and laugh at them.'

lyrical and grotesque catalogue of Dipsas' decrepitudes is funny in a way,[1] but it also leaves a bad taste. Even less pleasant is his resolution, when he hears that Dipsas has been restored to her rightful husband, to court none but old hags:

> I desire old Matrons. What a sight would it be to embrace one whose hair was as orient as the pearl! whose teeth shall be so pure a watchet, that they shall stain the purest turquoise! whose nose shall throw more beams from it than the fiery carbuncle! whose eyes shall be environed about with redness exceeding the deepest Coral! And whose lips might compare with silver for paleness![2]

It is not easy to account for this misogynist tendency that conflicts so sharply with the romantic elements in Lyly's work. Perhaps it was derived to some extent from his classical reading; more probably from Guevara, whose work, known to Lyly through North's translation,[3] was so closely imitated in *Euphues, Part I*. Also one suspects that it was not merely a literary pose but had its roots in Lyly's own psychology and experience. But, whatever its origins, this anti-romantic attitude towards women brought Lyly into obvious opposition with the romance tradition at two other points.

In the first place, we may observe in his writings sketches of a mode of love-making and courtship that is, by implication, a complete rejection of the spiritualised and sentimentalised fashion of romantic wooing. This mode we might describe as the machiavellian tactic of love-making: it is realistic, cynical, ruthless, egoistic, and quite divorced from any moral or spiritual sentiments. Woman, so its logic runs, is shallow, inconstant and filled with vanity; hence, to capture her, the successful lover must calculate, flatter, and deceive, and he is justified in using every trick and wile since women themselves set the example and are capricious and deceitful to the point of disdaining those who love them most.[4] An unusually sustained expression of this doctrine is Sibilla's advice to Phao:

> Flatter, I mean lie: little things catch light minds, and fancy is a worm, that feedeth first upon fennel. Imagine with thyself all are to be won.... It is impossible for the brittle metal of woman to

[1] *Endymion*, III. iii. 50 ff.
[2] Ibid., v. ii. 94-100.
[3] *The Dial of Princes* (1557).
[4] Cf. *Euphues*: 'they disdain them most that most desire them'.

withstand the flattering attempts of man. . . . Oh simple women! that are brought rather to believe what their ears hear of flattering men, than what their eyes see in true glasses.[1]

Occasionally Lyly's rejection of the romantic code of courtship is explicit rather than implicit. Twice at least, like Shakespeare after him, he aims at producing comedy by a burlesque of romantic courtship. The most obvious instance of this is Sir Tophas' fantastic infatuation for Dipsas, which is clearly to be taken as a parody of Endymion's soulful devotion to Cynthia.[2] A similar piece of burlesque occurs in *Mother Bombie* (Act II, Scene 3). In this scene Candius, true to the romantic convention, falls immediately in love with Silena's beauty, and, promising to 'practise all the art of love', at once tries to court her in the authentic romance language of 'I will always call on such a Saint that hath power to release my sorrows; yield, fair creature, to love'. But he is soon put clean out of his stride by Silena's rambling, half-witted talk, and the incident collapses into what Lyly intended as farce.[3]

With, at times, a misogynist picture of women and a cynical or humorous attitude towards courtship, it is not surprising to find that Lyly frequently opposes the romance tradition with a denigration of love itself. In this, three arguments constantly recur: that love is merely the product of idleness, a diversion from the serious affairs of life; that essentially, and stripped of its fine trimmings, it is often merely lust; and that its end is frequently disillusionment and unhappiness. Thus Alexander, after toying with love himself, admits its triviality: 'It is a children's game, a life for seamsters and scholars; the one pricking in clouts have nothing else to think on, the other pricking fancies out of books, have little else to marvel at'.[4] Hephestion in the same play, defining love as 'a word by superstition thought a god, by use turned

---

[1] *Sapho and Phao*, II. iv. 60-73. See also the following long speech where Sibilla describes the successful tactics of deceit and opportunism (l. 76 ff.).

[2] Lyly also uses the pages as a medium for the mocking and sceptical attitude. See especially Act II, Scene 2.

[3] It is worth noting in this connection that Lyly's work contains several digs at verse-writing as a part of courtship. See Parmenio's first speech in *Campaspe*, IV. iii.; *Gallathea*, III. iv. 46-68; and the following passage from *Euphues*, Vol. I, p. 252: 'What greater infamy than to confer the sharp wit to the making of lewd sonnets; to the idolatrous worshipping of their ladies, to the vain delights of fancy, to all kind of vice as it were against kind and course of nature.'

[4] *Campaspe*, v. iv. 135-138.

to a humour, by self-will made a flattering madness',[1] is more severe in his strictures: 'There is no surfeit so dangerous as that of honey, nor any poison so deadly as that of love; in the one physic cannot prevail, nor in the other counsel.'[2] Geron, sharing the sentiments of Alexander, rates love low beside true friendship: 'Love is a chameleon, which draweth nothing into the mouth but air, and nourisheth nothing in the body but lungs. . . . Desire dies in the same moment that Beauty sickens, and Beauty fadeth in the same instant that it flourisheth. When adversities flow, then love ebbs; but friendship standeth stiffly in storms.'[3] Diana reproves her infatuated nymphs to the strain of: 'You should think love like Homer's Moly, a white leaf and a black root, a fair show and a bitter taste. Of all trees the Cedar is greatest, and hath the smallest seeds: of all affections, love hath the greatest name, and the least virtue.'[4] And Martius castigates love as an enervating lust: 'Thy effeminate mind, Eristus . . . hath bred in all the court such a tender wantonness, that nothing is thought of but love, a passion proceeding of beastly lust, and coloured with the courtly name of love.'[5]

Since all these quotations are taken from the plays, we must not assume that they necessarily express Lyly's own conclusions. Martius, for instance, is a puppet, always speaking to his part as a warrior. Further, it is likely that the sentiments on love put into the mouth of Diana, Sapho and Cynthia were composed especially for the ear of Elizabeth, who, if she did not altogether disapprove of love, at least was often jealous of the love affairs of her courtiers and believed they should be under her own strict, if capricious, prerogative. But, with these allowances, we may fairly conclude from the plays that Lyly was conscious of an attitude towards love quite different from the romantic conception, and that there were perhaps times when this non- or anti-romantic outlook had his sympathy.

The significance of these generalisations on the conflicting attitudes to love evident in Lyly's plays may be sharpened and

[1] *Campaspe*, v. iv. 35-36.
[2] Ibid., II. ii. 73-76.
[3] *Endymion*, III. iv. 129-134.
[4] *Gallathea*, III. iv. 23-27. See also lines 41-46: 'Cast before your eyes the loves of Venus' trolls, their fortunes, their fancies, their ends. What are they else but Silenus' pictures: without, Lambs and Doves, within, Apes and Owls; who like Ixion embrace clouds for Juno, the shadows of virtue instead of the substance. Eagles' feathers consume the feathers of all others, and love's desire corrupteth all other virtues.'
[5] *Midas*, II. i. 59-63.

clarified by a closer focus on particular scenes. One especially apposite scene is the interview between Endymion and Tellus.[1]

This scene opens with a long soliloquy of Endymion, and most of this is pure romance rhetoric – the heavenly beauty of Cynthia, Endymion's eagerness to submit himself to any task for proving his prowess, his sighs and tears, his vows and service, his seven years' retreat into a solitary cell: 'thus mayest thou see every vein, sinew, muscle, and artery of my love, in which there is no flattery, no deceit, error, nor art'.[2] 'No flattery, no deceit' – it all seems the quintessence of the spiritual, disingenuous doctrine of romantic love. But not quite. When it serves his purpose Endymion does not contemn the machiavellian tactic of love. In the middle of his soliloquy he frankly admits, 'With Tellus, fair Tellus, have I dissembled, using her but as a cloak for my affections, that others seeing my mangled and disordered mind, might think it were for one that loveth me, not for Cynthia, whose perfections alloweth no companion, nor comparison;'[3] and, as he sees Tellus approach, he again announces his policy of double-dealing: 'I must turn my other face to her like Janus, lest she be suspicious as Juno.'[4]

We can sympathise with Endymion's behaviour, pursued as he is by a dangerous and passionate woman for whom he has no real affection. But the true romantic or chivalric hero would hardly stoop to dissembling; certainly he would not utter such warm and energetic protestations of insincere love. Earlier Tellus has complained of Endymion's feigned passion – 'Were thy oaths without number, thy kisses without measure, thy sighs without end, forged to deceive a poor credulous virgin?'[5] – and the scene we are examining proves that she had grounds for her complaint. Immediately she taxes him with his melancholy fancies he lies monstrously to her in the grand romantic manner: 'You know (fair Tellus) that the sweet remembrance of your love, is the only companion of my life, and thy presence, my paradise: so that I am not alone when nobody is with me, and in heaven itself when thou art with me.'[6] Nor would a lover of the perfect romantic type, taxed with deception, evade the issue so craftly or uncourteously as Endymion does when he tries to palm off dissembling as a

[1] *Endymion*, II. i.
[2] Ibid., II. i. 43-45.
[3] Ibid., 22-26.
[4] Ibid., 45-46.
[5] Ibid., I. ii. 7-8.
[6] Ibid., II. i. 53-56.

common vice of the female sex.[1] The nearest Endymion comes again to the doctrine of his opening soliloquy is when he tries to preserve the secrecy of his real love, though plainly this is not the genuine secrecy of his friend, Eumenides.

§

In both style and substance, then, Lyly's comedies reveal the influence not only of classical literature but also of the complex romantic tradition.[2] On the whole, the blending of these two disparate traditions is felicitous and successful, and, elaborated by Lyly's own bright, alert, and superficial intellect, this blend is the primary constituent of England's first substantial 'comedy of delight'. Intrinsically, this comedy may not be of great value, but without the inspiration of its experiments it is doubtful whether Shakespeare's comedy would have achieved such brilliant heights. However, in one major respect, in the treatment of love, where Lyly draws most heavily of all on the romance tradition, there is a sharp, unresolved conflict and contradiction between romantic conceptions and an attitude that, if it cannot be strictly defined as classical, is obviously not that of romance, the Italian poets or of the contemporary Petrarchians.

[1] Tellus, also, all too aware of Endymion's deception, and sparring with him through the scene, is hardly a romance type.
[2] There were, of course, a number of single plays before Lyly, like Edwards' *Damon and Pithias* and Gascoigne's *Supposes*, that were infused with romantic elements.

CHAPTER THREE

THE COMEDIES OF GREENE

AMONG ELIZABETHAN dramatists it was the writers of comedy[1] and tragi-comedy rather than those of tragedy who found the spirit of romance congenial and stimulating; and if – as seems inevitable – we continue to use the word 'romantic' in speaking of Elizabethan and Jacobean tragedy, its application must be altogether looser than when we are employing it with reference to comedy and tragi-comedy. So, among Shakespeare's predecessors, neither Marlowe nor Kyd is of much consequence in the assimilation of romance to drama. With Lyly, the figure who stands out most conspicuously for his part in this fusion is Greene, another writer of comedy.

Where Lyly was a maker of plots, Greene, setting an example for his successors, was a confirmed borrower, and for the substance of his narratives he went frequently to romantic sources. The stories of *Alphonsus, King of Arragon* and of *A Looking-Glass for London* (written in collaboration with Lodge) appear to have been largely original inventions, though *Tamburlaine* was certainly at Greene's elbow when he was writing *Alphonsus*. But in *Orlando Furioso*, which is probably the third of his surviving plays, he took a large draught from the stream of the Italian romantic epic; and in spite of considerable transformations, his action unmistakably follows Ariosto's poem of the same name, his Italian quotation[2] suggesting that he had read it in the original. In the composition of *James IV* he tapped another Italian source of romance, since much of his material is derived from Cinthio's *Hecatommithi*; and while he freely adapted his source, notably in his treatment of the villain Ateukin, who is a compound of pseudo-machiavellianism,[3] the Terentian flatterer, and the medieval wizard, his play is much closer to Cinthio's story than *Orlando Furioso* is to Ariosto's poem.

---

[1] This word is used in the wide Elizabethan sense of plays that end happily, with probably, though not necessarily, a certain amount of humorous material.

[2] *Orlando Furioso*, II. i. 685-692. Churton Collins, whose text of Greene's *Plays and Poems* is followed in this chapter, is of the opinion that Greene owed nothing to Harington's translation (1591), though he may have read it.

[3] See *James IV*, III. ii. 1227-1228: *Ateukin:* Where be my writings I put in my pocket last night? *Andrew:* Which, sir? your annotations upon Machiavel?

Nor, at this admittedly superficial level of origins, is Greene important merely for his work in putting Elizabethan drama in touch with Italian forms of the romantic tradition. He also successfully utilised native sources. In *Friar Bacon and Friar Bungay*, apart from the love-story, which he probably invented,[1] he borrowed all the other important episodes from an old English romance that Collins surmises was first written down at the end of the sixteenth century.[2] And if *The Pinner of Wakefield* is really Greene's work, here again he attempted to dramatise two other popular figures of English medieval romance and legend – George, the proverbial strong-armed Pinner of Wakefield and Robin Hood.[3]

Part of Greene's borrowings took him back to the oldest strata of romance, to what he himself describes as 'doughty deeds and valiant victories'. In *Alphonsus* his hero is a bold knight who, in a loose sequence of tedious scenes, re-establishes his right to the crown of Arragon 'achieved with honour in the field', conquers the Pagan dogs, and forces Amurack, Emperor of the Turks, to give him his amazonian daughter in marriage, with a promise of inheritance to the empire. This story, which contained enough fighting and sword-play to satisfy the most avid of Elizabethan appetites, is distinguished from similar tales of violent physical action, popular in every age, and including Marlowe's *Tamburlaine*, by its vaguely medieval setting and the medieval colouring of the language: the characters are constantly alluded to as 'knights', while resounding words of the old chivalric tradition like 'prowess', 'honour' and 'courtesy' crop up from time to time, as in the lines:

> Nor do I scorn, thou goddess, for to stain
> My prowess with thee, although it be a shame
> For knights to combat with the female sect.[4]

Much of the narrative of *Orlando Furioso*, with its knightly hero, Orlando, one of the twelve peers of Charlemagne, is of the same

[1] It is just possible that the story was taken from *Fair Em*. But the borrowing was probably the other way round.

[2] There is no certainty that Greene was familiar with this written version of the romance. The first printed edition, entitled *The Famous History of Friar Bacon*, is dated 1627.

[3] The chief literary sources of this play are the ballad – *The Jolly Pinder of Wakefield* and *The Famous History of George a Green*. There is a MS. version of the latter that Collins dates from the late sixteenth or early seventeenth century, but there is no evidence of a printed version in the Elizabethan period.

[4] *Alphonsus*, v. ii. 1595-1597.

kind. Hardly has Orlando been accepted by Angelica, daughter of the Emperor of Africa, as her future husband, when he is busy capturing a castle and putting to flight two of his disgruntled fellow-suitors. During his madness he kills Brandemart, one of these two rivals, in single combat; and later, when his wits have been restored, he slays in the same fashion Sacrepant, the author of all his misfortunes, and, as champion of Angelica's honour, measures swords with three of the peers of France. As in *Alphonsus*, most of these episodes are lightly embroidered with chivalric clichés.

However, this element of 'derring-do' in Greene's work is not of much account; there was little future for it in Elizabethan drama, and in *Orlando Furioso* it merges indistinguishably with the *Tamburlaine* motif. Much more important for the assimilation of romance to drama was Greene's attempt to put on to the stage stories of love adventure; and it was Greene rather than Lyly who first achieved impressive success in writing comedies that had a serious and substantial tale of human lovers as their core.

Even in *Orlando Furioso* the doughty deeds are subordinate to the love-story. This relates how Orlando, drawn far away from Charlemagne's court by the 'fame of fair Angelica', wins her favour against a host of princely rivals, who in the manner of knights, ready to fight for their lady in the lists, have arrived in Africa, 'to seek and sue for fair Angelica'. There is the familiar romantic crossing of true love: Sacrepant, whose own advances to Angelica are honourably repelled, manages by trickery to persuade Orlando that Angelica has another lover, with the result that Orlando is driven into madness through jealousy, and the unfortunate Angelica exiled by her father. But in the end all comes right in the usual romantic fashion: Orlando is cured of his lunacy by an enchantress and given a true account of Sacrepant's villainy; he arrives in the nick of time to vindicate Angelica's honour when she is about to be burnt by the peers of France; and, of course, the two lovers are reconciled and reunited.

There is a similar dramatisation of love adventures, with play on suspense and surprise, in Greene's two best works, *Friar Bacon and Friar Bungay* and *James IV*. The story of the latter in particular resembles that of several of Shakespeare's romances and romantic comedies, notably that of *Cymbeline*, for the heroine, Queen Dorothea, is forced to flee from court disguised as a young man in order to escape her husband's murderous intentions, is saved from death by the good knight, Sir Cuthbert, and in the end, when war breaks out between her husband and father, restores the peace by revealing herself and is reconciled to her repentant husband.

In all these love-tales that Greene dramatised there is, however, a striking absence of one outstanding romantic characteristic – courtship. There is no love-making at all in *Orlando*, where even Sacrepant, who needs all his powers of persuasion, refuses to play the role of the conventional lover in his attempt to win Angelica:

> Then know, my love, I cannot paint my grief,
> Nor tell a tale of Venus and her son,
> Reporting such a catalogue of toys:
> It fits not Sacrepant to be effeminate.[1]

In *Friar Bacon*, though there was obvious and abundant scope for courtship in the love-story had Greene wished to present it, there is singularly little. Prince Edward's love-making with Margaret is merely reported, while his wooing of Princess Elinor is of a purely ceremonial and public kind, larded with classical allusion:

> But see, Venus appears,
> Or one that overmatcheth Venus in her shape.
> Sweet Elinor, beauty's high-swelling pride,
> Rich nature's glory, and her wealth at once:
> Fair of all fairs, welcome to Albion.[2]

Even in the central episode of the love-story, Lacy's winning of Margaret, there is only a brief snatch of courtship, which (revealed through Bacon's magic glass) is broken by the presence and intrusion of Friar Bungay. In *James IV* the love-making between Eustace and Ida is a little more prominent, though even this is not much more noticeable than the discussion between the Countess of Arran and Eustace on the business side of her daughter's marriage.

---

[1] *Orlando Furioso*, II. i. 443-446.
[2] *Friar Bacon*, III. ii. 1274-1278. Much less dramatically appropriate are some of Margaret's lines in the classical vein, e.g.:

> How different is this farmer from the rest ...
> Proportioned as was Paris, when, in grey,
> He courted Oenon in the vale by Troy.
>   I. iii. 406-412.

Moreover, what courtship there is bears little trace of the romantic conventions and of the romantic attitude to love that we find in Lyly's plays. Orlando is described, and to some extent shown, in the manner of the romantic lover:

> Hard by, for solace, in a secret grove,
> The County once a day fails not to walk:
> There solemnly he ruminates his love.[1]

There is a hint of the convention of the lover's sleepless vigils in Lacy's remark:

> Thus watchful are such men as live in love,
> Whose eyes brook broken slumbers for their sleep.[2]

But, with one important and well-sustained exception, there is not much else. This exception, which, preluding many similar passages in Shakespeare, contains distinct traces of romantic sentiment and love-parlance, occurs in the first encounter of Ida and Eustace when Ida is busy with her needlework:

> *Eust.:* What work you here, fair Mistress? may I see it?
> *Ida:* Good sir, look on: how like you this compact?
> *Eust.:* Methinks in this I see true love in act:
> The woodbines with their leaves do sweetly spread,
> The roses blushing prank them in their red;
> No flower but boasts the beauties of the spring;
> This bird hath life indeed, if it could sing. –
> What means, fair Mistress, had you in this work?
> *Ida:* My needle, sir.
> *Eust.:* In needles, then, there lurks
> Some hidden grace, I deem, beyond my reach.
> *Ida:* Not grace in them, good sir, but those that teach.

---

[1] *Orlando Furioso*, II. i. 511-513.
[2] *Friar Bacon*, II, iii. 685-686. And, if Greene wrote *The Pinner of Wakefield*, there is a skit on romantic dolefulness in George's lines:

> Here sit thou, George, wearing a willow wreath,
> As one despairing of thy beauteous love:
> Fie, George, no more;
> Pine not away for that which cannot be.
> I cannot joy in any earthly bliss,
> So long as I do want my Beatrice.
>   III. ii. 684-689.

> *Eust.:* Say that your needle now were Cupid's sting, –
> But, ah, her eye must be no less,
> In which is heaven and heavenliness,
> In which the food of God is shut,
> Whose powers the purest minds do glut!
> *Ida:* What if it were?
> *Eust.:* Then see a wondrous thing;
> I fear me you would paint in Tereus' heart
> Affection in his power and chiefest part.
> *Ida:* Good lord, sir, no! for hearts but pricked soft
> Are wounded sore, for so I hear it oft.
> *Eust.:* What recks the wound, where but your happy eye
> May make him live whom Jove hath judged to die?
> *Ida:* Should life and death within this needle lurk,
> I'll prick no hearts, I'll prick upon my work.[1]

However, striking as this passage is, it is altogether exceptional, and even that form of the romantic love mode that consisted of extravagant tributes to feminine physical beauty, though prominent enough in Greene's poems,[2] is inconspicuous in his plays, apart from Prince Edward's ecstatic memory of the Fair Maid of Fressingfield:

> I tell thee, Lacy, that her sparkling eyes
> Do lighten forth sweet Love's alluring fire:
> And in her tresses she doth fold the looks
> Of such as gaze upon her golden hair:
> Her bashful white, mix'd with the morning's red,
> Luna doth boast upon her lovely cheeks:
> Her front is beauty's table where she paints
> The glories of her gorgeous excellence:
> Her teeth are shelves of precious margarites,
> Richly enclosed with ruddy coral cleeves.[3]

Possibly this marked limitation in Greene's treatment of the romantic love-story is to be explained by his state of mind in the period in which at least *Friar Bacon* and *James IV* were written, when, as his pamphlets show, he was possessed by a dark mood of penitence for his earlier dissolute life, and, to a lesser extent, for

---

[1] *James IV*, II. i. 723-749.
[2] E.g. *The Description of Silvestro's Lady, Doron's Description of Samela, Menaphon's Eclogue*, etc.
[3] *Friar Bacon*, I. i. 52-62.

his love-romances of those years.[1] The truth may well be that while as a professional dramatist he was not blind to the theatrical possibilities of a good story of love adventure, his penitential and religious feelings had converted him to a belief that the emotions and sentiments of love were trivial, vain, and misguided. So it may not be altogether fanciful to hear Greene's own voice in Margaret's renunciation of love:

> But now the touch of such aspiring sins
> Tells me all love is lust but love of heavens;
> That beauty us'd for love is vanity:
> The world contains naught but alluring baits,
> Pride, flattery, and inconstant thoughts.[2]

Yet this cannot be the whole truth of the matter, for his love-poems are nearly always of a superficial, pictorial, and fanciful sort, more Ovidian than Petrarchian in temper, with an occasional misogynist note. Further – and it is a difficulty we easily overlook – Greene may not have been altogether happy with the condition that any female lovers he chose to present had to be played by some squeaking boy.

However, if there is this one large omission in Greene's dramatisation of romantic love-stories, in most other respects his stories reveal the marks of their kind. Much of their action, for instance, derives from a situation in which love is subjected to some heavy and unusual strain. In *Orlando* the true and innocent Angelica is banished on a charge of adultery, is forced on one occasion to submit to the antics of her lover when he is so mad that he does not recognise her, and is later in danger of being burnt alive by the peers of Charlemagne in punishment for her believed treachery to Orlando. Margaret, in *Friar Bacon*, has to endure a double strain: first, when it seems that she can only retain her Lacy by dying with him at the hands of Prince Edward, and secondly, when she is led to believe that Lacy has abandoned her for a more advantageous match. All the way through *James IV* there is conflict in Dorothea between her love for James, which never falters, and her knowledge that he wishes to be rid of her, by murder if

---

[1] In his *Visions* (dated 1592, but composed in or before 1590) Greene wrote: 'They which heed Greene for a patron of love and a second Ovid shall now think him a Timon of such lineaments and a Diogenes that will bark at every amorous pen.' (Quoted in Churton Collins' Introduction to the *Plays and Poems of Greene*, Vol. I, p. 28.)
[2] *Friar Bacon*, v. i. 1868-1872.

necessary, while in the last part of the play Greene introduces the Zelmane-Gynecia motif when Lady Anderson falls in love with the disguised Dorothea.[1] Finally, though the potential drama of the situation is never really developed, we have in the relations of Edward and Lacy the conflict of love and friendship; and in the end, after some struggle with himself, Edward emerges as the magnanimous, chivalric comrade ready to surrender his love to a friend.

Again, these love-stories are whole-heartedly romantic in that they make no pretence to verisimilitude. Nothing, for example, could be more improbable than the way Orlando is driven literally mad with jealousy in such a short space of time, or than the way the expert cut-throat Jaques bungles his commission to murder Dorothea largely on the strength of her assertion that she is mortally wounded. In particular, the stories rely on an abundant and sustained use of coincidence, accident and chance. Orlando recovers just in time to save Angelica from death, in the same way as Lacy's friends arrive at the very moment when Margaret is about to enter a nunnery. Dorothea is providentially saved from murder the first time because the royal warrant for it has somehow or other become mixed up with the copy of a lease that Sir Bertram steals from Ateukin with the ready assistance of Slipper. And there are many such incidents.

As we should expect, the convention of disguise and mistaken identity is much exploited in these romantic stories. In the early *Orlando Furioso* we find one of Sacrepant's accomplices disguised as a shepherd, the two kings, Marsilius and Mandricard, roaming the country as palmers, Angelica making her way to 'woods and ways unknown' in the garb of a poor woman, and Orlando, once he has recovered his senses, fighting as a mercenary soldier. But there is just as much play with concealed identity in the late *Friar Bacon*, and each of Greene's works contains at least one example of this convention.

More than his successors – and probably to a large extent through the influence of Marlowe's *Faustus* – Greene also makes a considerable use of dream, magic, and the supernatural in the fabrication of his stories of romantic make-believe. Melissa, the good enchantress of *Orlando*, who restores the hero to sanity by means of a magic potion and charmed music, and reveals the

[1] Unfortunately one of the two scenes dealing with this episode, v. v., has come to us in a rather confused state.

truth to him, is a figure, like Lyly's Geron, straight from the pages of a romantic story. Closely related to her is the sorceress Medea in *Alphonsus*, who, with a similar spell-binding music, throws Amurack into a trance and conjures up the spirit of Calchas, through whose agency the future is revealed to Amurack in a dream; in the same play there is also the dream in which Carinus learns of the dazzling fortune of his son, and the treacherous message of Mahomet, speaking out of the brazen head. But the play whose story depends most of all on magic and the supernatural is *Friar Bacon*, where the Friar's talking, brazen head, his conjuring contest with Vandermast, and his 'glass prospective' through which Prince Edward learns of the love of Margaret and Lacy and the two young Oxford scholars see their fathers fighting a duel, occupy more of the play than the central love-story itself. In this comedy Bacon is made to abjure magic as alien to a truly religious life, and though this follows the text of *The Famous History*, one suspects, in view of Greene's penitential state of mind at the time, that he was using Bacon as a mouthpiece for his own views, as well as commenting on *Faustus*. One has only to glance through the pages of G. B. Harrison's *Elizabethan Journals* to realise that magic, white no less than black, was not just an interesting literary fiction to the typical Elizabethan mind, but a disturbing and (so men believed) real phenomenon.

With love-stories of this sort, deliberately extravagant and far-fetched as fairy-tales, prodigal in their employment of accident and coincidence, and frequently dependent on magic and the supernatural, it follows, as a corollary true also to romance, that the motivation is usually of a quite incredible kind. A father is supposed to acquiesce freely in a proposal to burn his daughter; a lover, to test his mistress, seriously pretends that he is deserting her for someone else; an abandoned wife never wavers for a moment in her love and loyalty to a husband who tries to murder her, and is always and instantly ready to condone his conduct as a passing youthful folly. Such examples of preposterous motivation could be multiplied many times. But it is not merely that the motives and attitudes of Greene's characters are inherently incredible; that, figures in a play, they are discovered to be impossible by the not altogether fair test of psychological realism. It is a weakness of Greene – or a sign of the immaturity of drama in his time – that he does very little to create an illusion of plausibility in the motivation of his characters. One moment

Orlando is sane, the next he is roaring mad: there is no serious effort to connect the two states, and we must either accept appearances[1] or excuse Greene's apparent shortcomings on the grounds that the text is a 'bad Quarto'. (No doubt if we were Elizabethan groundlings, amused by the mad antics of Orlando, we should be quite content with appearances.) And this crudity of motivation is as evident in Greene's best as in his worst plays. Nothing is wider of the mark than Boas' observation on the King in *James IV*: 'several of the male characters are well drawn, especially the King, whose unlawful passion, though too abrupt in origin, is powerfully portrayed'.[2] It is not simply the origin of James' love for Ida that is unconvincing, but all his conduct – his over-swift conversion to the idea of Dorothea's murder, his readiness to swallow Ateukin's promise of magic spells and his inability to see through Ateukin's trickery and unsubtle flattery, and the puppet-ease with which, at the end, he forgives himself for his adulterous and murderous conduct. So too with the motivation of Dorothea: had there been more doubt, more conflict in her, we might have been prepared to accept as a plausible dramatic fiction the spectacle of a woman who continues to love a man who wishes to murder her. As it is, her attitude all through the play is simply fantastic.

On the surface also, in the creation of personality, Greene's dramatic art is weak; for all the stimulus of dramatic presentation, most of his characters are as insipid and indeterminate as those of *Arcadia*. Yet there is a difference between Orlando and Angelica, woodenly passionless and incommunicative even in what should be their moments of greatest stress,[3] and some of the principal characters of *Friar Bacon* or *James IV*. What – in advance of Lyly – Greene was beginning to achieve was a certain sort of

---

[1] T. H. Dickinson, the editor of Greene's plays in the *Mermaid Series*, hints at parody and burlesque. Little need be said about the contention that Sacrepant is a parody of a Marlovian type, for plainly Sacrepant is not, as Dickinson alleges, 'the real hero'. The suggestion that Orlando's madness is a burlesque deserves more consideration, since it might imply that Greene was burlesquing the romantic love-story. But though Orlando's madness is inadequately motivated and ineptly handled, and though, in keeping with Elizabethan ideas, the madness is treated comically, Orlando is in no sense a parody of a romantic lover. However much he may have bungled it, Greene surely intended us to regard the love-story of Orlando and Angelica (including Orlando's madness) seriously. For a genuine parody of romance we must turn to Peele's *Old Wives' Tale*, which was probably hitting at such plays as *Orlando*.

[2] *Shakespeare and his Predecessors*, p. 81.

[3] Orlando's tirade against the female sex (II. i. 672-684) is an important exception to this generalisation. This speech has some of the vigour and passion, if crude, of the best sort of Elizabethan rant.

animation: he was learning to breathe at least the life of feeling into his lovers, and in Margaret, Dorothea and Ida he created figures of emotion, sentiment and, to some extent, of intelligence, with whom we can at times sympathise. In particular, there is some finely expressed and authentic feeling in the scene, rightly singled out for praise, where Margaret pleads with Edward to spare and forgive Lacy; and it would be hard to match from any previous English play the unstrained natural emotions and intelligence of such lines as

> 'Twas I, my lord, not Lacy, stept awry,
> For oft he sued and courted for yourself,
> And still wooed for the courtier all in green.
> But I whom fancy made but over fond,
> Pleaded myself with looks as if I loved;
> I fed mine eye with gazing on his face,
> And still bewitched loved Lacy with my looks;
> My heart with signs, mine eyes pleaded with tears,
> My face held pity and content at once;
> And more I could not cipher out by signs
> But that I loved Lord Lacy with my heart.
> Then, worthy Edward, measure with thy mind,
> If women's favours will not force men fall,
> If beauty, and if darts of piercing love,
> Is not of force to bury thoughts of friends.[1]

There is genuine pathos, too, in Margaret's feelings when she believes Lacy has deserted her.

Whatever may be said about the dramatic merits of Greene's three chief heroines, it would certainly be agreed that, with Angelica, they belong to the easily recognised romantic pattern[2] of the patient Grisilda: they are all loyal, long-suffering, tender, forgiving, and submissive. There is no definite proof, of course, that this type of heroine came ready-made to Greene from his reading of romantic literature. Indeed his poems leave a suspicion that women of this sort were psychologically attractive to him, while there may be something in Collins' suggestion that they are all reflections of his own ill-used wife whose image haunted his guilty mind.[3] Be this as it may, it remains true that this idealised feminine type belongs to the romantic tradition. Further,

[1] *Friar Bacon*, III. i. 959-973.
[2] This pattern is also common in Greene's novels.
[3] General Introduction, *Plays and Poems*, pp. 22-23.

the promotion of such admirable women as Margaret and Dorothea to the prominence they enjoy in the action of the plays was itself in keeping with the romantic spirit, as well as an important departure from the precedents of Latin comedy.

The social status of Greene's characters also bears the romantic hall-mark, for most of them are of the courtly type, kings and queens, lords and ladies. But much more than Lyly, and much more successfully, Greene diversified his last plays with the antics of low-life characters like Bacon's servant Miles, and Slipper, Andrew and Nano in *James IV*. In this respect Greene probably exercised a very considerable influence on Shakespeare: he had established and elaborated the Clown as a comic type and – of much greater significance – in *Friar Bacon* and *James IV* he had embodied the formula that Shakespeare was to follow in his comedies and romances. At the centre of the play there was a serious romance-story of human lovers, which might sometimes border on the tragic; attached to this, or superimposed on it, was a sub-plot or incidental scenes of broad comedy furnished by characters of a non-courtly type. This formula was a major contribution to the development of Elizabethan romantic comedy, and great as were Lyly's achievements, it is difficult to think of any that were of quite the same order of importance.

But while, with this notable variation, Greene follows the romantic fashion of aristocratic characters, in their setting, on the other hand, his plays derive much less than Lyly's from the conventional romantic background of woods and forests, mountains, streams, caves, castles and gardens. Occasionally, as when Orlando wanders madly through the woods or when the huntsmen encounter the Countess of Arran, Ida and Eustace in front of the castle, the backcloth reveals traces of the romantic brush. But Collins' remark that Greene took comedy 'into the woods and fields, and gave it all the charm of the idyll'[1] must be heavily discounted as poetic hyperbole. The truth is that the settings are often vague; and, unlike Shakespeare, Greene rarely employs his poetry for the sort of verbal scene-painting that we find in Orlando's lines –

> Sweet solitary groves, whereas the Nymphs
> With pleasance laugh to see the Satyrs play,
> Witness Orlando's faith unto his love.

[1] General Introduction to Greene's *Plays and Poems*, Vol. I, pp. 57-58.

> Tread she these lawns, kind Flora, boast thy pride.
> Seek she for shades, spread, Cedars, for her sake.
> Fair Flora, make her couch amidst thy flowers.
> Sweet crystal springs, wash ye with roses
> When she longs to drink.[1]

Even the country atmosphere of *Friar Bacon* is probably more a product of our imagination than it is of Greene's words or setting.

Finally, the spirit of Greene's work, which is gentle, full of grace, goodness, mercy and justice, owes much more to the romantic than it does to the classical tradition. There is little suffering and barely a glimpse, except perhaps in Ateukin, of wickedness in its all too real forms. The few bad characters, such as they are, receive their deserts; the virtuous and innocent are ultimately vindicated and rewarded in a system of poetic justice; and there is always the happy ending where all is made right in an atmosphere of forgiveness and reconciliation. T. H. Dickinson, the editor of Greene's plays in the *Mermaid Series*, was not far out when he described Greene's art as one of 'contemplative repose and genial humanity',[2] and essentially the spirit of his comedies is that of Shakespeare's, though it is simpler, cruder and less thoughtful.

On many important counts then, Greene is quite as significant as Lyly in the assimilation of romance to English drama and in the creation of a comedy of delight after Sidney's own heart. But there is this great difference between Shakespeare's two predecessors in romantic comedy: whereas the plays of Lyly are now chiefly of historical interest, a text for scholars and critics, Greene's *Friar Bacon* and *James IV* still compare favourably with all but the pick of Shakespeare's comedies and still merit stage-production.

[1] *Orlando Furioso*, II. i. 560-567.
[2] *Robert Greene*, Introduction, p. lxii.

CHAPTER FOUR

SHAKESPEARE'S 'ROMANTIC' COMEDIES

FOR NEARLY a hundred and fifty years now it has been a commonplace to refer to Shakespeare's early, non-historical plays as 'romantic' comedies. No other label can compete with this word in popularity, and its propriety passes without question. Yet even a slight acquaintance with Shakespearean criticism will reveal that the word is actually used in a wide variety of senses, and not infrequently with little sense at all. Some writers employ it, negatively, to distinguish Shakespeare's work from the neo-classical comedies of Jonson and the realistic Elizabethan and Jacobean comedies of lower- and middle-class life. With others it is a semi-poetic expression intended to suggest colour, youthful exuberance, kinship with the Romantic Revival; or perhaps it is a formal term, denoting looseness of structure, diversity of elements, freedom from the restraint of the 'rules'. Finally, there are those writers, by no means harmlessly confined to literary manuals and text-books, who squander the word as a mere emotional token of enthusiasm and approbation.

None of these usages of 'romantic', except the last, can be altogether reprehended. All the same, it is a pity that the label has become so worn and obscured through diverse and careless handling, for in reality Shakespeare's comedies are 'romantic' in the historical and most precise sense of the word. They are the climax, historically and aesthetically, of that assimilation of the romantic heritage into English drama that we have been tracing through its main phases.

It will help to clarify our understanding of the strictly romantic nature of Shakespeare's comedies if we approach our exposition by way of some negative definitions: if we attempt, that is, to mark off the obvious frontiers between the principal and homogeneous group[1] of them and the three oddities *The Comedy of Errors*, *The Taming of the Shrew* and *The Merry Wives of Windsor*.

Like *Titus Andronicus*, *The Comedy of Errors* belongs unmistakably to the drama of the previous generation, and because of this its

---

[1] For reasons that should become apparent in the course of this chapter, I include *Romeo and Juliet* and *The Merchant of Venice* in this group.

relationship to the rest of Shakespeare's comedies is rather like that of *Titus Andronicus* to the tragedies. It is an adaptation of Plautus the *Menaechmi*, elaborated with another episode from the Plautine comedy the *Amphitruo*; and if not so purely or cold-bloodedly the 'exercise in dramatic archaeology'[1] of J. Isaacs' phrase, it is certainly one of the closest imitations of Latin comedy that we have in English. For this reason it is clearly distinguished from the majority of Shakespeare's comedies, if not their antithesis as a type of drama.

Its setting follows the classical recipe. The scene is laid in a city, the busy port of Ephesus, while the social background (admittedly sixteenth-century in its details) against which the incidents of the story are played out is that of merchant life, with its docks, market-place, shops and legal system for the more serious business of life, and its taverns and domestic dining-rooms for diversion and recuperation. Moreover, there is very little movement of the characters, who are kept to the bounds of the market-place, the house of Antipholus and of the courtesan, and the nearby abbey. Only in *The Taming of the Shrew* and *The Merry Wives* can we find large and obvious parallels to this urban, bourgeois society and strict limitation of locality.

Nor is it merely the commercial activities of such figures as Aegeon, Antipholus of Ephesus and the goldsmith that link the characters to classical comedy. There is, for instance, the courtesan, who, though less obtrusive than in the *Menaechmi*, comes direct from a stereotyped mould of Latin comedy, with her sharp, uncompromising, mercenary sense and her unabashed self-confidence as an accepted part of society. Adriana, less harsh and a shade more sympathetic to us than her counterpart in the *Menaechmi*,[2] is still substantially a stock classical character – the shrew who drives her husband from bed and board with her clamorous tongue and suspicious jealousies. In the same line of dramatic descent stands her husband, a tough-skinned, violent fellow who, only too ready to fly to the softer endearments of a prostitute, almost deserves such a wife, and the two Dromios, sharp-witted, saucy bondservants who, while frequently chastised, enjoy a large measure of their masters' confidences. Admittedly,

---

[1] *Shakespeare As Man of the Theatre* (printed in *Shakespeare Criticism*, 1919-1935, p. 311).

[2] I cannot agree with H. B. Charlton's contention (*Shakespearian Comedy*, pp. 67-68) that Adriana is more shrewish than the wife in the *Menaechmi*.

the Dromios are among the forbears of Shakespeare's clowns, but, apart from this one resemblance, none of these types is encountered again in the main body of Shakespeare's comedy. And there is this further notable distinction between the characters of *The Comedy of Errors* and those of the other comedies: apart from the possible exception of Luciana, all of them are elderly or mature men and women.

The story, too, furnishes in almost all its chief features a sharp contrast with the majority of Shakespeare's comedies. Once we have swallowed the gross fiction of the twins so alike that they cannot be told apart, the tale is not unrealistic; and most of the incidents, like the merchant who is to be punished as a retaliatory political measure against his countrymen, the servant who is sent to fetch his master home to dinner, the business transactions over a goldsmith's chain and legal proceedings for non-payment, are drawn from the familiar stuff of everyday life. All these episodes, woven tightly together in a complicated entanglement full of cross-purposes, are treated in a boisterous, farcical spirit, with a good deal of crude, brutal and (in the literal sense) knockabout humour. Further, in place of the large love-interest of Shakespeare's other comedies, we have, as in Latin comedy, a sex and marital interest: there is little love-making, and the sex-interest is provided by the relations between a shrewish wife and her husband. In the background there is prostitution, an accepted institution of Roman society where marriage was primarily a business transaction.

Yet while in setting, characterisation and plot, *The Comedy of Errors* is a close imitation of Latin comedy, it contains two minor elements[1] that owe nothing to classical tradition and were to be prominently developed in Shakespeare's later comedies and romances.

In the first place there is the slightly-sketched love-story of Luciana and Antipholus of Syracuse. A virtuous and admirable young woman, a young man who falls hopelessly in love with her at first sight and has no other intention than the honourable one of matrimony – this is a pattern of love and love-making that has no precedent in classical comedy, where marriage is a purely financial affair and where illicit, intriguing amours are a pardonable part of a young man's worldly education as he sows his wild

---

[1] Both of these elements are admirably described by Charlton in his *Shakespearian Comedy*, pp. 69-72.

oats. Further, in Act III, Scene ii, Antipholus strives for a moment to burst through the tangle of misunderstanding and lay his heart at Luciana's feet, addressing her, the goddess, in notes of abject, adoring ecstasy that would have baffled the audience of Plautus and Terence like poetry from another world:

> Sweet mistress, – what your name is else, I know not,
>   Nor by what wonder you do hit of mine, –
> Less in your knowledge and your grace you show not
>   Than our earth's wonder; more than earth divine.
> Teach me, dear creature, how to think and speak;
>   Lay open to my earthy-gross conceit,
> Smother'd in errors, feeble, shallow, weak,
>   The folded meaning of your words' deceit. ...
> O! train me not, sweet mermaid, with thy note,
>   To drown me in thy sister's flood of tears:
> Sing, siren, for thyself, and I will dote:
>   Spread o'er the silver waves thy golden hairs,
> And as a bed I'll take them and there lie;
>   And in that glorious supposition think
> He gains by death that hath such means to die:
>   Let Love, being light, be drownèd if she sink![1]

All we can dispute in H. B. Charlton's sensitive exposition of this incongruous element in *The Comedy of Errors* is an occasional touch of exaggeration, as when he describes Luciana as 'a gentle-hearted girl whose lips speak in the sweet new style singers and sonneteers were consecrating to lovers and love-making'.[2] If Luciana does speak in this style, it must be the dumb language of lips, for Shakespeare affords her no opportunity of responding to Antipholus' courtship when it is cleared of the false appearance of adultery; and when one hears her reproving her sister and abusing Dromio like a fish-wife,[3] one is not altogether happy with the epithet 'gentle-hearted'. One further small point of qualification: Antipholus is thirty-three years of age, which is somewhat old for the typical Shakespearean lover, though it may be young enough for the matinée-idol who personates him.

The second unclassical element is furnished by old Aegeon and

---

[1] *Comedy of Errors*, III. ii. 29-52. (All the Shakespeare quotations are from the Globe edition.)
[2] *Shakespearian Comedy*, p. 20.
[3] *Comedy of Errors*, II. ii.

the Abbess and their mishaps.[1] It was no part of Latin comedy to deal pathetically, or even sympathetically, with old age. If fathers of marriageable sons and daughters, the elderly were to be intrigued against and ludicrously outwitted; if not, they were to be mocked at and satirised for such follies as miserliness, moroseness and senile lechery. In the *Menaechmi* the father of the twins is already dead, and there is no mention of his wife. The pathetic figure of old Aegeon, heavily stricken with grief, vainly wandering through the world in quest of his son, narrowly escaping an undeserved death, and ultimately restored to his wife and sons after a moment of bitter despair, provides a story altogether unclassical in spirit, while his adventures foreshadow several episodes in the later comedies and romances.

The Taming of the Shrew, derived to a considerable extent from an early sixteenth-century imitation of Latin drama, Ariosto's *Suppositi* (1509), is less classical in form than *The Comedy of Errors*. There is a larger range of characters; no attempt is made to keep to the unities of time and place; and the action is more complicated, with a main and a distinct subordinate plot. But in substance the play is pure Latin, though not always in the same way as *The Comedy of Errors*.

The setting of *The Taming of the Shrew* is slightly more varied than that of *The Comedy of Errors*. The action shifts from Padua to Petruchio's country house and back to Padua again; there is one open-air scene on a country road, and in the Induction there is some evocation of the open-air life of hunting. But these are really small points of difference: in the main, the setting is still bourgeois and urban, and there is comparatively little movement of characters or violent change of scene.

One of the most remarkable classical features of the characterisation is the prominence given to elderly folk. No less than four of the main characters, Baptista, Vincentio, Gremio and the Pedant, are old men. More than that, all of them – the two fathers, Baptista and Vincentio, who are gulled and (in the case of Vincentio) threatened with callous violence in order to effect the marriage of Bianca and Lucentio, Gremio, the rich, doddering old suitor, crafty but easily cheated himself, and the Pedant – to be made a tool and a fool of – are drawn direct from Latin comedy. But it is not merely these old men, with their traditional

[1] This part of the story seems to be derived from the romance *Apollonius of Tyre*, probably as related by Gower in *Confessio Amantis*.

dramatic functions, who are derived from this source. Katherine is obviously the stock shrew, sister to Adriana, while Petruchio is another Antipholus of Ephesus, even thicker skinned, more aggressive, blunt and self-confident, and (possibly accounting for these differences) but newly married in the play. Indeed, the truth is that there is hardly a character, apart from Sly, Bianca and Lucentio, who cannot be traced to a classical mould.

It is, however, in the substance of its plot that the play's Latin affinities are most marked and its contrast with the rest of Shakespeare's comedies most palpable.

In the first place, while a large part of the action concerns match-making and marriage, it is plain that the predominating conception of marriage is Roman (and sixteenth-century). Marriage is primarily an economic and social institution, and love has little to do with it. This attitude is manifested most boldly in the Petruchio-Katherine story. Petruchio, right from the outset, makes no bones about the blunt fact that 'wealth is burden of my wooing-dance',[1] and as soon as he has learnt from Baptista the size of Katherine's dowry, well-versed in the economics of match-making, he urges that a legal settlement should be speedily drawn up, with provisions for Katherine's widowhood. It is true that Baptista interrupts to remind him that Katherine may have something to say in the matter and that there follows a scene of courtship between Petruchio and Katherine; but this scene, farcical, full of irony, mocking wit-play and knockabout, has no meaning except for Petruchio to show that he will stand no nonsense, while Baptista's prompt acceptance of Petruchio afterwards, in spite of Katherine's expressed detestation of her proposed husband, suggests that Baptista's earlier deference to the wishes of Katherine was not meant to be taken seriously. No doubt, with acquaintance, Petruchio comes to appreciate the good looks, spirit and wit of Katherine; and doubtless wifely affection has a place in his ideas of a happy life. But so too has good food and drink, and he is never likely to forget the doctrine of 'She is my goods, my chattels'.

This attitude of Petruchio to love and marriage is not peculiar to him; on the contrary, it permeates the play. The Pedant, like Petruchio, knows how to strike the proper business-like note when, pretending to be Lucentio's father, he first encounters Baptista; Hortensio, after his failure to win Bianca, speedily comforts

[1] I. ii. 68.

himself with a rich widow, and it is soon apparent that no love has been lost on either side of the match; while – most blatant example of all of the purely mercenary attitude to marriage – there is the scene where Baptista virtually auctions Bianca off to the bidding of Gremio and Tranio.

Admittedly, as Charlton and other critics before him have pointed out, there are traces of a very different conception of love and marriage in the Lucentio-Bianca story.[1] While Lucentio is quite regardless of fortunes and marriage settlements until Baptista forces this consideration upon him (or at least upon his man Tranio), there is nothing in him of the reckless young libertine of Latin comedy: his love is pure, and from the first he intends to marry Bianca. Bianca, too, is chaste and honourable, and Shakespeare declines to follow the example of Ariosto in making the two young lovers live together in an irregular union. Further, like Antipholus of Syracuse, Lucentio falls in love with Bianca at first sight, and has learnt the same style of lyrical adoration:

> I saw her coral lips to move,
> And with her breath she did perfume the air;
> Sacred and sweet was all I saw in her.[2]

On the other hand, we should be misinterpreting Shakespeare to throw too much stress on this particular non-classical element. As Charlton remarks 'love remains more an intrigue than a religion', and in spite of the tone of Lucentio's first words Shakespeare does not afford him a chance to pour out his heart in any scene of genuine courtship. Moreover, our early impression of Lucentio and Bianca is largely effaced by their strange metamorphosis in the last scene of the play, where in an instant they have been transformed into jaded, bickering husband and wife, Bianca well on the way to becoming another Adriana and Lucentio promising to learn swiftly the response of giving as good as he gets.

Again, any flicker of the true romantic spirit there may be in the love of Bianca and Lucentio is all but extinguished in the boisterous, farcical whirlwind of Petruchio's treatment of Katherine, in which a full-blooded shrew of the authentic Latin mould is tamed by a series of torments and humiliations of the most unchivalric kind to complete submission, not to say

---

[1] Some scholars have ascribed this sub-plot to a collaborator.
[2] *Taming of the Shrew*, I. ii. 179-181.

subservience. How far Petruchio's behaviour had Shakespeare's approbation, how far Katherine's long and formal recantation in the last act represents Shakespeare's considered opinion on the proper relations between man and wife, are questions difficult to answer. Unless the play *The Taming of a Shrew* (1594) was by another hand and not an early rough draft or garbled version of his own play, the Petruchio-Katherine story is certainly Shakespeare's own invention. Again (and possibly an alternative explanation) we can regard the shrew-taming as a crude breath of social reality blowing for a moment into the fanciful and idealistic world of Shakespeare's comedy, for we must never forget, especially when we come to examine Shakespeare's growing dissatisfaction with romantic sentiment, that in Elizabethan times wife-beating was as prevalent in society as the refinements of chivalric and Petrarchian love were in literature. But these problems need not engage us deeply here. We may content ourselves with noting that the farcical and unsentimental episode of shrew-taming is as essentially classical in spirit as it is foreign to the temper of the main body of Shakespeare's comedy.

Apart from this predominating attitude to love, the action has two other prominent classical features that distinguish it from the romantic comedies. First, the Bianca-Lucentio story furnishes an abundance of complicated scheming in which the young, abetted by their servants, are out to circumvent the intentions of the old.[1] Indeed, this part of the play is likely to leave an impression of elaborate intrigue for intrigue's sake. There is, perhaps, some realistic point in Lucentio and Hortensio disguising themselves as teachers when Baptista declares a suspension of all further courting of Bianca until Katherine is wedded and off his hands. But once Lucentio wins Bianca's consent there seems little reason for all the trouble of passing the Pedant off as Lucentio's father or for arranging that Tranio, the Pedant, and Baptista are busy over the details of a marriage settlement while the two lovers are secretly married. Straightforward elopement would have been an easy dramatic expedient to avoid all these involved manœuvres.

Secondly, the plot contains a large amount of violent, knockabout humour. This is not, as in *The Comedy of Errors*, mainly a matter of

---

[1] When Grumio comments (I. ii. 138-140) 'See, to beguile the old folks, how the young folks lay their heads together', he gives us a text not only for *The Taming of the Shrew* but for a large part of Latin comedy as well.

drubbing and ill-treating servants. Katherine torments Bianca and cuffs Petruchio; Petruchio in one scene hurls food and platters across the stage. There are numerous incidents of this kind, though one or two, like Petruchio's outrageous behaviour to the priest and sexton at his wedding, are reported instead of being directly presented.

In all these characteristics *The Taming of the Shrew* is then, like *The Comedy of Errors*, the polar opposite of Shakespeare's romantic comedies. The third oddment among the comedies, *The Merry Wives of Windsor*, occupies an intermediate position, and for that reason no definition of it can be clear-cut.

The play certainly has some affinities with the romantic comedies. There is, in the last act, the outdoor setting of Windsor Forest and the fairy lore, though in this instance the fairies are children in disguise; the characters are originals, owing little to stock Latin types and bearing several resemblances to creations in the comedies and history plays; and of course there is the love-story and runaway marriage of Anne Page and the young courtier, Fenton. We see little of Fenton, but plainly, if by report, he is one of the amorous gallants who throng the world of the romantic comedies: 'he capers, he dances, he has eyes of youth, he writes verses, he speaks holiday, he smells April and May'.[1] On the other hand, this petty-bourgeois society of burgesses and their dames, doctor, parson and innkeeper, this small world of an English provincial town, is without counterpart in Shakespeare's other comedies. Nor are the main ingredients of the plot – the seedy knight, Falstaff, driven to the attempted seduction of two honest matrons through his lechery and dwindling purse, his farcical discomfitures, and the jealous, suspicious husband – to be paralleled in the other comedies.

Perhaps we shall not be so very wide of the mark if we regard this play as an odd and unspecialised prototype of Restoration comedy.

§

With these negative delimitations in mind, we may now more easily approach the main body of Shakespeare's comedies, including in this group the romantic tragedy *Romeo and Juliet* and perhaps *The Merchant of Venice*, though the latter play does not fall readily into any precise category.

[1] III. ii. 68-70.

All these comedies, with the exception of *A Midsummer Night's Dream* and of *Love's Labour's Lost* (the second play having no plot to speak of), are at least superficially romantic in the sense that they are adaptations and re-creations of stories and incidents borrowed from romance literature. The Proteus-Julia story of *The Two Gentlemen* comes from Montemayor's *Diana Enamorada*, from which pastoral romance Shakespeare may also have borrowed the love-juice device of *A Midsummer Night's Dream*; *Romeo and Juliet* is based on Brooke's narrative poem *Romeus and Juliet*, which derives, through Boisteau's French version, from Bandello's novel *Giulietta e Romeo* (1554);[1] the story of the Jew and the Merchant in *The Merchant of Venice* comes from Ser Giovanni's *Il Pecorone*, first printed in 1558, but written in the fourteenth century; the Hero-Claudio plot of *Much Ado* is taken from Bandello through the French version of Belleforest; *As You Like It* follows closely Lodge's pastoral romance *Rosalynde*, which is itself based to a large extent on the fourteenth-century poem *The Tale of Gamelyn*; and the story of *Twelfth Night*,[2] whose ultimate source is the Italian play *Gl' Ingannati* (1531), had been adapted as a novel by Bandello, Cinthio, and by Barnabe Riche in his *Apolonius and Silla* (1581). To these primary romance sources, mainly Italian, may perhaps be added slighter reminiscences of *Arcadia* in *The Two Gentlemen*, of the old French romance *Huon of Burdeaux* in the Oberon story of *A Midsummer Night's Dream*, and of Ariosto's *Orlando Furioso* and the second book of the *Faerie Queene* in *Much Ado*.

Of course it might well have happened that Shakespeare transmuted this romantic material out of all recognition. In one sense no doubt he did transform it, for the value of his comedies lies entirely in his own contribution – his power of animation, his poetry, his wit and humour. But in another sense there is no transformation; these adaptations and re-creations remain as typically romantic as the episodes and stories upon which they are founded.

---

[1] Though Bandello's novel is the most important Italian version of this story, it was not the first: the first printed version is a novel of Salernitano (1476). But the story is much older than its first literary recording: it was formed by an accretion of many widespread 'Separation' and 'Potion' romances, possibly deriving to some extent from two other famous medieval love-legends, Tristan and Isolt and Troilus and Cressida. (See J. J. Munro's Introduction to *Brooke's Romeus and Juliet*.)

[2] It is a vice of scholars to make too much of sources. All the same, it is a remarkable fact that although the story of *Twelfth Night* was easily accessible to Shakespeare in contemporary forms, there is clear proof that he was acquainted not only with *Gl' Ingannati* but with two other Italian imitations of this play called *Gl' Inganni*.

Apart from *Troilus and Cressida*, with its anachronistic 'knights' and Hector's vaunting challenge to the Greek host to deny the surpassing excellence of his lady – a challenge that culminates in an encounter between Hector and Ajax in the lists, there is nothing of the purely chivalric element in Shakespeare's comedies, though occasionally we are given a glimpse of the knightly exercises in which his heroes indulged. In *The Two Gentlemen*, for instance, part of Panthino's argument for sending Proteus to the Imperial Court is that 'There shall he practise tilts and tournaments'.[1] But if Shakespeare eschewed – and wisely – the deeds of derring-do that Greene unsuccessfully attempted to dramatise in his *Orlando Furioso*, he fully exploited the tale of amatory adventure that Greene had brilliantly utilised in *Friar Bacon* and *James IV*; to such an extent that every one of the eight plays in the group we are at present examining is primarily a love-story. It is this continuous and marked preoccupation with love that distinguishes Shakespeare's comedy sharply from that of his great contemporary Jonson – and perhaps as sharply from the whole of the main tradition of comedy that stretches from Aristophanes to Shaw. Not of course that Shakespeare's comedies are a monotonous repetition of the Greene formula, which he first experimented with in *The Two Gentlemen* and *Love's Labour's Lost*. There is a world of difference between the melodramatic incident of *The Two Gentlemen* and the discussions and sentiment-parade of *Love's Labour's Lost*, between the fantasy of *A Midsummer Night's Dream* and the near-tragedy of *Much Ado*. Above all, as we shall see in the next chapter, Shakespeare's attitude to love is a changing one. But always at the centre of the plot there is the love-story – sometimes, as notably in *As You Like It*, several love-stories – and one obvious effect of this is the overwhelming preponderance of young men and women among the characters. The elderly and middle-aged are rarely allowed into the picture, except in the necessary role of parents – as fathers and uncles mostly, since, apart from Juliet and Romeo, none of his heroes and heroines has a living mother.

Yet all these different and diversely treated love-stories fall, after all, into a limited class. They are characteristically romantic in that they deal, almost exclusively, with love-*making*. A youth and a maid, Valentine and Silvia, Romeo and Juliet, Orlando and Rosalind, Claudio and Hero, fall in love, more often than

[1] I. iii. 30.

not – following the familiar convention – at first sight; they court each other;[1] they are separated through various misunderstandings and thwarting circumstances and later re-united; and the comedy comes to a close with their marriage,[2] which is not simply a convenient curtain-ringer but also the natural consummation of love:

> Wedding is great Juno's crown:
> O blessed bond of board and bed!
> 'Tis Hymen peoples every town;
> High wedlock then be honourèd.
> Honour, high honour, and renown,
> To Hymen, god of every town![3]

Never in these plays does Shakespeare attempt to create comedy out of love that is already made, out of marriage that is to say, and rarely out of love that is not seriously intended, like coquetry or seduction. His restricted scope, the scope of the romantic writer, has been clearly set down by C. H. Herford in his essay *Shakespeare's Treatment of Love and Marriage*: 'The norm of love lent itself both to comic and to tragic situation, but only within somewhat narrow limits. The richness, depth and constancy of the passion precluded a whole world of comic effects. It precluded the comedy of the coquette and the prude, of the affected gallant and the cynical roué, of the calf-lover and the doting husband; the comedy of the fantastic tricks played by love under the obsession of pride, self-interest, meticulous scruple, or superstition. Into this field Shakespeare made brilliant incursions, but it hardly engaged his rarest powers, and to large parts of it his "universal" genius remained strange.'[4] And again: 'The immense field of dramatic motives based upon infringements of marriage, so fertile in the hands of his successors, and in most other schools

---

[1] The lack of physical love-making in this courtship is usually ascribed to Shakespeare's tact in working with his boy-actors. But E. E. Stoll (*From Shakespeare to Joyce*, Ch. IX, p. 157) prefers the explanation of a public sense of decorum: 'The Elizabethan audience, accustomed (like their fathers and forefathers and all the rest of the world) to no other players for the parts, would have been in danger of laughing or jeering only at the embraces or caresses, not at the actual boy who received them.'

[2] *Love's Labour's Lost* is an exception. But even here marriage for all the lovers is not far away.

[3] *As You Like It*, v. iv. 147-152. This idealisation of marriage cannot be wholly ascribed to late romantic ideas, since several of Shakespeare's plays, and notably *A Midsummer Night's Dream*, may have been commissioned for performance at a wedding.

[4] P. 20.

of drama, did not attract Shakespeare, and he touched it only occasionally and for particular purposes.'[1]

Naturally – for there could hardly be a play otherwise – the course of this love-making by Shakespeare's young heroes and heroines never runs smooth, and one familiar romantic complication that he takes over from his sources and employs on numerous occasions is the situation in which faithful love is subjected to some grievous, or otherwise abnormal strain, though none of these is ever so excruciating as the plight of Erona in *Arcadia*. Nor surprisingly, in view of the dead-on clash between romantic ideals and the business-like attitude to marriage prevailing in real life, the lovers frequently find themselves torn between their own wishes and submission or obedience to parents who have other, more worldly ideas about their marriage. Such is the plight of Valentine and Silvia, Lysander and Hermia, Romeo and Juliet. But the dilemma of these lovers is comparatively simple and true to life, as is also the banishment that separates Valentine from Silvia and Romeo from Juliet. More typical of the romantic love-story is the extravagantly strained, unrealistic situation of *Love's Labour's Lost*, where the king and his three young friends have to choose between new-found love and their sworn pledge to study for a year, isolated from the company of women. No less artificial and piquant is the strain imposed on Viola who, in love with Orsino, has not only to bear his love-messages to Olivia but to submit herself to the attentions of Olivia. This situation, though less fully elaborated, had already been employed with Julia in *The Two Gentlemen*, and there is something of a variant of it in *As You Like It* when Rosalind encounters her lover in the forest of Arden but cannot, owing to her necessary disguise, directly return his avowed and constant love. This episode is treated much more comically than the situation in which Julia and Viola find themselves involved, for it is Rosalind herself who proposes that she should pretend to be Orlando's own Rosalind and who mocks Orlando's love-making. But some element of strain is probably implied in the situation, and as soon as Orlando has gone Rosalind breaks out with her sincere heart-cry, 'O coz, coz, coz, my pretty little coz, that thou didst know how many fathoms deep I am in love!'[2] She does not find it easy to keep up the play-acting.

[1] Pp. 19-20.
[2] *As You Like It*, IV. i. 209-211.

Twice, too, Shakespeare makes considerable play with that strain, utilised by Sidney in the story of Philoclea and Pyrocles, in which one faithful lover is tormented by the believed infidelity or estrangement of the other. There is Hermia in *A Midsummer Night's Dream*, who not only believes that Lysander has deserted her but has to witness his importunate wooing of Helena; there is also Hero in *Much Ado* who thinks that Claudio, swallowing some fantastic slander on her honour, has abandoned her at the altar. A similar situation confronts Julia in *The Two Gentlemen* and Olivia in *Twelfth Night*, though this time the situation is somewhat varied, for Julia is actually thrown aside by Proteus, while Olivia's fear that she has been deserted by Sebastian arises only from mistaken identity.

In *The Two Gentlemen* occurs another common type of strained situation in romantic story, that of conflict between love and male-friendship. But Proteus surrenders to his passion (or lust) without much of a struggle, and the conflict is not elaborated so as to form an important part of the story, though Valentine, retaining his romantic ideal of friendship to the end, offers to surrender Silvia to Proteus even when he has recovered Silvia and Proteus is unmasked as a villian. However, with the exception of this play, Shakespeare makes no important use of the love-friendship conflict in his comedies. On the other hand, friendship, while passive from a dramatic point of view, is certainly very prominent in these early plays and as much a part of their spirit and atmosphere as it is in *Arcadia*. How far this characteristic was due to late romantic sentiment and how far – as Professor Dover Wilson would have it[1] – to Shakespeare's contact with the Southampton circle is not easy to settle.

However, the situation involving strain and anguish is only one form of the complications that beset the paths of Shakespeare's young lovers. There is also adventure, always the main element of 'fine fabling', and Shakespeare keeps faithfully to his romantic originals in making adventure rather than intrigue the mainspring of his story. This is not to say that there is no intrigue in the comedies: the gulling of Malvolio and the entanglement of Beatrice and Benedick furnish two large and obvious instances of Shake-

[1] 'Play after play at this period contains its party of dashing young bucks. ... Almost always too, like young men of whatever rank or period, they hunt in threes. ... So persistent is the triangle that it is hard to resist a suspicion that the same triangle existed among the "divers of worship" for whose eyes and ears they were primarily intended.'—*The Essential Shakespeare*, pp. 49-50.

speare employing his own invention to create a comedy of intrigue; and sometimes, as in the machinations of Oliver or Don John, the plotting and scheming was already present in his romantic source. But in the main it is what *happens* to the characters, their encounter with challenging and largely unexpected circumstances, rather than what they scheme or intend that forms the staple of Shakespeare's normal plot in the comedies.

As You Like It provides us with a typical example of Shakespeare's usual love-story. There is some intrigue certainly, such as Oliver's schemes to get rid of his brother and Rosalind's and Celia's to outwit Duke Frederick. But the main concern is adventure. Orlando, overcoming a famous wrestler, wins the love of Rosalind, but later, threatened by the murderous intentions of his brother, is forced to flee to the refuge of a forest. There, by chance (which is perhaps a synonym for 'adventure') he again encounters Rosalind, who has been banished, but he fails to recognise her through the accident that she has been forced to go disguised. Rosalind, because of her disguise, stumbles into another rare adventure when she attracts the attention of the shepherdess Phoebe. Oliver pursues Orlando, and – again by chance – Orlando encounters him while he is asleep, menaced by a serpent and a lion. By chance also the fates of Rosalind and Orlando are linked up with the fortunes of Rosalind's father, who happens (another key word) to be himself an exile in the same forest.

It would be wearisome to continue this plot-summary for the other comedies. What is true for *As You Like It* is true for most of the other plays under review. Apart from *Much Ado* and *Love's Labour's Lost* (the story of which is too slight to be characterised one way or the other) all of the plots are primarily love-tales of adventure, and this description applies no less to *Romeo and Juliet* and *The Merchant of Venice*[1] than it does to a comedy like *The Two Gentlemen* or *A Midsummer Night's Dream*. Indeed it is precisely because so much in *Romeo and Juliet* – Romeo's meeting with Juliet, the killing of Tybalt, Romeo's banishment, the undelivered letter from Friar Lawrence – does spring from chance, or at least is not deliberately intended, that the play is usually and accurately described as a 'romantic' tragedy, so to be distinguished from

---

[1] Even Shylock's ensnarement of Antonio hardly deserves the name of intrigue, since it is only Antonio's impossible bad luck in the wrecking of all his ships that brings into force the forfeiture clause of the bond.

Shakespeare's later tragedies where chance and adventure play a very insignificant part.

True also to the romantic manner the adventures dramatised in these plays are almost invariably of the far-fetched and incredible kind, demanding a whole-hearted, continuous suspension of disbelief. Probably because Shakespeare was combining romance with comedy there is much less intentionally harrowing suspense and less shock of surprise than in *Arcadia*;[1] and where the sensation, such as the reported death of Hero, might evoke feelings out of keeping with the spirit of comedy, we are usually let comfortably into the secret. But, with this important difference, the Shakespearean comedies are stuffed as full as *Arcadia* or any other romantic tale with coincidence and other preposterous incident. Where, except within the romantic and fairy-tale conventions, are to be found such obliging outlaws as those in *The Two Gentlemen* who, after refraining from robbing and murdering their captive, Valentine, appoint him their chief, with the most perfunctory inquiry into his qualifications? Where else can we find such lies, so patently shallow and yet at the same time so effective, as those that persuade Claudio into thinking that Hero is carrying on a sordid affair with a serving-man, that he has killed her with his accusations, and that her father – as a penance upon him of all things! – wishes to marry him to a niece, the very image of Hero? And the coincidences! – Valentine just on the spot, in a wide, lonely forest, to prevent Proteus ravishing Silvia; Friar John caught in a plague-house with his vital message to Romeo; Antonio losing every single one of his ships; Rosalind and Orlando both making their way to the same forest, and Duke Frederick providentially overcome by a religious conversion as he is on his way to crush the assembled 'outlaws'; Sebastian, believed to be drowned somewhere at sea, turning up without rhyme or reason at Olivia's house to be taken for his sister and bustled into a betrothal ceremony. ... Without these romantic licences, the plot of every Shakespearean comedy would fall to pieces. They are the lubrication and half of the machinery itself.

Yet while further dissection of all this make-believe would be as murderous as it would be easy, it is impossible to omit here all

[1] But our familiarity with Shakespeare's plots may mislead us here. Probably his own audiences were more gripped and excited by his stories than we allow; and this may be true of unsophisticated audiences to-day. Cf. Quiller Couch, New Cambridge *Measure for Measure*, p. xx: 'he wrote for us all; and he wrote so that any ordinary man follows almost every one of his plots with anxiety and interest'.

reference to Shakespeare's partiality to disguise, mistaken identity, and lack of recognition, since, with the possible exceptions of *A Midsummer Night's Dream* and *Much Ado*,[1] every one of the plays in our present group contains at least one instance of disguise. Rosalind's transformation is typical: merely because she assumes male attire, with her gallant curtle-axe upon her thigh, she is supposed to be quite unrecognisable to her father and lover, neither of whom is allowed a moment's suspicion of her true identity. No doubt much of Shakespeare's fondness for this device is to be explained by the fact that he had only boy-actors to perform his female parts; certainly it must have seemed an attractive solution to his difficulties to change his heroines, Julia, Portia, Rosalind, and Viola, into youths or young men. But the convention itself, of miraculous[2] disguise, was thoroughly in keeping with the spirit of romantic story.

All these narrative conventions and artificialities are woven – and sometimes loosely fumbled together – into the common romantic climax of the happy ending, in which love and right triumph in an ideal, poetic justice. The conclusion of *As You Like It*, in which all the lovers are united (Touchstone under some protest), Oliver, the villain, repents and surrenders the family estate to his wronged brother, the exiled Duke recovers his dominions and the usurping Duke, after his timely conversion, joins a religious fraternity, is a fair sample of what we find in the last act of the other comedies. There are certain variations, admittedly. Sometimes, for instance, there is a villain to be disposed of, and sometimes there is not. But in the main the winding-up of each story follows a stereotyped pattern: the lovers obtain their hearts' desire, wrongs are redressed, and the villian, if there is one, exposed and punished – lightly punished.

Such, in rough outline, is the pattern of the stories that Shakespeare dramatises in his comedies, and it is perhaps appro-

---

[1] Titania's blindness to the appearance of Bottom is hardly a true example of this convention since it is produced by magic, while the mistaken identity in *Much Ado* is only reported.

[2] The way in which Shakespeare and his contemporaries employ disguise might perhaps be regarded as a kind of magic. But magic in the strict sense of the word, though common enough in romantic story, is rare in Shakespearean comedy. With the one exception of *A Midsummer Night's Dream*, the adventures in the comedies are never controlled by magical or supernatural agencies, and, apart possibly from the death-simulating potion in *Romeo and Juliet*, the only example of a magical device is the love-juice in *A Midsummer Night's Dream*. We hear rumours of Rosalind's magician uncle, but this suggestion is not seriously developed.

priate at this point to face one important objection that may very well be levelled against the foregoing analysis of it. Some readers, while admitting the accuracy of the description, may be inclined to deny that, apart from the emphasis on adventure, there is anything specifically 'romantic' about such plots. They may argue that all the features we have isolated – the strained, artificial situations, the far-fetched incidents and episodes, the coincidences, mistaken identities, the happy endings – are the normal stuff of comedy and melodrama, are in fact nothing more than the primary reference of the word 'theatrical'. Such an objection cannot be dismissed or completely controverted, for it is largely true. At the same time there is a difference between the comedies of Shakespeare and those of Jonson, Sheridan, Wilde and Shaw; and the term 'romantic' is a useful measure of this difference, not only because so much of Shakespeare's plot-material is taken direct from actual romance sources, but because his comedies represent as pure and extreme a type of the love-story of adventure in drama as the romances do in narrative. It is certainly true, also, that Shakespeare was first and foremost a practical dramatist, always thinking primarily of theatrical effect, and that any 'romantic' influence upon him that we care to talk about must have been quite secondary. But there is no need to weigh these influences against each other in the balance: the simple fact is that romantic literature was there to provide Shakespeare with some excellent raw material full of dramatic possibilities,[1] and, shrewd as always, he did not look a gift-horse in the mouth. He seldom did.

These love-stories of adventure, much more than the tale of intrigue, imply movement: for in order that surprising things may happen to the heroes and heroines they must venture abroad. That is one of the main reasons why the comedies reveal the further romantic characteristic of abrupt and violent changes of scene: 'men and women are tossed from land to sea, from city to forest and desert, from court to country, from a civil and cultured to a rustic and simple life'.[2] *As You Like It,* one of the latest of the comedies, with Orlando running away from home to court, returning home again and then fleeing to the forest, and Celia, Rosalind and Touchstone escaping from the court to the forest, follows the pattern of *The Two Gentlemen,* one of the earliest

---

[1] This ready adaptability of romance to theatrical situation and effect is another answer to the question posed at the end of Chapter 1.
[2] Croce, *Ariosto, Shakespeare and Corneille,* p. 187.

comedies, which starts with the journeys of Valentine and Proteus to court (the latter being followed by his mistress in disguise), and, after certain adventures at court, including an attempted elopement, concludes with the flight of Silvia, pursued by all the other main characters, to the forest where her banished lover is living. In most of the intervening plays, *A Midsummer Night's Dream, Romeo and Juliet* and *The Merchant of Venice*, there are similar and numerous examples of excursions, flights and pursuits that boldly ignore the classical precept of unity of place.

Since the comedies are dramatisations of such typically romantic adventures it follows that their motivation is often weak and sometimes lacking altogether. We have already referred to the automatic way in which so many of the lovers fall utterly in love at first sight. But this lack of subtle or realistic motives is not to be confined to the classifiable conventions – to the love at first sight, the sudden repentances, the happy ending; it is everywhere in the comedies. Obviously there must be a start to the surprising adventures: hence we must not ask, or ask too closely, why the old duke in *As You Like It* should have allowed his daughter to stay with the man who had exiled him or why Duke Frederick, having entertained Rosalind in his family so many years, should suddenly and pitilessly send her packing after her father. And, once started, the adventures must go on: it is irrelevant, for instance, to complain that Sebastian's acceptance of Olivia's hand is utterly unconvincing. We are informed by Sebastian, in a well-turned speech,[1] that he is in a whirl of enchantment, ready to believe and accept anything. We must simply take his word for it and be content with that, since his ready compliance with Olivia's wishes produces an entertaining complication for the last Act. So with Sir Eglamour's promptness to assist Silvia, Valentine's decision to become chief of a band of brigands, and a score of other incidents that any reader will easily recall.

Overlapping all this, there is the strained and often fantastic psychology that must necessarily accompany these extraordinary incidents and situations. No one genuinely in love has ever voluntarily surrendered his sweetheart to a friend, especially when that friend stands revealed as a perfidious, lustful wretch. Valentine in *The Two Gentlemen* makes such an offer. But then Valentine was never intended as a study in realistic psychology: he is simply a romantic hero prepared to put into practice one of

[1] *Twelfth Night*, IV. iii. 1-21.

the high ideals of his faith.[1] In any case, his behaviour does not suddenly jolt us into some unfamiliar dimension: he is merely acting consistently with the Valentine who guilelessly allows the duke to trick him into divulging all the details of his intended elopement with Silvia.

This unrealistic behaviour of Valentine could be paralleled by numerous examples from the other comedies, as when Orlando, supposed to be desperately and seriously in love, willingly submits himself to the mockery of Rosalind, or when Helena plans to win the gratitude of Demetrius by letting him into the secret of the elopement of Lysander and Hermia, in spite of the fact that it is so obviously to her advantage to get Hermia married off as soon as possible. But further instances of unconvincing psychology and deficient motivation are unnecessary, for both of these features must be subsumed in something far more fundamental to Shakespeare's romantic comedies. Like the characters in *Arcadia*[2] and most of those in Greene's plays, a very large proportion of Shakespeare's young lovers, Valentine and Silvia, Lysander, Demetrius, Hermia and Helena, Bassanio (and much of Portia), Sebastian and Olivia, Claudio and Hero, along with their necessary friends, rivals and parents, are simply pasteboard. They merely act out their tale of love-adventure. The tale is the thing, and Shakespeare never intended us to worry ourselves with their personalities and motives. In the main – though there are certain important exceptions to be made – he was not much interested in the comedy of character.

In spite of the vigorous, persistent and energetic criticism of E. E. Stoll, with his Aristotelean insistence on action, situation,

[1] This episode, which is as consistent with the chivalric code as Valentine's earlier willingness to write an affectionate letter for Silvia, to a rival (as he believes), out of duty, is a puzzle only to those who attempt, absurdly, to apply a realistic psychology to Shakespeare's comedy. C. H. Herford's comment (*Shakespeare's Treatment of Love and Marriage*, pp. 28-29) is not without interest: 'A second mark of unripeness is the conception of love as extravagant magnanimity. This, like other kinds of unnatural virtue, was a part of the heritage from medieval romance, fortified with Roman legend. The antique exaltation of friendship concurred with the Germanic absoluteness of faithful devotion, and for the medieval mind the most convincing way of attesting this was by the surrender of a mistress. . . . But the humanity and variety of the mature Shakespeare rejected these extravagances as the cognate genius of the mature Chaucer had done before him.' See also 'Some Matters Shakespearean', John Munro, *Times Literary Supplement*, 13th September, 1947.

[2] E. M. W. Tillyard (*Shakespeare's Last Plays*, p. 33) appears to hold a different view: 'But Sidney, granted his inferior powers, makes a better job of the very same problem that faced Shakespeare, the problem of blending the human and the symbolic treatment of character.' (Tillyard is referring here to the Shakespeare of *Cymbeline*.)

and (in the tragedies) the emotion that is communicated through and by the situation,[1] the Bradleian habit of detailed psychological interpretation dies hard. Even against the comedies the psychologisers lay their text-books, and their influence is to be traced right down to those examination papers in English literature where luckless candidates are still sometimes compelled to attempt a description of Sebastian's 'character', to work out an elaborate contrast between Hermia and Helena, or to write about Rosalind as though she were a three-dimensional creation like Emma Bovary.

An appreciation of the romantic nature of Shakespeare's comedies (using 'romantic' in its strict sense) should help to expose the crudity and irrelevance of most attempts to interpret the comedies from the standpoint of realistic psychology or even from the predominantly psychological approach that we might make to Jonson or Molière. The core of every comedy consists of a romantic tale of love-adventure, and the interest of this lies in its piquant or unusual incidents and situations and in its romantic love-sentiments. Both of these interests are dependent on artificiality and make-believe, and not even Shakespeare's genius could have worked the miracle of infusing fairy-tale with depth, realism or complexity of characterisation. This inevitable limitation upon his powers of character creation can be demonstrated in two other ways: first, by the fact that his greatest comic character has his being outside the world of the romantic comedies altogether, and, secondly, by the fact that many of his most vital characters in the comedies, Jaques, Malvolio, Sir Andrew and Sir Toby, Beatrice and Benedick, Bottom and Dogberry, are his own original creations and exist in non-romantic episodes and stories that he had invented for himself. There is an obvious parallel to all this in the lyric love-poetry of the time: if we are looking for psychological penetration and realism, for the passionate utterance of intense emotion, we shall not go to those poets like Sidney and Spenser who are in the main romantic tradition, but to Donne who had broken clean away from it.

[1] Stoll's last book, *From Shakespeare to Joyce*, furnishes several clear and categorical statements of his view: ' "In tragedy and comedy both," I have said elsewhere, "life must be, as it has ever been, piled on life, or we have visited the theatre in vain." It is not primarily to present characters in their convincing reality that Shakespeare and the Greeks have written, nor in an action strictly and wholly of their doing, but to set them in a state of high commotion, and thus to move and elevate the audience in turn' (pp. 305-306). Again: 'Drama and even the novel at its best are primarily or ultimately emotional, more concerned with the situation and poetry than with the portrayal of character' (p. 235).

This does not mean we must go all the way with Stoll, though his argument is often a tempting sword for cutting through some of the tangles of Shakespearean criticism.[1] Extremism is the vice of reformers, in literary criticism and politics, as vigorous honesty is their virtue; and Stoll is as much inclined to underrate the significance of 'character' in drama as he is the contribution that psychology can make to literary criticism. While it may be true that few, and perhaps none, of Shakespeare's comedy figures are projected with the psychological realism and rich, subtle observation of a great novelist, of Jane Austen for instance, it is impossible to deny 'character' to figures like Malvolio, Mercutio, Beatrice and Benedick, who live on as creations in our minds and must obviously be distinguished from such labelled shadows as Sebastian, Hero and Claudio. What appears to divide these characters from the pasteboards is their *animation*:[2] they have a clear shape and colour, certain idiosyncratic and recognisable traits that is to say; they move – in so far as they react with and on the events of the play to some extent; and, above all, they are quickened (and usually individualised) by the enchanting wit and poetry that Shakespeare has put into their mouths.[3] They give the actor or actress who is to represent them something to bite on, but they are still, in a considerable measure, dependent for their vividness and vitality on the personality and histrionic skill of their performer.

Among these successfully animated characters in Shakespeare's comedies we must certainly include, however vigorously we eschew the sentimentalities of Mrs. Jameson, many of his heroines, who, in the last phase of Rosalind, Viola and Helena, dominate

[1] See, for instance, his essay on Falstaff, Ch. 12, *From Shakespeare to Joyce*.

[2] Apart from the 'animated' character in drama I should distinguish – probably in opposition to Stoll – the memorable and significant character who is usually the projection of some acute original reading of the human heart or reflects some profound enigma or contradiction of human nature or symbolises and personifies some deep philosophic truth. Such a 'character' is not necessarily more realistic than the animated type, for he may be, as in Shakespearean tragedy, simplified, poetically intensified, often unrealistically motivated, and involved in melodramatic situations that we must merely accept as given. Such a character lives on in our minds, haunting, fascinating, long after any performance of the play in which he occurs, and, independent of the actor's art for his essential vitality, is a challenge to the actor's utmost powers of imagination. In Shakespeare this type of character, apart from Falstaff, is confined to the tragedies; but the type is not exclusively tragic.

[3] Cf. Stoll, ibid.: 'Like the ancients, less interested in anything that can be called a psychology, in motives or mental processes, and vastly more resourceful in expression, Shakespeare presents the character, minor or major, chiefly by the form and tone of speech.'

their world not only in a formal heroine capacity but as 'the efficient force which resolves the dilemma of the play into happiness'.[1] Such heroines are too vital, active, and at times shrewd and worldly to belong to the 'charming nonentity' species of romantic heroine. On the other hand, even if the conclusion savours of paradox, these admirable, idealised women owe much to the long romantic tradition, including of course the plays of Greene, which Shakespeare inherited.

It is this same tradition, and not any anachronistic anti-democratic bias, that accounts for the social status of the characters, which is predominantly aristocratic. Uninfluenced by the work of such contemporaries as Jonson, Shakespeare stuck to the usual romantic social types – kings, dukes, lords, princesses, highborn ladies, and gentlemen of leisure. Even *The Merchant of Venice*, the social framework of which might easily have been the same as that of the *Comedy of Errors*, is primarily a play of aristocrats – of Portia, the rich heiress of Belmont, Bassanio, 'a scholar and soldier' and a member of the entourage of the Marquis of Montferrat, Gratiano and Lorenzo, his friends, and of Antonio, who is only formally a merchant and plainly, by the tone of his conversation and his friendship with Bassanio, of the same social type. Admittedly, a few characters, varying in number from play to play, are drawn from other social strata, for Shakespeare was quick to exploit Greene's successful comedy formula of a tale of courtly personages, diversified with the humour of 'low-life' characters. But these characters are never allowed to steal the play, though Bottom comes very close to doing so in *A Midsummer Night's Dream*, and they exist only for some ancillary and (in a non-pejorative sense) parasitical function: they are servants, clowns, constables, and occasionally temporary actors for some show to be performed before the lords and ladies.

Intimately connected with the social environment of the comedies is their scenic background. We have already shown that the *Comedy of Errors* conformed to the classical model in the urban nature of its setting, while romance usually employed a background of castles, courts, and the open air, which it retained even when Europe had evolved an extensive town-civilisation. Such a romantic background is the broad setting of Shakespeare's comedy also, though the details of the canvas are painted with a local colour that is sometimes English, sometimes Italian and

[1] H. B. Charlton, *Shakespearian Comedy*, p. 285.

often both. One popular setting of romance was the untamed, mysterious wood or forest, with its fays, hermits, magicians, outlaws and wild beasts, and this was a favourite background with Shakespeare, who employed it in *The Two Gentlemen*, *A Midsummer Night's Dream* and *As You Like It*, and also for an odd hunting-scene in *Love's Labour's Lost*. Of these four examples the most richly romantic is the Forest of Arden in *As You Like It*. This wood, apart from the stray and unfounded reference to Rosalind's uncle –

> . . . a great magician,
> Obscured in the circle of this forest –[1]

certainly lacks the mystery, moon-steeped magic and fairy-lore of the Athenian wood. But it has its outlaws, its hunting-festivals and its kinship with the greenwood of Robin and his merry men; and its life and scenic details present an amazing medley and phantasmagoria. At moments, as when Jaques is sprawling

> Under an oak whose antique roots peep out
> Upon the brook that brawls along this wood,[2]

or when we are listening to the songs of the greenwood tree and the green cornfield, we are transported to Shakespeare's native Warwickshire. At other times, while Orlando is decking the trees with his poems, or such images are evoked as

> A sheepcote fenced about with olive trees,[3]

we are in the suave, artificial landscape of the pastoral. Then, a minute or two later, the background changes suddenly to an older romance type, to the 'desert place'[4] of deadly, exotic serpents and fierce lionesses of the medieval bestiary, a 'desert inaccessible'[5] not only to the imagination of Orlando but to the knowledge of any human geographer.

---
[1] *As You Like It*, v. iv. 33-34.
[2] Ibid., II. i. 31-32. Gray at least must have felt this as a typically English image when he assimilated it into his *Elegy*:
> There at the foot of yonder nodding beech
> That wreathes its old fantastic roots so high,
> His listless length at noontide would he stretch,
> And pore upon the brook that babbles by.
[3] Ibid., IV. iii. 78.
[4] Ibid., IV. iii. 142.
[5] Ibid., II. vii. 110.

Castles are never used by Shakespeare as a setting for his comedies. But he is fond of its contemporary real-life equivalent – the court of king or duke, or, approaching this in magnificence and lavish scale of entertainment, the estate of some rich and noble person like Portia and Olivia. This type of background is by no means invariably an indoor one; for the whole of *Love's Labour's Lost* the court of the King of Navarre is his park, and the court scenes in the early part of *As You Like It* have a similar open-air setting. Further, the courts and great estates in which so many of the comedies are set enabled Shakespeare to exploit one particular type of scene with a long romantic association. This was the garden, or 'orchard' as it was frequently called – a background that is used in *Romeo and Juliet*, *Much Ado*, *The Merchant of Venice* and *Twelfth Night*. The abbey or hermitage too, which Shakespeare had already used in the *Comedy of Errors*, was not only a characteristic feature of the romantic landscape, but a useful piece of dramatic machinery for retirements and secret meetings, as he demonstrates in *The Two Gentlemen* and *Romeo and Juliet*.

§

> Well, I will love, write, sigh, pray, sue and groan –
> (*Love's Labour's Lost*, III. i. 206.)

A close examination then of the characteristic features of the stories dramatised in Shakespeare's comedies reveals one important reason why we are justified in describing these plays as 'romantic' in the primary and most exact sense of the word. A very large part of their plot-material was borrowed from romantic literature, and in adapting this Shakespeare usually kept close to the traditions and conventions of romantic narrative.

But there is another important reason why the term 'romantic' gives us an exact classification. This is that the comedies, particularly the early ones, provide a rich and almost complete anthology of the doctrine and poetry of high romantic love in its late Elizabethan form. Not even Lyly's comedies are so word-perfect in the liturgy of romantic love, for Lyly's normal measure is prose, not verse.

The first and fundamental article of the romantic doctrine is clearly proclaimed in Shakespeare's comedies, where love is commonly represented as a transcendant experience, an actual re-creation of being that sets the imagination aflame, stimulates a heightened sensibility, reveals the exhilarating poetry of life, and brings to perfection the fine flower of almost every virtue. Nowhere in English poetry, unless in Spenser's *Hymns*, is there a more passionate or eloquent affirmation of this faith than in Berowne's famous speech, 'Have at you then, affection's men-at-arms',[1] the pith of which is in the lines:

> But love, first learned in a lady's eyes,
> Lives not alone immured in the brain;
> But, with the motion of all elements,
> Courses as swift as thought in every power,
> And gives to every power a double power,
> Above their functions and their offices.
> It adds a precious seeing to the eye;
> A lover's eyes will gaze an eagle blind;
> A lover's ear will hear the lowest sound,
> When the suspicious head of theft is stopp'd:
> Love's feeling is more soft and sensible
> Than are the tender horns of cockled snails;
> Love's tongue proves dainty Bacchus gross in taste:
> For valour, is not Love a Hercules,
> Still climbing trees in the Hesperides?
> Subtle as Sphinx; as sweet and musical
> As bright Apollo's lute strung with his hair;
> And when Love speaks, the voice of all the gods
> Make heaven drowsy with the harmony.
> Never durst poet touch a pen to write
> Until his ink were temper'd with Love's sighs.[2]

The obverse, or negative side of this affirmation is the lament of utter desolation, of a world emptied of all its meaning and beauty, when the beloved mistress is absent. Such is Valentine's plaint when he hears news of his banishment:

> To die is to be banish'd from myself;
> And Silvia is myself: banish'd from her
> Is self from self: a deadly banishment!
> What light is light, if Silvia be not seen?

[1] This speech may have been composed as a retort to the 'School of Night', some of whose members seem to have regarded love as a hindrance to learning (see M. C. Bradbrook, *The School of Night*, Ch. 7 and passim). But whatever the initial impulse, in asserting the value of love Shakespeare advanced the highest romantic claims.
[2] *Love's Labour's Lost*, IV. iii. 327-347.

> What joy is joy, if Silvia be not by?
> Unless it be to think that she is by
> And feed upon the shadow of perfection.
> Except I be by Silvia in the night,
> There is no music in the nightingale;
> Unless I look on Silvia in the day,
> There is no day for me to look upon;
> She is my essence, and I leave to be,
> If I be not by her fair influence
> Foster'd, illumined, cherish'd, kept alive.[1]

And such is Romeo's prostrate grief when Friar Lawrence informs him that he has been banished:

> Heaven is here,
> Where Juliet lives.[2]

The condition of such transcendant experience is complete and devout self-dedication. The lover must live entirely for his love, counting all time wasted, all activity vain, unless he is paying court to his lady and meditating on her matchless beauty and virtue. So the Duke in *Twelfth Night* boasts himself to be the model of every true lover,

> Unstaid and skittish in all motions else,
> Save in the constant image of the creature
> That is beloved.[3]

Formerly this unswerving devotion had been derived from the code of chivalry, upon which early romantic love had been largely modelled, but now love was its own justification for the dedicated life:

> Love's a mighty lord,
> And hath so humbled me as I confess
> There is no woe to his correction,
> Nor to his service no such joy on earth.
> Now no discourse, except it be of love;
> Now can I break my fast, dine, sup and sleep,
> Upon the very naked name of love.[4]

---

[1] *Two Gentlemen*, III. i. 171-184.
[2] *Romeo and Juliet*, III. iii. 29-30.
[3] *Twelfth Night*, II. iv. 18-20.
[4] *Two Gentlemen*, II. iv. 136-142.

In earlier times, as we have indicated, this dedication had been manifested in a life of 'courtesy', of service and gracious deeds, and it is interesting to note some reminiscences of the old chivalric love-code in *A Midsummer Night's Dream,* which chimes with words like 'loyalty', 'gentleness', 'knight', and 'courtesy'. There is, for instance, Lysander's vow as he lies down to sleep, a chaste and guardian knight, a little apart from Helena:

> And then end life when I end loyalty![1]

Shortly afterwards, when Lysander has been bewitched by the magic juice, Helena reproves him for making love to her with a direct appeal to his sense of courtesy:

> I thought you lord of more true gentleness,[2]

while, unadmonished, Lysander concludes his love-speech with a reference to the same code:

> And, all my powers, address your love and might
> To honour Helen, and to be her knight![3]

Later, to rid herself of the pestering attentions of Lysander, Helena makes yet another appeal to his duties as a knight:

> If you were civil and knew courtesy,
> You would not do me thus much injury.[4]

But, interesting as these lines in *A Midsummer Night's Dream* are, they represent nothing more than an odd survival. Shakespeare was writing at the end of the sixteenth century and, like Lyly, the dedication he chiefly reflects is not to a life of courtesy and chivalry but to the cult of dejection.

This fashion of love-affirmation is described or exhibited time and again in all its chief forms. There are, for example, numerous references to the lugubrious vein of sighs, tears and groans. Thus Valentine, in the first scene of *The Two Gentlemen,* swears that he will never fall in love

> ... where scorn is bought with groans;
> Coy looks with heart-sore sighs; one fading moment's mirth
> With twenty watchful, weary, tedious nights;[5]

---

[1] *A Midsummer Night's Dream,* II. ii. 63.
[2] Ibid., II. ii. 132.
[3] Ibid., II. ii. 143-144.
[4] Ibid., III. ii. 147-148.
[5] *Two Gentlemen,* I. i. 29-31.

and Montague describes how many a morning Romeo has been seen

> With tears augmenting the fresh morning's dew,
> Adding to clouds more clouds with his deep sighs.[1]

(Presumably – for the symptoms of the romantic lover are so clearly described by Montague and Benvolio – we must put Montague's ignorance of his son's state down to dramatic exigency.) Lysander, when he wishes to convince Helena of the sincerity of his sudden, new-found love for her, can think of no better or more eloquent proof than his tears:

> Why should you think that I should woo in scorn?
> Scorn and derision never come in tears:
> Look, when I vow, I weep; and vows so born,
> In their nativity all truth appears –[2]

which same method of proof Viola attempts when, hoping to convince Olivia of the intensity of her master's passion, she protests that he loves Olivia

> With adorations, fertile tears,
> With groans that thunder love, with sighs of love.[3]

Alongside this lachrymose part of the ritual went of course the trial and penance of sleeplessness, fasts and vigils. Valentine himself, after he had fallen in love with Silvia, came to welcome the discipline of the 'twenty watchful nights', even to exult lyrically in it:

> I have done penance for contemning Love,
> Whose high imperious thoughts have punished me
> With bitter fasts, with penitential groans,
> With nightly tears and daily heart-sore sighs;
> For in revenge of my contempt of love,
> Love hath chased sleep from my enthralled eyes
> And made them watchers of my own heart's sorrow.[4]

Not unnaturally such tearful griefs and penitential exercises often led Shakespeare's heroes, like true romantic lovers, to the cultivation of solitude. Romeo, for instance, in his earliest,

---

[1] *Romeo and Juliet*, I. i. 138-139.
[2] *A Midsummer Night's Dream*, III. ii. 122-125.
[3] *Twelfth Night*, I. v. 274-275.
[4] *Two Gentlemen*, II. iv. 129-135.

affected period as a lover, had been in the habit of haunting
solitary places, and Benvolio's report on him to his father –

> So early walking did I see your son:
> Towards him I made, but he was ware of me
> And stole into the covert of the wood –[1]

reminds us at once of Sidney's description of Pyrocles in the first
ecstasies of love:

> Every morning early going abroad, either to the garden, or to
> some woods towards the desert, it seemed his only comfort was to be
> without a comforter.[2]

Duke Orsino, too, displays a marked fondness for solitude in his
love-fever –

> ... for I myself am best
> When least in company –[3]

while Valentine's chief consolation for his outcast life as a forest
outlaw is that it gives him undisturbed leisure to brood upon his
unhappy love:

> This shadowy desert, unfrequented woods,
> I better brook than flourishing peopled towns:
> Here I can sit alone, unseen of any,
> And to the nightingale's complaining notes
> Tune my distresses and record my woes.[4]

In this last line Valentine is presumably thinking of poetic
composition, and Shakespeare's romantic lovers run true to type
in their penchant for verse-making. Proteus gives us perhaps the
most complete account of this part of the lover's role when, as he
is pretending to advise Thurio how to win Silvia, he emphasises
the value of sonnet-making, especially as a permanent record of
the tears and sighs:

> You must lay lime to tangle her desires
> By wailful sonnets, whose composed rhymes
> Should be full-fraught with serviceable vows. . . .
> Say that upon the altar of her beauty

[1] *Romeo and Juliet*, I. i. 130-133.
[2] *Arcadia*, Bk. 1, Ch. 9 (Vol. I, p. 54).
[3] *Twelfth Night*, I. iv. 40-41.
[4] *Two Gentlemen*, v. iv. 2-6.

> You sacrifice your tears, your sighs, your heart:
> Write till your ink be dry, and with your tears
> Moist it again, and frame some feeling line
> That may discover such integrity.[1]

But there are several other explicit references to the same habit: Mercutio twits Romeo for his verse-making; Egeus, giving the parent's point of view, accuses Lysander of bewitching his daughter with 'verses of feigning love' sung at her window; and Viola, invited by Olivia to describe how she would make love to her, declares that she would

> Write loyal cantons of contemned love
> And sing them loud even in the dead of night.[2]

In *Love's Labour's Lost* and *As You Like It* indeed, we have more than descriptive references; the verse-making of the King, Longaville and Dumaine in the one play, and of Orlando in the other, form an actual part of the story, and we are forced to hear out their insipid efforts.

However, one of the sonnets in *Love's Labour's Lost* – Longaville's sonnet – if not inspired, is certainly of some interest, for it furnishes a good example of the religious phraseology in romantic love-poetry. There are several other instances of this style of writing in Shakespeare's comedies. Sometimes it merely occurs in small phrases, as in the already quoted 'upon the altar of her beauty'; sometimes it is so slight and delicate that we may easily overlook it:

> But truer stars did govern Proteus' birth:
> His words are bonds, his oaths are oracles,
> His love sincere, his thoughts immaculate,
> His tears pure messengers sent from his heart,
> His heart as far from fraud as heaven from earth.[3]

But sometimes this pseudo-religious vein is bold and unmistakable, as in the lines:

> When the devout religion of mine eye
>   Maintains such falsehood then turn tears to fires;
> And these, who often drowned could never die,
>   Transparent heretics, be burnt for liars![4]

---
[1] *Two Gentlemen*, III. ii. 68-77.
[2] *Twelfth Night*, I. v. 289-90.
[3] *Two Gentlemen*, II. vii. 74-78.
[4] *Romeo and Juliet*, I. ii. 93-96.

An even more sustained example of this manner, perhaps the most sustained in all Shakespeare, occurs later in the play when Romeo first speaks alone with Juliet:

> *Romeo:* If I profane with my unworthiest hand
>   This holy shrine, the gentle fine is this:
>   My lips, two blushing pilgrims, ready stand
>   To smooth that rough touch with a tender kiss.
> *Juliet:* Good pilgrim, you do wrong your hand too much,
>   Which mannerly devotion shows in this;
>   For saints have hands that pilgrims' hands do touch,
>   And palm to palm is holy palmers' kiss.
> *Romeo:* Have not saints lips, and holy palmers too?
> *Juliet:* Ay, pilgrim, lips that they must use in prayer.
> *Romeo:* O! then, dear saint, let lips do what hands do;
>   They pray, grant thou, lest faith turn to despair.
> *Juliet:* Saints do not move, though grant for prayers' sake.
> *Romeo:* Then move not, while my prayers' effect I take.
>   Thus from my lips, by thine, my sin is purged.[1]

Such lines as these, which, in England at least, could not have been written before the late sixteenth century, remind us that parts of the substance and expression of romantic love were constantly changing. On the other hand, there were some elements that hardly changed at all in the three to four hundred years dividing Shakespeare from Chretien of Troyes. Such was the importance attached to the virtues of chastity, purity, and even to denial and asceticism. This attitude was strong in romance in the beginning and, as we have indicated in Chapter I, it was powerfully and intellectually reinforced by the work of the Petrarchians and neo-platonists.

It would of course be untrue to say that this side of romantic love is emphasised by Shakespeare. Quite obviously chastity and the sublimation of physical love have neither the value nor fascinating mystery for Shakespeare that they have for Spenser or the Milton of *Comus*:

> So dear to Heav'n is Saintly chastity,
> That when a soul is found sincerely so,
> A thousand liveried Angels lacky her,
> Driving far off each thing of sin and guilt,
> And in clear dream, and solemn vision
> Tell her of things that no gross ear can hear,

---

[1] *Romeo and Juliet*, I. v. 95-109.

> Till oft converse with heav'nly habitants
> Begin to cast a beam on th' outward shape,
> The unpolluted temple of the mind,
> And turns it by degrees to the soul's essence,
> Till all be made immortal.[1]

Shakespeare's was a robust, full-blooded sensibility that appears to have been quite unaffected by the theories and abstractions of neo-platonism, and his constant attitude to the physical side of love – repeated again and again – is always that of the *Sonnets*:

> From fairest creatures we desire increase,
> That thereby beauty's rose might never die,
> But as the riper should by time decease,
> His tender heir might bear his memory.[2]

Occasionally a romantic attitude is reflected through the comedies, as when Claudio passionately denies Leonato's imputation that he has had sexual intercourse with Hero before their marriage, or when Hermia demurely reproves Lysander for proposing to lie beside her in the wood:

> But, gentle friend, for love and courtesy
> Lie further off.[3]

But such responses are purely dramatic, and Shakespeare never chooses to elaborate them as Spenser or Milton might have done. On the other hand, our total impression of Shakespeare's lovers, of the heroines in particular, certainly includes a sense of purity and chastity, and this sense is produced to a large extent by the absence of physical love-making. Admittedly, there is a salacious humour in the comedies that is by no means confined to the 'low-life' characters: in *Love's Labour's Lost*, for instance, the Princess and her attendants sometimes talk as 'greasily' as Costard, while Rosalind and Celia indulge in occasional obscenities. But, measured against the comedy of other periods and against the comedy of the other Elizabethans, Shakespeare's plays have only a slight bawdy element; and, apart from the interludes where Beatrice and Benedick (quite *un*romantic lovers as we shall see) are brought together, this element does not enter into the courtship scenes, which take their tone from the spiritual

---

[1] *Comus*, 453-463.
[2] *Sonnet* 1.
[3] *A Midsummer Night's Dream*, II. ii. 56-57.

and soulful atmosphere of the main romantic tradition. Further, the type of indecency that is occasionally exchanged between a Rosalind and Celia is light, witty and ungloating, uttered and gone almost before we have had time to notice it, and in a way innocent, like the talk of children who only half understand what they are alluding to.

Finally, there is in the comedies the romantic note of rhapsody over female beauty. True, this type of lyricism is rare and more fleeting than one might at first imagine before making a close scrutiny of the text, for our impressions tend to be coloured by the opulent, sensuous descriptions in *Venus and Adonis* and *The Rape of Lucrece*. However, there is one passage in *A Midsummer Night's Dream* that vies in rich hyperbole with anything in the poems:

> O Helen! goddess, nymph, perfect, divine!
> To what, my love, shall I compare thine eyne?
> Crystal is muddy. O! how ripe in show
> Thy lips, those kissing cherries, tempting grow!
> That pure congealed white, high Taurus' snow,
> Fann'd with the eastern wind, turns to a crow
> When thou hold'st up thy hand: O! let me kiss
> This princess of pure white, this seal of bliss.[1]

[1] *A Midsummer Night's Dream*, III. ii. 137-144.

CHAPTER FIVE

SHAKESPEARE'S DETACHMENT FROM ROMANCE

NONE OF SHAKESPEARE's comedies is more deeply infused with romantic elements than *The Two Gentlemen of Verona*, which, if we exclude *The Comedy of Errors*, is probably the first or second of this group in order of composition. By itself it furnishes an almost complete anthology of that doctrine of romantic love which, in the previous chapter, we compiled from the comedies as a whole, while its narrative, wholly concentrated on a serious love-story, is pure romance. As H. B. Charlton comments: 'its actions are conducted to a conventional etiquette and are determined by a particular creed; and every feature of it, in matter and sentiment, is traceable to the romantic attitude of man to woman'.[1]

Yet *The Two Gentlemen* is not merely a romance; it is also a comedy. Further, as Charlton clearly perceives, there is a vital connection between the comedy and the romance: the play is not just a serious romantic story with detached or loosely connected scenes of comic relief. The romance element itself generates humour. But, according to Charlton, this humour is largely unconscious, the fumblings of an apprentice hand intent on manipulating the dangerous material of romance into drama: 'Clearly, Shakespeare's first attempt to make romantic comedy had only succeeded so far that it had unexpectedly and inadvertently made romance comic'.[2]

No doubt the serious romantic story of the play does produce such instances of inadvertent humour as Charlton demonstrates – the hero, who ought to be something of a superman, exhibiting himself as a dolt with less wit than the official fool of the play, the impossible forest outlaws with no parallel in literature except the Pirates of Penzance. But Charlton's analysis is deficient, if not mistaken. He fails to notice the abundant signs that even at this early stage in his development Shakespeare was capable of standing in conscious and amused detachment from the romantic mode and tradition. So far from the comedy of the piece being merely a matter of inadvertent humour, Shakespeare deliberately

[1] *Shakespearian Comedy*, p. 27.
[2] Ibid., p. 43.

uses Speed and Launce – as he later uses Touchstone – to guy romantic sentiment through the realistic and occasionally satiric chorus of the clown.

Admittedly this function of Speed is not much in evidence at his first entry, for though he brings the soulful image of the typically dejected Proteus –

> Thou, Julia, thou hast metamorphosed me,
> Made me neglect my studies, lose my time,
> War with good counsel, set the world at nought –[1]

down to the cruder and (for the gallants in the audience) the more realistic level of laced 'muttons' and bawdy jokes, this note is soon smothered in a riot of punning and back-chat. But when Speed next comes on to the stage his purposes are obvious enough. In the first place, he is employed to ridicule Valentine, who, having in the meanwhile fallen in love himself, is now as absurdly 'a votary to fond desire' as ever Proteus was. The material-minded Speed, in love only with his bed, finds his master easy game and banters him with what is in effect a comic outsider's view of the cult of dejection:

> Val.: Why, how know you that I am in love?
> Speed: Marry, by these special marks: first, you have learned, like Sir Proteus, to wreathe your arms, like a malcontent; to relish a love-song, like a robin-redbreast; to walk alone, like one that had the pestilence; to sigh, like a schoolboy that had lost his A B C; to weep, like a young wench that had buried her grandam; to fast, like one that takes diet; to watch, like one that fears robbing; to speak puling, like a beggar at Hallowmas. You were wont, when you laughed, to crow like a cock; when you walked, to walk like one of the lions; when you fasted, it was presently after dinner; when you looked sadly, it was for want of money: and now you are metamorphosed with a mistress, that, when I look on you, I can hardly think you my master.[2]

Secondly, Speed remains on the stage to keep up a mocking commentary that flickers over the encounter of the lovers, which is conducted to the stilted code of romantic courtship, with its 'Mistress' and 'Servant', its lady's absolute commands and knight's unquestioning obedience. His words at his exit have the

---

[1] *Two Gentlemen of Verona*, I. i. 66-68.
[2] Ibid., II. i. 17-33.

decisive ring of his own mundane conclusions: 'though the chameleon Love can feed on the air, I am one that am nourished by my victuals and would fain have meat'.[1]

The meeting between Speed and Launce (Act II, Scene v), coming between Valentine's extravagant tributes to the peerless divinity of his mistress and Proteus' perjured, though equally high-flown, dedication of himself to her, has a similar effect of comic deflation:

> *Speed:* But, Launce, how sayest thou, that my master is become a notable lover?
> *Launce:* I never knew him otherwise.
> *Speed:* Than how?
> *Launce:* A notable lubber, as thou reportest him to be.
> *Speed:* Why, thou whoreson ass, thou mistakest me.
> *Launce:* Why, fool, I meant not thee; I meant thy master.
> *Speed:* I tell thee, my master is become a hot lover.
> *Launce:* Why, I tell thee, I care not though he burn himself in love. If thou wilt, go with me to the alehouse; if not, thou art an Hebrew, a Jew, and not worth the name of a Christian.[2]

However, it is in the coarse, peasant realism of Launce's own love affair that the anti-romantic note is struck most audibly. Not for Launce the rosy spectacles or lyricism of religious devotion; the maid whom he has an eye on can be reduced to the business-like points of a bare catalogue – to a list of practical virtues and defects: 'Item, she brews good ale. ... Item, she can wash and scour. ... Item, she is not to be kissed fasting, in respect of her breath. ... Item, she hath no teeth.'[3] What makes this episode (which foreshadows Touchstone's pursuit of Audrey) particularly striking is that it occurs immediately after Valentine's banishment – that is to say, precisely at the point in the narrative when we ought to be most concerned with the fate of the lovers of the romance.

Naturally an acute Shakespearean critic like Charlton does not altogether overlook the anti-romantic significance of Launce. 'A sheer clod of earth, Launce by name, will ... expose the unsubstantiality of the romantic hero with whom the play throws him into contact.'[4] But he mars that perception by slipping in between

---
[1] *Two Gentlemen of Verona*, II. i. 182-185.
[2] Ibid., II. v. 42-58.
[3] Ibid., III. i. 304-344.
[4] Charlton, op. cit., p. 34.

'will' and 'expose' the peculiar phrase 'quite unwittingly'. 'Quite unwittingly' to Launce himself, no doubt; but to Shakespeare . . .? The suggestion is fantastic. Shakespeare had not 'unexpectedly and inadvertently made romance comic' when he created Launce. Launce was one mask of a dramatist who had already learnt to laugh at the romantic conception of love.

But though this burlesque or choric satire of Speed and Launce provides the chief criticism of romance in the play, there are one or two slighter notes of depreciation. For instance, there is a gratingly obvious discord against the dominant romantic harmonies of the play in Act III, Scene i, where Valentine is advising the Duke on courtship. Here we have – the more remarkable in that it is spoken by the hero, and with little dramatic necessity – a description of what in our study of Lyly we defined as the cynical, machiavellian tactics of courtship. This sentiment is so rare in Shakespearean comedy that Valentine's speech deserves quoting in full:

>A woman sometimes scorns what best contents her.
>Send her another;[1] never give her o'er;
>For scorn at first makes after-love the more.
>If she do frown, 'tis not in hate of you,
>But rather to beget more love in you:
>If she do chide, 'tis not to have you gone;
>For why, the fools are mad, if left alone.
>Take no repulse, whatever she doth say;
>For 'get you gone', she doth not mean 'away!'
>Flatter and praise, commend, extol their graces;
>Though ne'er so black, say they have angels' faces.
>That man that hath a tongue, I say, is no man,
>If with his tongue he cannot win a woman.[2]

We should wantonly distort the meaning of the play if we threw an exaggerated stress on passages of this kind, isolated as they are and few in number. They are momentary variations, undeveloped themes, faint undertones. But, like the prominent chorus of the clowns, they do show us that even in his youthful and most enthusiastic days, when romance was the main inspiration of his work, Shakespeare, with the comprehensiveness of true genius, was capable of smiling at what he cherished, was critical of romantic doctrines (especially of love) and perhaps

[1] Another (present, gift).
[2] *Two Gentlemen of Verona*, III. i. 93-105.

already had a glimpse of their shallowness and falsity. When the repentant Proteus cries out:

> O heaven! were man
> But constant, he were perfect. That one error
> Fills him with faults; makes him run through all the sins,[1]

he may be merely speaking in part. But if Shakespeare shared those sentiments, he was on his way to question, though not necessarily to reject, one of the basic assumptions of the romantic attitude to love.

Whatever may be said of *The Two Gentlemen*, there is certainly nothing inadvertent about the amalgam of romance and comedy in the sophisticated *Love's Labour's Lost*. Romance is certainly present: the moral, which is the folly of those who war against their affections and 'the huge army of the world's desires', at least supports the romantic attitude, and the King, Longaville, Dumain and even Berowne behave as typical romantic lovers once they surrender to their passion. When Berowne says, 'By heaven, I do love; and it hath taught me to rhyme and to be melancholy',[2] he is speaking for them all. Also, the most impressive passage of the play is the long speech,[3] running to over seventy lines, in which Berowne elaborates the central and loftiest doctrine of romantic love. But *Love's Labour's Lost* differs conspicuously from *The Two Gentlemen* in that the romantic element is treated in a consistently comic spirit. The scene in which the lovers confess themselves against a background of eavesdroppers is pure comedy for all the soulful sonneteering:

> O, what a scene of foolery have I seen,
> Of sighs, of groans, of sorrow, and of teen;[4]

while the courtship of the lovers is adapted to a 'civil war of wits' – pun-capping, logic-chopping, raillery and verbal fireworks of every sort. This particular adaptation, which was to be fully and continuously exploited as a fundamental part of the pattern of the later comedies, had been first tried out in *The Two Gentlemen* (assuming this was the earlier play of the two); but there is nothing in *The Two Gentlemen* comparable with the prolonged episode of the 'Russians', in which the disguised king and his followers are

[1] *Two Gentlemen of Verona*, v. iv. 110-112.
[2] *Love's Labour's Lost*, IV. iii. 13-14.
[3] Ibid., IV. iii. 290-365.
[4] Ibid., IV. iii. 163-164.

baffled and mercilessly derided by the princess and her ladies. Clearly, Shakespeare had no scruples about handling romance lightly, and even irreverently, when he was assimilating it to comedy.

Occasionally, as notably in the lines:

> What, I! I love! I sue! I seek a wife!
> A woman, that is like a German clock,
> Still a-repairing, ever out of frame,
> And never going aright, being a watch,
> But being watch'd that it may still go right![1]

Berowne is allowed licence to deny the high romantic doctrine that he is able at other times to maintain so eloquently. Again, though he can pour out his lyrical hyperbole to a lady with the best –

> Who sees the heavenly Rosaline,
> That, like a rude and savage man of Ind,
> At the first opening of the gorgeous east,
> Bows not his vassal head and strucken blind
> Kisses the base ground with obedient breast?
> What peremptory eagle-sighted eye
> Dares look upon the heaven of her brow,
> That is not blinded by her majesty? –[2]

in his heart he knows the fundamental falsity of this sentiment

> which makes flesh a deity,
> A green goose a goddess.[3]

But in this play Shakespeare has not yet developed his later mode of mocking at romantic love through characters who are themselves within the courtly and romantic world. What we have instead is an exterior, anti-romantic burlesque, with Don Armado as the main figure, similar to that employed in *The Two Gentlemen*. There is a large difference between the two burlesques of course. Launce is a low-bred fellow with a materialistic, peasant outlook, Don Armado a gentleman and a parody of the romantic lover, who affects all the sighing, moping melancholy of his kind, including the cult of poetry: 'Assist me, some extemporal god of rhyme, for I am sure I shall turn sonnet'.[4] Where Launce is comic

---

[1] *Love's Labour's Lost*, III. i. 191-195.
[2] Ibid., IV. iii. 221-228.
[3] Ibid., IV. iii. 74-75.
[4] Ibid., I. ii. 188-189.

for his grossness and prosaic calculation, Don Armado is comic for the extravagance and folly of his love. But just as Launce serves to remind us that the attitude of Valentine and Proteus to love is after all a singular one, and perhaps hopelessly divorced from the realities of everyday life, so Armado's infatuation for the country baggage Jaquenetta, who belongs to Launce's world, reflects upon the loves of the King and Princess and their followers and causes us to regard these loves less seriously than we should do were there no Armado and Jaquenetta. The note of sheer earthiness may not be so prominent in Don Armado's affair as it is in Launce's. But it is there, notably when – in a delightful anti-climax to the Pageant of the Worthies – Costard bursts out unceremoniously that Jaquenetta is two months gone with child.

However, it is not merely the sentiments of romantic love that Shakespeare lightly and occasionally mocks at in *Love's Labour's Lost*. Not surprisingly in this play that is characterised by so much parody of various artificial styles of speaking and writing, he also reveals himself as an alert critic of the manner of contemporary romantic love-poetry.

As far as the King's poem – a sonnet with two extra lines, in the lugubrious vein – is concerned, it is difficult to say definitely whether the effort is intended as a parody or not. Certainly the similes of the octave are violently strained, and there is a most awkward transition to the fantastic conceit of the 'coach' in lines nine and ten. On the other hand, there are too many Petrarchian sonnets with similarly grotesque figures for us to say that these crudities were deliberately manufactured by Shakespeare in order to be laughed at, while the conclusion of the sonnet proper:

> But do not love thyself; then thou wilt keep
> My tear for glasses, and still make me weep[1]

is no more perversely ingenious than many of the W. H. Sonnets.[2] Yet if we must doubt Shakespeare's intentions in the King's poem, we may feel more confident about Longaville's sonnet. This, though its two opening lines:

---

[1] *Love's Labour's Lost*, IV. iii. 38-39.
[2] I agree with John Palmer's comment (*Shakespeare's Comic Characters*, p. 16) on this sonnet, though not with his praise for the last part of it: 'If this be parody, it is such that only a poet, indulgently smiling at a brother's extravagance would write. It is written in sport, but might have fallen from the sheaf inscribed to Mr. W. H.'

> Did not the heavenly rhetoric of thine eye,
> 'Gainst whom the world cannot hold argument[1]

might come straight from the W. H. Sonnets, is certainly a travesty of the religious phrasing and imagery used in so many of the amatory poems of the late sixteenth century. We can hardly miss Shakespeare's deliberate parody when we have the immediate comment of Berowne to guide us:

> This is the liver-vein, which makes flesh a deity,
> A green goose a goddess: pure, pure idolatry.[2]

However, the hardest blow against the extravagant style of romantic love-poetry and love-making is reserved to the last scene of the play where, shamed by the behaviour of the King and his other companions and by the way the Princess and her ladies have fooled them all, Berowne abjures not merely verse of the strained and artificial type but all wooing

> ... in rhyme, like a blind harper's song!
> Taffeta phrases, silken terms precise,
>   Three-piled hyperboles, spruce affectation,
> Figures pedantical; these summer-flies
> Have blown me full of maggot ostentation:
> I do forswear them; and I here protest
> By this white glove,– how white the hand, God knows! –
> Henceforth my wooing mind shall be express'd
> In russet yeas and honest kersey noes.[3]

But perhaps there is a comment on romantic love in the final act of the play that goes much deeper than Berowne's rejection of 'taffeta phrases'. Most audiences find the last part of this act an oddity and something of a puzzle, for in a bewildering instant the gay, sunlit scene is plunged into cold shadow that utterly transforms it. It is not simply the news of the death of the Princess's father that effects this change. This report might have been but a passing cloud. What shocks and sobers us is the abrupt and decisive change in the characters, especially in the Princess, to seriousness, the unfamiliar note of gravity in the speeches, the evocation of a world of suffering – of sick-beds, hospitals, death.

It is difficult to say what exactly Shakespeare meant by this unexpected development. Perhaps he intended nothing more

---

[1] *Love's Labour's Lost*, IV. iii. 60-61.
[2] Ibid., IV. iii. 74-75.
[3] Ibid., V. ii. 405-413.

than the surface meaning of the speeches of the Princess and Rosaline: that partly as penance, partly to prove the reality of their love, the King and Berowne were to be sent on a quest, this time to experience some of the ineluctable hardness of life. But the passage is so sustained and some of the lines so intense –

> To move wild laughter in the throat of death?
> It cannot be; it is impossible:
> Mirth cannot move a soul in agony –[1]

that another effect is produced. Whether Shakespeare intended it or not, we feel – not happy to be bundled out of our enchanted circle of make-believe – that we are in the real, complex world of pain and mortality, where all love, romantic or otherwise, is but a part of our human experience, and perhaps nothing more than a sweet momentary diversion.

§

No one can miss the romantic elements in *A Midsummer Night's Dream* – its courtly love adventures in the enchanted wood near Athens, its tissue of romantic love-sentiment, its idealisation of marriage, its fairies,[2] hunting-scene and delicate evocation of the dewy May morning, so rich with old romantic associations. The play is, though in a different way, as pure a specimen of romance as *The Two Gentlemen*. For all this, it contains a strong note of criticism and interrogation, which is announced insistently, even monotonously, in the very first scene.

This note is struck when Lysander openly accuses Demetrius, a 'spotted and inconstant man', of having broken his plighted troth to Helena. We might expect to hear no more of it, for a few moments later the true lovers, Lysander and Hermia, whose passionate and unquenchable devotion to each other we have witnessed in the first part of the scene, draw together. But hardly are they in each others' arms before Lysander, so confident and courageous before, is lamenting the precarious mortality of love:

> Or, if there were a sympathy in choice,
> War, death, or sickness did lay siege to it,
> Making it momentany as a sound,

---

[1] *Love's Labour's Lost*, v. ii. 865-867.
[2] These fairies owed something to the fays of romance as well as to the elves of popular tradition; but in the main they are re-creations. The benign fairy-world of modern literature is almost entirely Shakespearean in inspiration.

> Swift as a shadow, short as any dream;
> Brief as the lightning in the collied night,
> That, in a spleen, unfolds both heaven and earth,
> And ere a man hath power to say 'Behold!'
> The jaws of darkness do devour it up:
> So quick bright things come to confusion.[1]

– a mere straightforward response to the dramatic situation from a lover who is threatened with the loss of his mistress? Perhaps. But why does Hermia, when she is trying to convince Lysander that she will keep her promise to elope with him, swerve so curiously from Cupid's strongest bow and Venus' doves to inconstancy and broken vows? –

> And by that fire which burn'd the Carthage queen,
> When the false Troyan under sail was seen,
> By all the vows that ever men have broke,
> In number more than ever women spoke,
> In that same place thou hast appointed me,
> To-morrow truly will I meet with thee.[2]

This theme is developed by the soliloquy of Helena on Demetrius, which concludes the scene, for one of the main reasons for this precariousness of love and fickleness of lovers is, so Helen maintains, the complete irrationality of our passion:

> And as he errs, doting on Hermia's eyes,
> So I, admiring of his qualities:
> Things base and vile, holding no quality,
> Love can transpose to form and dignity:
> Love looks not with the eyes, but with the mind;
> And therefore is wing'd Cupid painted blind:
> Nor hath Love's mind of any judgement taste;
> Wings and no eyes figure unheedy haste:
> And therefore is Love said to be a child,
> Because in choice he is so oft beguiled.
> As waggish boys in game themselves forswear,
> So the boy Love is perjured everywhere.[3]

Analysed then, the opening of *A Midsummer Night's Dream* reveals two distinct and contrasting subjects, both of which are woven into the substance of the sentimental main plot – first, the passionate loyalty and devotion of romantic love which will

[1] *A Midsummer Night's Dream*, I. i. 141-149.
[2] Ibid., I. i. 173-178.
[3] Ibid., I. i. 230-241.

fight against all obstacles, and secondly, the changefulness, frenzied irrationality and brevity of love. What Shakespeare is surely, if delicately, hinting is that unswerving constancy is a rare and more fragile quality than romance commonly admits. We recall Proteus' words at the close of *The Two Gentlemen*:

> O heaven! were man
> But constant, he were perfect. That one error
> Fills him with faults; makes him run through all the sins.[1]

This second, counter theme, which is perhaps more accurately described as a correction than a criticism of romantic love, is elaborated in two directions. In the first place, the elopement of Lysander and Hermia is complicated by the mistakes of Puck, who, by misusing the magic juice that Oberon has given him, causes Lysander to desert Hermia and, with Demetrius, to transfer his affections to Helena. Admittedly these two examples of fickleness are produced by a purely mechanical means. All the same there is good reason to believe that Shakespeare intended the episode to be more than a piece of pantomimic business. We remember that one of the inconstant lovers, Demetrius, 'the spotted and inconstant man', has already once before – and without any supernatural compulsion – changed the object of his affection. We notice that Shakespeare does not treat the episode in a spirit of near-tragedy, as one who held seriously to the doctrines of romantic love would probably have done; on the contrary, the transformation of Lysander and Demetrius, though they are characters in the main and (on the whole) serious romantic plot, is to be regarded comically. Above all, we must be struck by Shakespeare's mischievous sense of fun in keeping for Demetrius and Lysander the same 'votary's' attitude to love before and after the enchantment. Lysander in particular is outrageously brazen in wooing Helena with the same terms of frantic and rhetorical devotion as he had previously employed towards Hermia. Only, it appears, has the physical form of the 'goddess' and 'mistress' changed. Small wonder that Puck excuses his carelessness on the grounds that it has, after all, merely produced a situation that Fate normally ordains:

> Then fate o'er-rules, that, one man holding troth,
> A million fail, confounding oath on oath.[2]

[1] *Two Gentlemen of Verona*, v. iv. 110-112.
[2] *A Midsummer Night's Dream*, III. ii. 92-93.

There is, of course, no way of proving conclusively that the entanglement caused by the magic juice has a significance and meaning of the kind we have just indicated, or indeed of proving conclusively that it has any meaning and significance at all. But the story of the Athenian lovers must not be viewed in isolation; it must be linked with the quarrel between Oberon and Titania, which contains a fairy-world, but unmistakable variation of the same theme of fickleness and inconstancy. It is not merely that Titania deserts her husband and comes, under the influence of the magic juice, to dote upon an ass. The whole fairy atmosphere – in the first part of the play at least – is thick with rumours of infidelities: Oberon, disguised as Corin, has been wooing Phillida and is now casting an amorous eye on Hippolyta; Titania, so Oberon alleges, is in love with Theseus. Even Theseus, who might otherwise have passed as the one solid, constant and commonsense lover of the play, is degraded by the wrangle between the Fairy King and Queen, since, in his anxiety to prove Titania's fondness for Theseus, Oberon drags up Theseus' unsavoury past of treachery and broken vows:

> Didst thou not lead him through the glimmering night
> From Perigenia, whom he ravished?
> And make him with fair Aegle break his faith,
> With Ariadne, and Antiopa?[1]

However, the Theseus who is exhibited to us in these lines is a momentary and soon-forgotten figure. The Theseus that we remember is the mature, rational, self-possessed husband (or husband-to-be) who, in a speech that repeats the theme of Helena's earlier soliloquy, brackets the lover with the lunatic, and so, indirectly, utters the play's own comment on the fantastic adventures of its heroes and heroines:

> Lovers and madmen have such seething brains,
> Such shaping fantasies, that apprehend
> More than cool reason ever comprehends.
> The lunatic, the lover and the poet
> Are of imagination all compact:
> One sees more devils than vast hell can hold,
> That is, the madman; the lover, all as frantic,
> Sees Helen's beauty in a brow of Egypt . . .[2]

[1] *A Midsummer Night's Dream*, II. i. 77-80.
[2] Ibid., v. i. 4-11.

Such, too, appears to be the attitude of Bottom who, recovering from his surprise at hearing Titania's declaration of love for him, balances himself with the reflection – 'to say the truth, reason and love keep little company together now-a-days'.[1]

However, Bottom has more significance for our present inquiry than this one passing remark. It is likely – particularly if we keep *A Midsummer Night's Dream* in the context of the other comedies and remember the recurrence of situations, themes, methods of treatment – that Shakespeare intended Bottom, like Speed and Launce, to embody a mundane, broadly comic antithesis to the romance world. Perhaps that is not his significance in the middle scenes of the play, for if his affair with Titania reduces love to the level of farce and furnishes a ludicrous contrast with the romantic love-making of Lysander, Demetrius, Hermia and Helena, it is love in general rather than love in the romantic form that, directly and by implication, he renders comic. Where Bottom does surely emerge as a distinctive antithesis to romance is in the *Pyramus and Thisbe* Interlude, of which he is the central figure. It is, of course, possible that Shakespeare's choice of the Pyramus and Thisbe story for the play of the mechanicals was entirely fortuitous. But when we think of the scores of suitable tales at hand for Shakespeare's purpose it is somewhat remarkable that he should have utilised one of the most famous of all love romances. And even if his choice of the story was unpremeditated, it is in effect a murderous burlesque of a romance, so murderous indeed that it is impossible to believe that its author could ever regard romantic love with a serious, uncritical, undivided attitude.

Bringing together these various themes that we have traced, we may attempt to state the 'meaning' of the play, which in so delicate a piece of work is not a 'moral' but the shaping attitude behind it. Young love, as Shakespeare here presents it, is passionate, intense, permeated with lyrical wonder and indefinable magic; but it is transient, irrational, full of frenzy and fantasy. The absurdities and extravagances of such love are often ludicrous, and it does no one any harm, least of all the lovers themselves, that we should occasionally laugh at it. But love of this kind is real and true to human nature, and its reality, which we should tolerate, is the truth of the romantic attitude. On the other hand, the romantic conception of love is an inadequate

[1] *A Midsummer Night's Dream*, III. i. 146-148.

one:[1] first, because it ignores or too lightly dismisses the changefulness, selfishness and unfaithfulness of human beings in their sexual relations; and secondly, because it is essentially a reflection of youthful and pre-marital love. The loves and fancies of Lysander, Demetrius, Hermia and Helena are natural enough, but they represent only a phase, the phase of courtship. The love of marriage, which is the consummation of courtship, should be something cooler, more substantial and rational – an 'everlasting bond of fellowship' as Theseus calls it.

There is also, by implication at least, a third criticism of the romantic attitude: if love is so irrational, then the romantic claims for its moral and spiritual elevation, the contention of Berowne in his great speech, are grossly exaggerated.

§

Romeo and Juliet, written about the same time as *A Midsummer Night's Dream*, falls naturally into this discussion of Shakespeare's attitude towards romantic love, for though conventionally described as a tragedy, two-thirds of it belongs unmistakably to the world of the comedies. Certainly, apart from its *dénouement*, it is both in spirit and substance as much a comedy as *Much Ado About Nothing*. Moreover, its main theme is love, and the forms of love represented have much to do with the romantic ideal.

In the first place, the Romeo of the opening act is a portrait and – as far as we can be definite about these matters of impression – almost certainly a caricature of the typical romantic lover. He is introduced to us indirectly through the account of his companion, Benvolio, who relates how he has seen Romeo in the early morning seeking the solitude of a nearby wood. Romeo's father describes other familiar symptoms: his son weeps and sighs; he locks himself up in his room during the daytime, making an artificial night for himself. Both Benvolio[2] and Montague affect ignorance of the cause of Romeo's condition, for like a true romantic lover Romeo cherishes the precept long before laid down by Andreas Capellanus – 'Qui non celat, amare non potest':

---

[1] Charlton (op. cit., p. 235) is not afraid to stress this element of 'meaning' in the play: 'The light-hearted comedy of *A Midsummer Night's Dream* is as complete an exposure of the foundations of romantic love as *Troilus and Cressida*.'

[2] But, as is evident later in the scene, Benvolio has an accurate suspicion of the true cause of Romeo's behaviour.

> But he, his own affections' counsellor,
> Is to himself – I will not say how true –
> But to himself so secret and so close,
> So far from sounding and discovery,
> As is the bud bit with an envious worm.[1]

When Romeo himself appears, all that he says and does only adds to the outlines of the caricature. He is woefully sad; desperate to madness. He rails (but a willing slave) against the torment of love; and he is utterly hopeless, out of favour, for his Rosaline is of course one of the proud and scornful fair ones:

> She'll not be hit
> With Cupid's arrow; she hath Dian's wit;
> And, in strong proof of chastity well arm'd,
> From love's weak childish bow she lives unharm'd.[2]

Reluctant, he accompanies Benvolio and Mercutio to the Capulet feast; but, while the thoughts of his friends run all on dancing and merry-making, he can think of nothing except his own dearly-cherished gloom:

> I cannot bound a pitch above dull woe:
> Under love's heavy burden do I sink.[3]

Even Mercutio's high-spirited mockery is incapable of raising him an inch out of his lugubrious humour.

To deepen the lines of exaggeration and caricature Shakespeare invests Romeo's speech with all the conventional rhetoric of contemporary love-poetry. He habitually talks in oxymoron, hyperbole and extravagant conceit,[4] and he is always close to the sonnet vein. On one occasion Shakespeare actually gives him a sonnet sestet to speak, while his first words to Juliet form a sonnet in the pseudo-religious style, in the recitation of which Juliet joins.

All this strained and sham-poetic artificiality of speech can have but one effect, which Shakespeare certainly intended: we are convinced of the utter shallowness of Romeo's believed passion

---

[1] *Romeo and Juliet*, I. i. 153-157.
[2] Ibid., I. i. 214-217.
[3] Ibid., I. iv. 21-22.
[4] E. Dowden points out (*Romeo and Juliet*, Arden edition, p. 14, footnote) that such lines as 'Why then, O brawling love! O loving hate!', &c., 'could be illustrated endlessly from Elizabethan sonneteers and earlier poets, English and foreign'.

for Rosaline. Even before Friar Lawrence reminds us, we realise that it is mere 'doting'.

But, though Juliet shares the speaking of the 'If I profane with my unworthiest hand' sonnet, she is no Rosaline. Refracted to us at first through the memories of the nurse – memories of suckling, of childish, innocently indecent remarks – an earthiness that surrounds but does not sully Juliet – she is a spontaneous, passionate child of nature, whose speech and heart are always one. She is not ignorant of the conventional frowns and perverseness of the lady of romantic love; indeed she protests that she would have aped that style had not Romeo caught her unawares:

> I should have been more strange, I must confess,
> But that thou overheard'st, ere I was ware,
> My true love's passion.[1]

But one is certain she would never have been able to keep up this demureness and make-believe for long.

Meeting such a woman, falling in love with her at first sight, Romeo experiences real passion for the first time, and the experience transforms his whole being, indeed turns him from a caricature into a human being. There is scarcely a single correspondence between the Romeo of the first act and the Romeo of the rest of the play, who is as unlike his prototype as the Falstaff of *Henry IV* is unlike the Falstaff of *The Merry Wives*. His speech (usually a significant index of Shakespeare's characters[2]) is completely changed as we can realise at once if we compare such lines as

> O, she doth teach the torches to shine bright!
> It seems she hangs upon the cheek of night
> Like a rich pearl in an Ethiope's ear;
> Beauty too rich for use, for earth too dear![3]

with

> O, she is rich in beauty, only poor,
> That when she dies with beauty dies her store.[4]

This is not to deny the considerable amount of conceit and hyperbole in Romeo's courtship of Juliet; nor can we make an exception of such lines as those in the first quotation on the

---

[1] *Romeo and Juliet*, II. ii. 102-104.
[2] A similar change of speech, a poetic heightening and intensifying, is to be observed between the Cleopatra before Antony's final defeat and the Cleopatra afterwards.
[3] *Romeo and Juliet*, I. v. 46-49.
[4] Ibid., I. i. 221-222.

grounds that Romeo has still not completely shaken off his old self, since such artifice is found everywhere, even in the superb aubade that he speaks with Juliet. But this artifice is no longer frigid or perfunctory; and it is rarely conventional. It is, we are convinced, a lyrical fervour that flames from deep and genuine love.

This initial caricature of Romeo, and his transformation, certainly show that by the time Shakespeare wrote this play (1595?) he was able to regard the conventional lover of the romantic school with complete detachment; also that he realised the conventions and poetry of the romantic tradition did not correspond with the realities of human passion. But is this all?

To make any sort of answer to this question we must recognise that while the Romeo of the last four acts is no longer the lover of contemporary sonnet and Petrarchian love-poetry, he is certainly a type, one of the supreme types, of the more modern ideal of the 'romantic' lover. His characteristic mood is emotional, ecstatic, unanalytical, and, therefore, uncomplicated; he prefers death to separation from Juliet; and love is his chief, if not his only value. For love he is prepared to sacrifice everything.

Now the play cannot be described as a tragedy of this ideal. Strictly speaking – and certainly if we take Shakespeare's other tragedies as a criterion – we cannot admit *Romeo and Juliet* as a tragedy at all, for the catastrophe depends on chance, the undelivered letter of Friar Lawrence. Without that accident, all might have been well. But, even if we ignore this objection, we never feel, as we do in *Antony and Cleopatra*,[1] that the element of unrestrained passion inherent in the romantic ideal is necessarily destructive and disruptive. True, there is a unique stress on doom in *Romeo and Juliet* and much play with premonition; but these are poetic and dramatic effects, something external and imposed that is not to be confused with the inevitable tragedy that is within Antony and Cleopatra. The fundamental theme of *Romeo and Juliet*, which is imaginative not moral, is the unending conflict between Eros (love and life) and the forces of death. This conflict is developed dramatically by the story of sexual love arising out of family feud, challenging it, triumphing over it, and finally destroyed by it, and developed poetically by the powerful imagery of strife, contrast, contradiction and paradox.

[1] Of course, even in *Antony and Cleopatra* the moral judgments, and indeed much of the moral issue, are oblique and implied. For a deliberate treatment of the Antony and Cleopatra story in moral terms we must turn to Dryden's version, *All For Love*.

does this mean that Shakespeare was completely uncritical
at has become the *modern* ideal of romantic love?

Our answer to this question must depend primarily on our conception of Friar Lawrence, and in particular on our interpretation of Act II, Scene iii.

Now there are two clear-cut and opposing attitudes to this character. The first, an emphatically moral one, was satisfactorily stated by Gervinus. 'By Friar Lawrence who, as it were, represents the part of the chorus in this tragedy, the leading idea of the piece is expressed in all fulness ... that excess in any enjoyment, however pure in itself, transforms its sweet into bitterness, that devotion to any single feeling, however noble, bespeaks its ascendancy; that this ascendancy moves the man and woman out of their natural spheres; that love can only be a companion in life, and cannot fill out the life and business of the man especially.'[1]

Edward Dowden, on the other hand, would have nothing of these 'well-meant moralisings' of Gervinus. He flatly denied that Friar Lawrence is a chorus to the tragedy and regarded him as a type of interfering, middle-aged prudence – something of a milder, more gracious Polonius in fact. 'The amiable critic of life as seen from the cloister does not understand life or hate or love; he is not the chorus of the tragedy, but an actor whose wisdom is of a kind which may easily lead himself and others astray.'[2]

There is undoubtedly considerable force in these objections of Dowden. For instance, he is obviously right in insisting on the importance of Friar Lawrence as an actor in the drama and on the disastrous outcome of his hopeful attempt to reconcile the Capulet and Montague families. Again, as we have already said, it is a gross distortion of the play to turn it into some sort of moral drama and to argue that any ethical or philosophical idea embodied in Friar Lawrence is the 'leading idea of the piece'. But a character, active in the drama to some extent, may have a choric function without fulfilling the role of chorus in the formal Greek sense of the word – Horatio is such a character; and characters like Speed, Enobarbus, Thersites may perform a choric function without voicing Shakespeare's simple or settled convictions.

The central idea of Friar Lawrence's long soliloquy is definite

---

[1] Quoted in the Introduction to the Arden *Romeo and Juliet*, p. xxxii.
[2] Introduction, Arden *Romeo and Juliet*, p. xxxiii.

enough and fairly expressed by Gervinus' paraphrase: that any single good, pursued blindly in isolation and to extremes, is dangerous and may, by a dialectical process, give rise to its opposite; that every virtue (including love by implication) has its particular good, but no more:

> For nought so vile that on the earth doth live
> But to the earth some special good doth give,
> Nor aught so good but strained from that fair use
> Revolts from true birth, stumbling on abuse:
> Virtue itself turns vice, being misapplied;
> And vice sometimes by action dignified.[1]

This same idea, it should be noticed, is repeated by Friar Lawrence, with an explicit reference to love, just before the marriage of Romeo and Juliet:

> These violent delights have violent ends
> And in their triumph die, like fire and powder,
> Which as they kiss consume: the sweetest honey
> Is loathsome in its own deliciousness
> And in the taste confounds the appetite.[2]

Of course, this soliloquy of Friar Lawrence is to a large extent simply a piece of dramatic artifice: it bridges the awkward interval between Romeo's exit at the end of the previous scene and his appearance in this, while its references to 'baleful weeds and precious-juiced flowers' prepare us for some necessary business of the play that is to follow. But why the length of the soliloquy, why its grave, sincere accent (which is not to be compared with the platitudinous moralisings of Polonious in his 'Give thy thoughts no tongue' speech[3]) unless Shakespeare intended it as a significant comment – and a critical one – on the extravagance of the romantic ideal?

But there is no need to leave this objection to Dowden's analysis in mid-air, suspended on an interrogation mark. A few scenes later, in the main current of the play, the attitudes of Romeo and Friar Lawrence are brought into direct conflict, and there can be no doubt which is presented to us in the more favourable light. We cannot, assuredly, be quite unsympathetic to Romeo's retort

[1] *Romeo and Juliet*, II. iii. 17-22.
[2] Ibid., II. vi. 9-13.
[3] *Hamlet*, I. iii. 59-80.

to the Friar's well-meaning words of comfort and wisdom when
he is informed of his banishment:

> Heaven is here,
> Where Juliet lives; and every cat and dog
> And little mouse, every unworthy thing,
> Live here in heaven and may look on her;
> But Romeo may not.[1]

Philosophy may, as the Friar states, be adversity's sweet milk;
our minds allow the proposition. But who ever drank that milk
at the right time, in actual and felt adversity? It is the old, old
story – the philosopher vainly attempting to assuage a grief he has
never, and can never, feel himself; and part of us, rebellious
always against the woes of life, applauds when Romeo cries out
impatiently:

> Hang up philosophy!
> Unless philosophy can make a Juliet,
> Displant a town, reverse a prince's doom,
> It helps not, it prevails not: talk no more.[2]

This is the moment when we are inclined to agree with Dowden's
dismissal of Friar Lawrence as an 'amiable critic of life seen from
the cloister' who 'does not understand life or hate or love'. Yet all
this is merely a transient reaction. Our total impression of the
scene is of an extravagant, pitiful, even ludicrous Romeo reduced
to a state of emotional deliquescence like Troilus at the opening
of *Troilus and Cressida*. He blubbers, he rolls on the ground, he is
hopeless and incapable of stirring a finger to help himself. And
this is not the Romeo of the first act – pitiful and absurd in a
different, a more callow way – but the grand romantic lover of
the Balcony scene and, in a few hours, of the great dawn-farewell
to Juliet. The Friar, on the other hand, is altogether admirable:
he rises to and dominates the situation. His reproof of Romeo's
unmanly despair and desperation, besides pulling Romeo
together with the right sort of appeal, is entirely just, and without
wasting words he maps out a practical and hopeful course of
action for the lovers. By word and deed he completely refutes
Dowden's interpretation of him, and Romeo, as always, except
when he is grief-distraught, appreciates his sterling worth:

[1] *Romeo and Juliet*, III. iii. 29-33.
[2] Ibid., III. iii. 57-60.

> But that a joy past joy calls out on me,
> It were a grief, so brief to part with thee.[1]

The sorry spectacle that Romeo, the romantic lover, makes of himself in this scene should not be regarded in isolation, for it points directly forward to the catastrophe. Admittedly, he does not bear the responsibility for that catastrophe that Othello and Anthony bear for the disasters in which they are overwhelmed. But if the efficient cause of the catastrophe in *Romeo and Juliet* is an accident, this catastrophe is hastened by Romeo himself who, when he hears the false report of Juliet's death, reveals the same weaknesses that he had shown when Friar Lawrence had informed him of his banishment – reckless impulsiveness, an incapacity to think, and a despair that turns instantly to thoughts of suicide. But this time there is no Friar Lawrence to stand beside him, and he perishes miserably.

There is a further point of significance to be appreciated in Shakespeare's elevation of Romeo from the lugubrious, literary lover of the first act. When Mercutio strikes off his lively picture of Romeo in this pose –

> Romeo! humours! madman! passion! lover!
> Appear thou in the likeness of a sigh:
> Speak but one rhyme and I am satisfied –[2]

his caricature, though he does not know it, is already out of date. Romeo has met Juliet, and the morose knight of Rosaline is no more. But though the Romeo of the rest of the play is a different sort of romantic lover, sincere, mature, a hero to be sympathised with in the main, Shakespeare does not allow him, or Juliet, to exist in the rarified, ideal atmosphere of romance. Less affected now, he is less a butt for his friends, and it is a tribute to his new love for Juliet, not a criticism of it, that Mercutio can praise him for a new-found bonhomie: 'Why, is not this better now than groaning for love? now art thou sociable, now art thou Romeo; now art thou what thou art, by art as well as by nature: for this drivelling love is like a great natural, that runs lolling up and down to hide his bauble in a hole'.[3] But he must still endure the good-natured jesting of his friends; and if most of this glances off him – even such an excellent stroke as 'Now he is for the numbers that

[1] *Romeo and Juliet*, III. iii. 173-174.
[2] Ibid., II. i. 7-9.
[3] Ibid., II. iv. 92-98.

Petrarch flowed in: Laura to his lady was but a kitchen wench'[1] – he and Juliet are to the end constantly submitted to the clown-commentary, this time of a woman, the racy, much-experienced, bawdy-minded Nurse, for whom love is primarily a matter of 'the chinks', copulation, and bed-sports. Her commentary is not, of course, Shakespeare's; but it is *a* commentary, and a criticism, and, because of Shakespeare's detachment from the doctrines of romantic love, which is manifest in his creation of such characters as the Nurse and Mercutio, we see the lovers through earthy as well as their own divine eyes.

There are the bright festal torches that lead Romeo to Juliet; there are the 'baleful weeds and precious-juiced flowers' that induce death and a sleep like death. There is the lyricism; there is the tragedy; and there is also that grief-softener from commonplace, humble life – the Nurse's flask, so often called for, of *aqua vitae*.

§

Much Ado About Nothing, *As You Like It* and *Twelfth Night* may conveniently be taken together not only on account of their dates of composition (1598-1601) and level of excellence as the peaks of Shakespeare's comedy, but also because of certain broad similarities in their attitudes towards the romantic tradition.

Up to the time of this trilogy, the 'romantic' comedies had followed a fairly consistent formula: the core of each one had been a love romance, serious in the main, though often treated comically and frequently lightened with wit. Woven in and around this romantic centre there had been comic diversions and incidents, sometimes serving as a burlesque or anti-masque to the main love romance.

Now one of the chief points to be noticed about these three great comedies that Shakespeare composed at the turn of the century – probably in the order *Much Ado*, *As You Like It* and *Twelfth Night* – is the shift of dramatic gravity away from the love romance. It would obviously be incorrect to say that Shakespeare rejected the romantic narrative, since *As You Like It* is an almost perfect specimen of a dramatised romance. But *Much Ado* and *Twelfth Night* do afford the first clear signs that he was growing – temporarily at least – tired or dissatisfied with this type of story.

---

[1] *Romeo and Juliet*, II. iv. 40-41.

This shift of gravity is plainly discernible in *Much Ado*. The Hero-Claudio story, which Shakespeare took from Bandello with some suggestions from Spenser and Ariosto, belongs clearly to the romantic type. But, to say nothing of the fact that this story contains several romantic elements that Shakespeare could have elaborated, particularly if he had been more susceptible to suggestions in his sources, the tale of Hero and Claudio is not the centre of the comedy. All audiences from Elizabethan times to the present have recognised the entanglement of Beatrice and Benedick as the dramatic heart of the play, and Shakespeare, who poured all his wit, powers of characterisation, gusto, and sense of enjoyment into the tale of Beatrice and Benedick, must have been thoroughly conscious of what a playgoer like Digges easily perceived:

> Let but Beatrice
> And Benedick be seen, lo in a trice
> The Cockpit, Galleries, Boxes, all are full.[1]

This story of Beatrice and Benedick contains two points of outstanding significance for understanding the development of Shakespeare's comedy: in the first place, the plot is entirely Shakespeare's own invention, and in the second, this invention is one that owes very little to romantic tradition. The narrative is certainly a love-story, but in almost every one of its main characteristics it is distinct from the typical romance. The protagonists are mature, sophisticated, three-dimensional (the woman no less than the man); there is little love-making, but instead scintillating clashes of wit; and the action is one of intrigue rather than adventure, for the lovers are brought together, not by any love-at-first-sight miracle but by a piece of pure theatrical artifice. Further, the whole of this part of *Much Ado* is orchestrated in prose – prose as vivid and lively as anything Shakespeare ever wrote.[2]

In *Twelfth Night* the romantic part of the plot is admittedly rather more to the foreground. But at least as prominent as this, and certainly more entertaining, is again Shakespeare's own

---

[1] Quoted E. K. Chambers, *William Shakespeare*, Vol. II, p. 253.

[2] A slighter point, though not one to be overlooked, is that the ripe humour of the Dogberry-Verges interlude, while related to that of the mechanicals in *A Midsummer Night's Dream*, has no reference to love, romantic or otherwise. It is the humour of comic caricature, combined with some mild and delightful satire on the Elizabethan police system.

invention – the gulling of Malvolio, Sir Toby's confidence tricks on Sir Andrew, and Sir Andrew's duel with Viola. Once more this original creation has little to do with romance. The action in these episodes is farcical intrigue; love is a subsidiary factor completely lacking the romantic spirit; the main characters are middle-aged men and women; and the comedy is to a large extent satirical, a mocking exposure of human foibles and weaknesses. With Sir Andrew the satire is light-hearted and kindly enough. But when we contemplate the great satiric portrait of Malvolio and the harsh indignities to which he is subjected, we feel ourselves transported from the genial atmosphere of the earlier comedies to a region not very far removed from the raw, vigorous and unromantic comic world that Jonson was about to create.

Nor is it merely that the dramatic centre of gravity in these three comedies is shifting away from the romantic story. Love-making, so essential a part of romance, is dwindling too – even in the romantic parts of the comedies. In *Much Ado*, as a number of critics have pointed out, Claudio and Hero hardly deserve the name of lovers. We are, on the contrary, back in the domain of classical comedy and of *The Comedy of Errors* and *The Taming of the Shrew*, for one of Claudio's first concerns is to discover whether Leonato has any son who will inherit his fortune, while the match is entirely arranged through the good offices of his patron, Don Pedro. There is, it is true, a considerable amount of love-making in *As You Like It*, but it is all very indirect, and, as we shall demonstrate more fully in a moment, Shakespeare goes much further than he had ever gone before in transforming courtship into mock-courtship – so far indeed that there is actually a burlesque marriage ceremony with Celia officiating as priest. In *Twelfth Night* the love-making is by proxy and constantly interrupted by the raillery of Olivia, while there is no courtship between Viola and the Duke or between Olivia and Sebastian, who are all united in a somewhat perfunctory manner.

Linked with this decline of courtship in the action is another important change, which is perhaps to be first discerned in the courtship scene of *Henry V*, a play written in the months immediately preceeding these three comedies. In this scene the emphasis is definitely on Henry as the 'plain soldier' speaking in 'soldier terms'; hence the bluntness and forthrightness of Henry's conversation, his reference to his own plainness of feature, and his touches of crudity (to us more than to the Elizabethans). He is, as Professor

Shakespeare's Detachment from Romance

Dover Wilson says,[1] a Berowne practising the precept of 'russet yeas and honest kersey noes'. But it is significant that he is not simply the plain outspoken soldier; by implication he several times attacks the manner of romantic love-making, with its poetry, its eloquence, and its extravagant declarations:

Marry, if you would put me to verses . . . you undid me.[2]

These fellows of infinite tongue, that can rhyme themselves into Ladies' favours, they do always reason themselves out again.[3]

I cannot look greenly nor gasp out my eloquence, nor I have no cunning in protestation.[4]

To say to thee that I shall die, is true; but for thy love, by the Lord, no; yet I love thee too.[5]

There is no need to go so far as Dover Wilson in his suggestion that this was the kind of wooing Shakespeare himself admired, but it may well be that, granted the dramatic necessity of making Henry woo Katherine in 'soldier terms', Shakespeare seized the opportunity to express a changed, or changing attitude to the romantic manner of love-making.

Whether or not this is a valid interpretation of Henry's courtship, it is certainly a remarkable feature of the three main comedies that the high romantic liturgy of love almost disappears from them.

Since there is little scope for love-making in *Much Ado* there is no need to say much about this play, though it is perhaps worth noticing that even when the plot affords Claudio a chance for a lyrical outburst in the old style he singularly fails to seize his opportunity. So, after Don Pedro has done his wooing for him, he greets his good fortune merely with a few words of prosaic formality: 'Silence is the perfectest herald of joy: I were but little happy, if I could say how much. Lady, as you are mine, I am yours: I give away myself for you and dote on the exchange.'[6] The nature of the Beatrice-Benedick story precludes any expression of strained amatory sentiment from either of these two characters, and when,

---
[1] Introduction, Cambridge *New Shakespeare* edition of *Henry V*., p. xliii.
[2] *Henry V*, v. ii. 137-139.
[3] Ibid, v. ii. 164-167.
[4] Ibid., v. ii. 149-151.
[5] Ibid., v. ii. 158-160.
[6] *Much Ado*, II. i. 316-320.

towards the end of the play, Benedick does try his hand at sonneteering, he swiftly comes to the conclusion that this is not his line: 'No, I was not born under a rhyming planet, nor I cannot woo in festival terms.'[1]

More interesting to examine is *As You Like It*, for the plot of this did not prevent Shakespeare from indulging freely, if he chose, in the romantic and Petrarchian vein. But while the hero is allowed to follow the sonneteering convention of the romantic lover, those effusions of his that we are allowed to listen to are sorry stuff, and he is well trounced for them by Jacques. Touchstone, too, on one occasion when Rosalind recites a lyric of Orlando's, counters it with a poem,[2] which in its realistic sensualism belongs in spirit, if not in achievement, to Donne's robust assault on the Petrarchian mode. Yet the most significant feature of Orlando's love-making is that in all his interviews with Rosalind he is confined to matter-of-fact prose. Where the old religious, extravagant style does come pat is from the lips of the namby-pamby Silvius. 'Tell . . . what 'tis to love', invites Rosalind, and Silvius at once bursts out into the hyperbolical parlance of a long line of comedy heroes, Valentine, Proteus, Ferdinand of Navarre and Lysander:

> It is to be all made of fantasy,
> All made of passion and all made of wishes,
> All adoration, duty, and observance,
> All humbleness, all patience and impatience;
> All purity, all trial, all obeisance.[3]

This decline in the status of the precentor is surely one symptom of Shakespeare's growing dissatisfaction with the liturgy of romantic love. Another is Jaques' picture of the typical lover in his catalogue of the seven ages:

> Sighing like furnace, with a woeful ballad
> Made to his mistress' eyebrow.[4]

Then there is Phoebe's crushing retorts to the conceits of Silvius – and, indirectly, to the whole school of poetry that engendered them:

[1] *Much Ado*, v. ii. 40-41.
[2] *As You Like It*, III. ii. 107-118.
[3] Ibid., v. ii. 100-104.
[4] Ibid., II. vii. 148-149.

> Lie not, to say mine eyes are murderers!
> Now show the wound mine eye hath made in thee:
> Scratch thee but with a pin, and there remains
> Some scar of it . . .
>   but now mine eyes,
> Which I have darted at thee, hurt thee not,
> Nor, I am sure, there is no force in eyes
> That can do hurt.[1]

There are some few passages of the old romantic love parlance in *Twelfth Night*, but these are spoken either by the Duke, who is momentarily in love with love's mood rather than with any woman, or by Viola, who recites them to Olivia, only to be mocked at for her pains. Not that Viola can have been greatly grieved by Olivia's response, for all her fine love speeches have usually a casual note, sometimes even a suggestion of parody. Moreover, there is a good deal of contradiction in the Duke's attitude. If we can believe his opening words, there is a part of him that would really prefer not to be in love, while he seems to share Duke Theseus' conviction that love is 'high fantastical'. Certainly, for all his indulgence, he does not believe in the romantic doctrine of the elevating powers of love, which is, he states, like the sea:

> Nought enters there,
> Of what validity and pitch soe'er,
> But falls into abatement and low price.[2]

Later, in conversation with Viola, he utters two further heresies: he has no faith in the lover's fidelity –

> Our fancies are more giddy and unfirm,
> More longing, wavering, sooner lost and worn
> Than women's are –[3]

and, in spite of this, he has a low, unchivalric opinion of a woman's love that none of the earlier romantic lovers would have shared:

> Alas, their love may be call'd appetite,
> No motion of the liver, but the palate,
> That suffer surfeit, cloyment and revolt.[4]

---

[1] *As You Like It*, III. v. 19-27.
[2] *Twelfth Night*, I. i. 11-13.
[3] Ibid., II. iv. 34-36.
[4] Ibid., II. iv. 100-102.

However – to return to *As You Like It* – it is not only the traditional rhetoric of romantic love-making that is scoffed at in the play. This comedy also contains some of Shakespeare's most withering, though always genial, comment on the central doctrines of romantic love.

Once again this rarified and idealised attitude to love is submitted to the earthy, irreverent scrutiny of a clown, Touchstone. A capital instance of this shift of viewpoint occurs in the scene where Rosalind, Celia and Touchstone first arrive in the Forest of Arden. We are given a brief glimpse of the absurd, sentimental lover of the pastoral manner in the overheard conversation between Silvius and Corin. Even Rosalind seems affected by Silvius' soulful lament. But Touchstone instantly punctures the inflation with his ludicrous reminiscences: 'I remember, when I was in love I broke my sword upon a stone and bid him take that for coming a-night to Jane Smile; and I remember the kissing of her batlet and the cow's dugs that her pretty chopt hands had milked; and I remember the wooing of a peascod instead of her, from whom I took two cods and, giving her them again, said with weeping tears "Wear these for my sake". We that are true lovers run into strange capers.'[1]

What is still more striking than this kind of humorous commentary on the extravagances of the romance heroes and heroines is the fact that Touchstone's own love-affair is not merely indicated, as Launce's is, but is played out in front of us as an integrated and important part of the plot. While Orlando finds Rosalind in the Forest of Arden and Oliver falls in love with Celia, Touchstone pays court to the goat-maid, Audrey. But a 'material fool', as Jaques calls him, Touchstone is burdened with no sentimental, romantic illusions: his attitude is simply one of cynical, but always good-humoured, sensualism. He is not so blind as not to realise that Audrey is a foul slut. Indeed, he is constantly poking fun at her and also at himself for his weakness. But 'man hath his desires', and he hopes that if he can cover his seduction with the flimsy marriage ceremony of some hedge-priest he will have a good excuse for deserting her when he is tired of the game. Certainly, under pressure, he is forced into a more formal marriage service, but he remains a good fellow, and Shakespeare condemns him no more severely than in Jaques' parting words:

[1] *As You Like It*, II. iv. 46-55.

> And you to wrangling; for thy loving voyage
> Is but for two months victuall'd.[1]

Even more indicative of Shakespeare's increasing emancipation from the doctrines of romantic love is his treatment of Rosalind. Adapting courtship far more boldly for comic purposes than he had ever done before, he uses Rosalind, in her interviews with Orlando, for questioning and ridiculing from a realistic standpoint several of the most sacred articles of romantic love. Twice at least she sketches a picture of her own sex that completely gives the lie to the idealised 'lady' and 'mistress' of romantic writing: there is her comparison between the 'effeminate, changeable, longing and liking, inconstant' youth and the girl in love,[2] and her speech in Act IV, Scene i: 'Maids are May when they are maids, but the sky changes when they are wives. I will be more jealous of thee than a Barbary cock-pigeon over his hen, more clamorous than a parrot against rain, more new-fangled than an ape, more giddy in my desires than a monkey: I will weep for nothing, like Diana in the fountain, and I will do that when you are disposed to be merry; I will laugh like a hyen, and that when thou are inclined to sleep.'[3]

Nor is this cautionary and unflattering confession all. So far from the romantic ideal of faithfulness having any wide validity, wives as well as husbands are commonly untrue – so commonly in fact that a wife is a witless fool and lacks an indispensable qualification if she cannot lie and bluff her way out when she is intercepted by her husband on her way towards some neighbour's bed. For the moment, as we listen to Rosalind's witty raillery, we are transported from romance into the world of Restoration comedy, where there is no scope for moral stricture or the lament of outraged idealism. After all, 'love is merely a madness, and, I tell you, deserves as well a dark house and a whip as madmen do: and the reason why they are not so punished and cured is, that the lunacy is so ordinary that the whippers are in love too'.[4]

Further, in what is probably her most devastating broadside of all, Rosalind shatters the romantic legend of fanatical, entire devotion: 'The poor world is almost six thousand years old, and in all this time there was not any man died in his own person,

---
[1] *As You Like It*, v. iv. 197-198.
[2] Ibid., III. ii. 427-443.
[3] Ibid., IV. i. 148-157.
[4] Ibid., III. ii. 420-424.

videlicet, in a love-cause. Troilus had his brains dashed out with a Grecian club; yet he did what he could to die before, and he is one of the patterns of love. Leander, he would have lived many a fair year, though Hero had turned nun, if it had not been for a hot midsummer night; for, good youth, he went but forth to wash him in the Hellespont and being taken with the cramp was drowned; and the foolish chroniclers of that age found it was "Hero of Sestos". But these are all lies: men have died from time to time and worms have eaten them, but not for love.'[1]

These tonic moments of good-natured scepticism and realism do not give us the entire Rosalind (still less the entire Shakespeare), for Rosalind is herself extravagantly, and at times sentimentally, in love. 'I'll tell thee, Aliena,' she confesses, 'I cannot be out of sight of Orlando: I'll go find a shadow and sigh till he come'; and it is Celia who provides the prosaic 'And I'll to sleep.'[2] But there is no denying that the comedy in these interviews between Rosalind and Orlando is provided chiefly by Rosalind's realistic criticisms of romantic love, that these criticisms are more sustained and trenchant than most of the mocking in the earlier comedies, or that – for the first time if we pass over Mercutio – romantic love is here ridiculed by one of the main courtly figures as well as by the licensed Clown.

It is symptomatic of Shakespeare's unfailing talent for successfully fusing a diversity of materials that a play so full of geniality and affirmation as *As You Like It* should at the same time contain so much criticism and semi-satirical writing; and besides this comic treatment of romantic love there is also some burlesque and implicit satire on a particular and contemporary form of romance – the pastoral. We have already mentioned the caricature of the love-sick shepherd swain and his cruel mistress in the persons of Silvius and Phoebe. But this is only one of the several directions of Shakespeare's satire on the pastoral. There is also the slow, timorous, rustic clod William, whom Shakespeare surely introduced, by way of contrast, as a sketch of the real English countryman of the time that he himself knew. There is the contradiction between the words and actions of the exiled Duke, who, while he can poeticise the severities of an open-air life, and, finding 'sermons in stones and good in every thing', can swear he would not change his condition, has no qualms about

---
[1] *As You Like It*, IV. i. 95-107.
[2] Ibid., IV. i. 222-225.

returning to the civilised comforts of court life as soon as a favourable opportunity presents itself. There is the united front of Jaques and Touchstone, the first perceiving clearly that the exiled Duke and his followers are merely playing at the Arcadian life, the second never really swerving from his first forthright opinion – 'Ay, now am I in Arden; the more fool I'.[1]

It would be a mistake to exaggerate this satire. The tone is too light-hearted and kindly, the strokes too often oblique. Moreover, if we envisage Shakespeare as seriously rejecting pastoralism in this play, we create the problem of accounting for his use of the pastoral in his later 'romances'. On the other hand, the pastoral theme in *As You Like It* is certainly not a pointless piece of decoration woven in as a concession to popular taste. Shakespeare revealed the pastoral, critically, for what it really was – a precious and highly artificial form of writing and a fashionable mode of escapism from the court-life of the time, which most courtiers of sensibility and intelligence discovered from experience to be more sordid, exhausting and dangerous than it appeared from a distance.

Finally, to appreciate the total effect of these three masterpieces of Shakespeare's comedy and their attitude towards the romance tradition we must be attentive to a wide range of fleeting, random and easily missed notes like the recurrent 'horns' infidelity joke in *Much Ado*, the words of such songs as 'Sigh no more, Ladies' or 'What shall he have that killed the deer?' and snatches of dialogue like –

Rosalind: You have heard him swear downright he was [in love].
Celia: 'Was' is not 'is'.[2]

In isolation such notes do not mean much, if indeed we consciously notice them at all. Yet in innumerable small ways they combine together to form a background that re-echoes and sustains those larger unromantic themes and passages that we have traced in the centre of these comedies. If, for instance, we isolate such a song-refrain as 'most loving mere folly'[3] it will seem to lack any significance. But if we become familiarly acquainted with *As You Like It* we shall realise that this refrain is a delicate echo repeated

[1] *As You Like It*, II. iv. 16-17.
[2] Ibid., III. iv. 31-33.
[3] Ibid., II. vii. 181.

from the background – first, and most immediately, of Jaques' lover 'sighing like furnace', with a 'woeful ballad made to his mistress' eyebrow', described only a minute or two before, and secondly, in anticipation, of Rosalind's 'Love is merely a madness'.

§

There is one particular aspect of *Much Ado* which, if not directly bearing on the main theme of this chapter, has some relevance to it and deserves separate attention.

When, after an interval of several years, the play was brought back to the London stage by Robert Donat's company in the late autumn of 1946, almost all the dramatic critics revealed a similar uneasy reaction in their notices. They opined that the play was losing some of its long popularity; they felt, often vaguely, there was something unpalatable about it to modern taste; they argued – and they might almost have been speaking of the traditional 'problem' comedies, *Measure for Measure* and *All's Well* – that it is a difficult play, taxing the resources of producer and actor. And – of great interest to our present inquiry – most of their stricture and uneasiness was focused on the romantic part of the story.

This response was genuine enough, but the elaboration and analysis of it was shallow and timid, perhaps because the critics felt a little guilty in questioning what has always been considered one of the greatest of Shakespeare's comedies. In general, objection to the Hero-Claudio story followed the obvious realistic line: that the behaviour of Claudio is preposterous and the disgrace of Hero an utterly incredible business. Yet this explanation of the difficulty of successfully putting *Much Ado* over to a modern audience does not really get us very far. It must of course be admitted that *Much Ado* is somewhat exceptional among the comedies in the heavy weight of romantic story that its last two acts have to bear. But if we are to object merely to unreality of incident and character in the romantic story, then *As You Like It* and *Twelfth Night* are wide open to the same charge and are, presumably, in a similar danger of losing their popularity with modern audiences.

Actually, the real source of the trouble lies elsewhere. In the first place, it is probable that Shakespeare made the mistake of choosing a romantic story that could never be completely assimilated to the spirit of a comedy, for all romance stories are not alike in spirit, some being more suited to tragic than to comic dramatisation. The romantic story in *Twelfth Night* is in the main serious and has one or two slight tragic potentialities – in Olivia's situation when she falls in love with Cesario, in the Duke's jealous threat to kill Cesario. Yet there is not the slightest discord between this story and the rest of the play, since Olivia, while in no sense a comic character, not even as we may regard Malvolio as a comic character, fits in harmoniously with the world of comedy. She is making absurd mistakes, she is misunderstanding things, she is to some extent to blame for the situation, amusing from one angle, in which she is involved. Hero is more like Desdemona or Ophelia: she is caught helplessly in undeserved suffering; her plight is never, from any angle, amusing.

But the chief weaknesses of this play arise from Shakespeare's treatment of his romantic subject rather than from his choice of it.[1] One of the chief secrets of his success in blending romance and comedy had been that he had allowed wit and humour to blow freely through the romantic part of the play, much of this comic zephyr consisting, as we have already shown, of mockery and mild satire on the extravagances of romantic love. This is indeed the method employed in the first part of *Much Ado*: for instance, no sooner has Claudio fallen in love with Hero, no sooner is he ready to declare his love, than he has to submit to the chaff of Benedick. Similarly, Claudio's bitterness and chagrin when he believes that Don Pedro has played him false with Hero is never allowed to develop or to work upon us, since it is at once swamped by the boisterous humour of Benedick. There is another convincing fusion between the romantic and the comic when Claudio joins in the plot to deceive Benedick. But what humour there is in the last part of the play (excluding of course the final scene) is extraneous, the 'comic relief' of Dogberry and Verges; and the introduction of the essentially comic figure of Benedick into these near-tragic scenes only imposes a strain and an aggravated sense of incredibility upon us, as well as calling for great powers of sustained adaptability from the actor who is playing Benedick's part.

More hazardous than this is the fact that Shakespeare, depart-

---

[1] John Palmer, on the contrary, praises *Much Ado* for its excellent dramatic craftsmanship: 'It is one of Shakespeare's greatest triumphs as a dramatic craftsman, showing what he can do when his genius is not half engaged and he falls back on his technical skill as a playwright'. (*Shakespeare's Comic Characters*, p. 135.)

ing from the precedent of his earlier romantic comedies, has in in the last two acts of the play infused a large breath of life into it. No doubt the shattered marriage-service (the model for a hundred such melodramatic scenes), the lament of Leonato, and the scene of the exequies sung over Hero's tomb are 'theatrical' in the worst sense of the word. They exist simply for dramatic effect; they are all part of a sham. But these serious scenes are at the same time filled with powerful, plausible emotions, notably the sense of disgrace, grief and anger of Leonato, and with some impressive speeches like Leonato's 'I pray thee, cease thy counsel'[1] or

> Tush, tush, man; never fleer and jest at me:
> I speak not like a dotard nor a fool,
> As under privilege of age to brag
> What I have done being young, or what would do
> Were I not old. Know, Claudio, to thy head,
> Thou hast so wrong'd mine innocent child and me
> That I am forced to lay my reverence by
> And, with gray hairs and bruise of many days,
> Do challenge thee to trial of a man.
> I say thou hast belied mine innocent child;
> Thy slander hath gone through and through her heart,
> And she lies buried with her ancestors;
> O, in a tomb where never scandal slept,
> Save this of hers, framed by thy villainy![2]

There is perhaps a touch of rant in these lines; there is certainly counterfeit emotion, since Hero is not dead. Yet this passage might assuredly have come out of one of the tragedies.

Here is the crucial, and probably insoluble, problem for the producer, who is impaled by Shakespeare on a dilemma. Either – as is a common practice – he may try to hurry and huddle through these scenes as so much dead wood, hoping his audience will tolerate them in return for the fine comic episodes, or – as with the Robert Donat version – he will make the most of the emotional opportunity that these scenes present. With the first alternative, the producer incurs certain tediousness, though a good Dogberry and Verges may save the situation to some extent; with the second, he will undoubtedly intensify the discord between this part and the rest of the play.

[1] *Much Ado*, v. i. 3-32.
[2] Ibid., v. i. 58-71.

This is essentially a dramatic problem, but it has two distinct bearings on our present subject of inquiry. In the first place, it reminds us of something that Shakespeare's great success elsewhere causes us to overlook, namely that the combination of romance and comedy, so far from being an inevitable and easily effected one, was always a tricky one for the dramatist. In particular, it reminds us of the debt that Shakespeare owed to earlier experimenters like Lyly and Greene.

In the second place, this difficulty that Shakespeare creates for himself (and for his producer) may be another piece of indirect evidence, as important as his treatment of the Beatrice and Benedick story, on his growing, if temporary, dissatisfaction with the romantic type of story. He was moved to express deep and genuine emotion in his comedies, as in his later histories, so much so that he attempted to infuse it into a romantic story whose characters and situations were never intended to carry realism or profound feeling.

A few years later, in his so-called 'romances', Shakespeare made another and more sustained attempt to turn romance into serious and weighty drama. So doing, he produced two or three major plays. But, as we shall see, when judged as drama rather than fireside poetry, these plays are flawed with large weaknesses. *The Tempest* apart, they might even be described as dramatic failures; and perhaps they fail for the same reason that the last two acts of *Much Ado* fail – that Shakespeare was essaying the impossible.

CHAPTER SIX

THE 'DARK' COMEDIES

OF THE SO-CALLED 'dark' or 'problem' comedies two – *All's Well That Ends Well* and *Troilus and Cressida* – have a significant and direct relevance to our present inquiry. Moreover, a consideration of the positive and negative attitudes to romance manifested in all three will help us considerably in the solution of several outstanding problems raised by these plays.

Whatever its exact position in the sequence of Shakespeare's plays,[1] *All's Well* is certainly the nearest in spirit and dramatic structure to the three comedy masterpieces. At the centre there is once more a story, borrowed through Painter's *Palace of Pleasure* (1566) from Boccaccio, of a youth and a maid; and this tale has a large number of the usual romantic features. There are adventures, journeys and pursuits, miraculous events, strange coincidences, disguises and mistaken identities. In the last act, out of all this tangle, the youth and the maid are united, and all ends well – at least by the superficial standards of romantic justice.

Yet in spite of these characteristics the tale of Bertram and Helena is the least romantic of all the serious love-stories we have so far examined in the Comedies. To begin with, even in its original Boccaccio form, the story is a singular one, since by making the heroine the pursuer – and an energetic and determined one at that – Boccaccio completely inverts one of the main postulates of romantic love-narrative. If Shakespeare merely followed this unromantic inversion, he at least followed it of his own choice. At the same time, while the nature of the main story precluded any scenes of courtship or any expression of the romantic love-liturgy, which had been evolved for the male wooer, there was certainly some scope, if Shakespeare had cared to exploit it, for a display of romantic sentiments in Bertram's attempt to win Diana. As it is, the play is as bare of romantic

[1] The order and date of these plays has been much disputed. Charlton, in his *Shakespearian Comedy*, pp. 211-212, even controverts the traditional view that they fall as a group between the rest of the Comedies and the Tragedies. So far as their sequence is concerned, most critics place *Measure for Measure* last, and though E. K. Chambers puts *Troilus and Cressida* before *All's Well*, many authorities hold the opposite opinion.

love-speech as *Much Ado*, and in the one scene where Bertram does try to woo Diana he is a pathetic figure who can only overcome her dialectical skill and worldly wisdom by bribing her with a valuable heirloom.

On the other hand, if no attempt is made to revive the literary manner of romantic courtship, the clown-mocking of love and women is still present, full of bawdy and more cynical than ever: 'an we might have a good woman born but one every blazing star, or at an earthquake, 't would mend the lottery well: a man may draw his heart out, ere 'a pluck one'.[1] Like Touchstone too, Lavache, the clown, has his desires, and, 'driven on by the flesh', is contemplating marriage. But he renounces his folly after he has had the chance to compare his country Isbell with the Isbells of court: 'the brains of my Cupid's knocked out, and I begin to love, as an old man loves money, with no stomach'.[2]

However, it is in Shakespeare's general treatment of his hero and heroine that his alienation from romance strikes us most forcibly. Bertram is the meanest and most fatuous romantic hero he ever drew, the Claudio of *Much Ado* not excepted, and Johnson's description of him is no worse than he deserves:[3] 'a man noble without generosity, and young without truth; who marries Helen as a coward, and leaves her as a profligate: when she is dead by his unkindness, sneaks home to a second marriage, is accused by a woman whom he has wronged, defends himself by falsehood, and is dismissed to happiness'.[4] But what is more significant than this is that Shakespeare has transformed the Beltramo of Boccaccio into an altogether more contemptible figure. In two ways in particular he has debased the hero: he has made him the blind callow patron of the unspeakable Parolles, and he has so altered the story that his exposure is far more ignominous and protracted than Beltramo's.[5] There is nothing in Boccaccio of the second ring, palmed off on Bertram by Helena in Florence, which entangles him more hopelessly in a web of lies, and drags out his exposure. Nor is the King present in the conclusion of Boccaccio's

---

[1] *All's Well*, I. iii. 90-93.
[2] Ibid., III. ii. 16-18.
[3] Notwithstanding Coleridge's defence. (See *Table Talk*, 1st July, 1833.)
[4] *Johnson on Shakespeare*, ed. Walter Raleigh, p. 103.
[5] Primarily this exposure is for simple dramatic effect, the suspense of the last act. But it is significant that Shakespeare should throw so much stress on dramatic effect to the exclusion of romantic sentiment.

story. Beltramo is giving a feast, and Gilletta appears with her two sons, simply claiming her lawful rights as his wife.

Helena, on the other hand, is a much more sympathetic figure than Boccaccio's heroine. Certainly she is not among the loveliest or most entrancing of Shakespeare's creations; but no less certainly she is not the disagreeable or despicable woman that some critics have made her out to be. She has a warm affectionate heart, and is inherently intelligent, shrewd of judgment and determined. The three wisest and most admirable characters in the play, the Countess, the King and Lafeu, all have a high opinion of her and regard her with affection. To the Countess, likely to be her severest critic, she has become by adoption a favourite child.

It must not be imagined that the effect of this amelioration of the heroine's character is an intuitive stroke of Shakespeare's to restore some of the romantic spirit of the story lost in the debasement of Bertram. What is admirable in Helena is, as we guess from a few odd glimpses, and the opinion of such characters as the Countess, her normal essential self; for most of the play, a dupe to her emotions, she is blindly and stupidly in love with a worthless young fellow, prepared to stoop to any shift and humiliation to win him. In other words, she too is degraded, but, with her, degradation springs from the irrationality of love. If we appreciate this, we shall avoid the extremes of idealisation and disparagement to which she has been distorted.

Such a situation, stripped of its romantic plot-elaboration like the miraculous cure of the King, or Helena's device to lie with her husband, is common enough in real life. But it is a reading of love that has no place whatever in the romantic tradition.

Even with this realistic twist to the central romance Shakespeare was not satisfied. Accordingly, he weighted it by adding to the Countess two other solid, mature characters – the re-created King and the original figure of Lafeu. These three characters are more prominent than the strict dramatic necessities of the plot require, and two of them, the King and the Countess, are used as mouthpieces for the increasingly reflective and philosophic turn of Shakespeare's mind. Such lines as the Countess' confession –

> Even so it was with me when I was young:
> If ever we are nature's, these are ours; this thorn
> Doth to our rose of youth rightly belong;
> Our blood to us, this to our blood is born;

> It is the show and seal of nature's truth,
> Where love's strong passion is impressed in youth:
> By our remembrances of days foregone,
> Such were our faults, or then we thought them none.[1] –

or the King's –

> For we are old, and on our quick'st decrees
> The inaudible and noiseless foot of Time
> Steals ere we can effect them –[2]

create, if only for a moment, an illusion of resonant substantiality unknown in Shakespeare's earlier comedies.[3]

But the chief measure Shakespeare employed to give weight and reality to the play was to repeat the pattern of *Much Ado* and *Twelfth Night*: that is to say, to work into the romance a non-romantic story of his own invention. The central figure of this, the boastful, lying, cowardly Parolles, who because he has a tough guttersnipe resilience possesses a certain impressive vitality, is a compound from several sources: he is partly the classical parasite, partly the *miles gloriosus*, and partly the contemporary real-life 'Captain' who did so much to vitalise this second type. He is a caricatured, or in the language of the time a 'humorous', portrait; is treated in a spirit of mordant satire, and his exposure is a scene of merciless and brutal farce, in which any amusement we may feel is qualified by a sense of shame that human nature could sink so low. Composed of broad humours and ruthlessly stripped of his pretensions, he has clear affinities with Malvolio; like Malvolio, too, he reminds us of the Jonsonian comic world. Certainly there is nothing remotely romantic in the grim bleak comedy he provokes, where laughter is mingled with scorn and disgust.

There is another feature of the Parolles story that may throw some light on Shakespeare's abandonment of romance. We have some grounds for believing that the scenes in which Parolles featured, like the non-romantic portions of *Twelfth Night* and *Much Ado*, formed the most popular part of the play with contemporary audiences. We cannot prove this so easily as we can the popularity of Malvolio and of Beatrice and Benedick. But it is

---

[1] *All's Well*, I. iii. 134-141.
[2] Ibid., V. iii. 40-42.
[3] This ripe wisdom and reflection is not confined to the King or Countess. It is also in the mouth of the unnamed lord who declares, 'The web of our life is of a mingled yarn, good and ill together. Our virtues would be proud, if our faults whipped them not; and our crimes would despair, if they were not cherished by our virtues.'– IV. iii. 83-87.

significant that Charles I, in his copy of the play, substituted the title *Parolles* for *All's Well*, just as he substituted *Malvolio* for *Twelfth Night*.

§

If *All's Well* marks a further stage in Shakespeare's alienation from romance, it is at the same time characterised among the 'dark' comedies by its strong family resemblances to *Twelfth Night* and *Much Ado*. Its colours are more cold and sombre; its laughter rarer and more scornful. But reading it immediately after *Much Ado* and *Twelfth Night*, we are not conscious of any abrupt transition, and there is that strange, sad, wistful song of Feste at the close of *Twelfth Night* to prepare us for the slight change of key.

Troilus and Cressida, on the other hand, is a unique, isolated creation. It is the extreme of Shakespeare's recoil from romance – his most deliberate, sustained and scarifying satire on the whole romantic code of love and honour.[1] How such an acute critic as Saintsbury could ever have let fall the pathetically naïve remark that Shakespeare 'has not availed himself of Chaucer's beautiful romance so fully as he might'[2] passes comprehension – unless it indicates how little Shakespeare's relation to romance has been understood. The beauty of romance was the last thing Shakespeare felt at the time of composing *Troilus and Cressida*. What he was undoubtedly trying to express was his sense of the shallowness and sham of the doctrines of romantic love and the code of chivalric honour.[3]

[1] There is no reason to believe that Shakespeare was an isolated critic. As H. B. Charlton writes (*Shakespearian Comedy*, p. 235): 'Even the sixteenth century had reached a stage in humane progress sufficient to suggest the questionings of a merely martial heroism: just as it had become humanely conscious enough to question the medieval assumptions on which the creed of romantic love was reared.'

[2] *Cambridge History of English Literature*, Vol. V, Ch. viii, p. 196, 'Shakespeare: Life and Plays'.

[3] This is not to say that Shakespeare in his denigration of Cressida, Pandarus, and the Greek heroes owed nothing to such treatments of the Troy legend as those of Henryson in his *Testament of Cresseid* and Caxton in his *Recuyell of the Historyes of Troye* (the first possibly and the second probably to be counted among Shakespeare's sources). A. L. Attwater was certainly right when he pointed out (*A Companion to Shakespeare Studies, Shakespeare's Sources*, p. 234): 'those who like Swinburne criticize Shakespeare for "brutalising" the character of the great Achilles, whom they know from Homer, are forgetting the material on which Shakespeare had to work'. But there is no precedent for the width and intensity of Shakespeare's disillusionment; and it is this fact that gives us grounds for thinking that Shakespeare was not merely following a tradition or fashion but expressing a strong personal mood in *Troilus and Cressida*.

Just how decisive Shakespeare's recoil from romance was in this play is best appreciated if we compare it with Chaucer's *Troilus and Criseyde*, which, almost certainly Shakespeare's main source for the love-story, was undoubtedly the most characteristically romantic version of this extremely popular legend.

On the surface level one of the most obvious changes and symptoms of Shakespeare's scepticism is his depreciation of the heroine. Not, of course, that Chaucer's Criseyde belongs to the most idealised type of romantic heroine. But she is an amorous, warm-hearted young woman (not a coquette) who is for the time genuinely in love with Troilus. There is even the suggestion that, like a true lady of romance, she is partly in love with Troilus for his chivalric qualities:

> Ek gentil herte and manhod that ye hadde,
> And that ye hadde, as me thoughte, in despit
> Every thing that souned into badde,
> As rudenesse and poeplissh appetit,
> And that your reson bridleth your delit:
> This made, aboven every creature
> That I was youre, and shal whil I may dure.[1]

We are almost certainly intended to take this confession as truth, for in Chaucer's eyes Criseyde too is an embodiment of admirable virtues –

> ... men mighte in her gesse
> Honour, estat, and wommanly noblesse.[2]

How could she be otherwise than virtuous when she was so beautiful? –

> ... passing every wight,
> So angelik was hir natif beaute,
> That lik a thing inmortal semed she,
> As is an hevenissh parfit creature
> That down were sent in scorning of nature.[3]

Her chief weakness, admirably demonstrated by C. S. Lewis in *The Allegory of Love*,[4] is her timidity and constant need for a strong protector: 'She was the ferfulleste wight that mighte be.'[5]

[1] *Troilus and Criseyde* (Globe edition), Book IV, 1674-1680.
[2] Ibid., Book I, 286-287.
[3] Ibid., Bk. I, 101-105.
[4] Pp. 182-190.
[5] *Troilus and Criseyde*, Bk. II, 450-451.

Even her ultimate infidelity is treated by Chaucer reluctantly, and in a spirit of gentle 'compassioun'. For a long time she feels genuine grief for her parting from Troilus; Diomede is forced to use all his wiles to overcome her resistance; and when she at last surrenders herself to Diomede she is not without sorrow for her conduct:

> And if I mighte excuse her any wise,
> For she so sory was for her untrouthe,
> Y-wis, I wolde excuse her yit for routhe.[1]

'Routhe' has no place at all in Shakespeare's delineation of his Cressida, who is one of the most repulsive female characters he ever drew, a kind of meaner, unredeemed Cleopatra, though completely lacking in Cleopatra's mischievous sense of fun. Her portrait has no suggestion of beauty, certainly not of the 'angelik' romantic sort. Some physical charms and sex-appeal she must have possessed, but they are self-conscious and deliberately flaunted; even in her exhibition of grief she cannot forget them:

> I'll go in and weep . . .
> Tear my bright hair and scratch my praised cheeks,
> Crack my clear voice with sobs and break my heart
> With sounding Troilus.[2]

Her one resemblance to the heroine of romance is the aloofness and 'cruelty' she displays in the early part of the play, but even this Shakespeare cynically reduces to the level of cold-blooded, whorish calculation by her soliloquy at the end of Act I, Scene ii. Certainly there is nothing in her beyond youth and sexual attraction to justify Troilus' delirious infatuation: she is a shallow, sensuous, theatrical, utterly selfish creature, whose every other word or gesture is a pose sultry with suggestiveness – the instinctive whore in fact. Ulysses, one of the first of the Greeks to win a kiss from her, has her taped to a nicety as a daughter of the game:

> There's language in her eye, her cheek, her lip,
> Nay, her foot speaks; her wanton spirits look out
> At every joint and motive of her body.[3]

And so far from exerting, as Chaucer's Criseyde does, any resistance to Diomedes, it is she who entreats him.

---

[1] *Troilus and Criseyde*, Bk. v, 1097-1099.
[2] *Troilus and Cressida*, IV. ii. 111-115.
[3] Ibid., IV. v. 55-57.

However, if this denigration of the heroine is the change that strikes us most immediately, it is not the most significant pointer to Shakespeare's attitude, for after all Cressida was always the least typically romantic element in the legend.[1] Much more revealing is his re-creation of Troilus.

One transformation of the Shakespearean Troilus follows almost inevitably from the refashioning of Cressida. In Chaucer's poem Troilus is brought from 'wele' to 'wo' partly through the weakness of Criseyde, but more through the sudden inexorable turn of Fortune's wheel. With a typical medieval outlook, Chaucer is continually reminding us of –

> Fortune, which that permutacion
> Of thinges hath,[2]

of Fortune –

> That seemeth trewest whan she wil bigile;[3]

and there can be no doubt that he intended us to sympathise with Troilus (and no less with Criseyde) as two doomed, star-crossed lovers. We cannot feel this sympathy with Shakespeare's Troilus since he is himself largely responsible for his misery and suffering. Unlike Chaucer's hero, but like Helena in *All's Well*, he is the dupe of his own blind infatuation and chooses to found his happiness on a creature who stands confessed to everyone else as a worthless trull. Even at what should be the poignant moment of the lovers' parting, Shakespeare deliberately emphasises Troilus' blindness by contrasting it with Diomedes' instantaneous and correct appraisal of Cressida. So rapidly does Diomedes measure the whore and the greenhorn, trusting lover that he can risk a speech impudent with irony and double-meaning:

> The lustre in your eye, heaven in your cheek,
> Pleads your fair usage; and to Diomed
> You shall be mistress[4]

– a shrewd prophecy that Troilus only understands as a piece of gratuitous praise!

Apart from this contingent change there are two fundamental differences between Chaucer's Troilus and the Troilus of Shake-

---
[1] Also much of this blackening of Cressida may have been traditional, notably from Henryson's *The Testament of Cresseid*.
[2] *Troilus and Criseyde*, Bk. v, 1541-1542.
[3] Ibid., Bk. IV. 3.
[4] *Troilus and Cressida*, IV. iv. 120-122.

speare. In Chaucer's hero we have a perfect specimen of the medieval ideal of lover *and* chivalric knight: he is zealous to win favour in his lady's eyes by his exploits in battle, and once he has been accepted as her servant his entire moral being is changed for the better:

> And most of love and vertu was his speche,
> And in despit hadde alle wrecchednesse;
> And douteles, no nede was him biseche
> T'honouren hem that hadden worthinesse,
> And esen hem that weren in distresse.[1]

Shakespeare's Troilus is more the feverish lover of late romantic poetry, practising the cult of Dejection; and so far from his love acting as a spur to deeds of chivalry, it is not till he has witnessed Cressida's faithlessness that he really flings himself whole-heartedly into Troy's fight. When we first see him he is ravaged by his own delirious passion, and his attitude is fairly described by his own confession:

> But I am weaker than a woman's tear,
> Tamer than sleep, fonder than ignorance,
> Less valiant than the virgin in the night.[2]

Had Shakespeare intended us to sympathise much with Troilus, it would have required some of his most cunning strokes of art to erase the unfortunate impression that his hero creates in the opening scene.

The second original feature of Shakespeare's Troilus is his deep-rooted doubt and uncertainty as a lover. Though at times, as notably in his speech 'I tell thee I am mad in Cressid's love',[3] he can declare his passion and devotion with all the single-hearted vehemence of the typical romantic lover, his heart is gnawed by a restless scepticism – not so much of Cressida in particular as of the permanence of love and the strength of the romantic ideals of devotion and constancy. At the very moment when Cressida accepts him as her lover that astringent doubt carks him, and he gives expression to it in some of the finest lines of the play:

> O! that I thought it could be in a woman –
> As, if it can, I will presume in you –
> To feed for aye her lamp and flames of love;

[1] *Troilus and Criseyde*, Bk. III, 1786-1790.
[2] *Troilus and Cressida*, I. i. 9-11.
[3] Ibid., I. i. 51-52 ff.

> To keep her constancy in plight and youth,
> Outliving beauty's outward, with a mind
> That doth renew swifter than blood decays!
> Or that persuasion could but thus convince me,
> That my integrity and truth to you
> Might be affronted with the match and weight
> Of such winnowed purity in love;
> How were I then uplifted! but, alas!
> I am as true as truth's simplicity
> And simpler than the infancy of truth.[1]

The same pessimistic doubt thrusts its way to the surface in the parting between the two lovers, though Cressida (and Troilus himself) endeavour to staunch it. 'Be thou but true of heart', Troilus begins; he is reproved and pretends that his words are a mere form of speech, but he returns to his fears of what may happen when Cressida finds herself among the courtly Grecian youths. Cressida then, quite naturally, asks him point-blank whether he thinks she will fall to such temptation, and though Troilus gives an equally direct 'No', his answer is only a half-truth, or a hope rather than a conviction, for his fearful intuition of human frailty still persists:

> Something may be done that we will not:
> And sometimes we are devils to ourselves,
> When we will tempt the frailty of our powers,
> Presuming on their changeful potency.[2]

There is one more glimpse of this contradiction between his hope and his intuition when, at the time of truce between the two armies, he is arranging for Ulysses to lead him to the tent of Calchas. His words should remind us of a point frequently overlooked in interpretations of his character: that is, that, however much the surface of his mind was dazed with incredulity at Cressida's fickleness, part of him had always been prepared for such infidelity:

> She was belov'd, she lov'd; she is, and doth:
> But still sweet love is food for fortune's tooth.[3]

---
[1] *Troilus and Cressida*, III. ii. 165-177.
[2] Ibid., IV. iv. 95-98.
[3] Ibid., IV. v. 292-293.

F

Naturally, Chaucer's Troilus, too, is afraid of what may happen once he and Criseyde are parted, and he entreats Criseyde to pledge herself with oaths of loyalty. There is even a moment when, like the Troilus of Shakespeare, he expresses his fear of the charm of the Greek youths. But the vital root of his uneasiness is his suspicion that Calcas 'in sleighte as Argus yed' will outwit his daughter in her scheme to return to Troy and will compel her into marriage with one of the Greeks. Certainly there is nothing in him of the doubtful or sceptical element that is defined in Shakespeare's play by such a speech as 'O! that I thought it could be in a woman'. He is what we should expect from a poet who referred to himself as 'I, that God of Love's servants serve' – an innocent, simple, single-hearted lover, who is pledged to the doctrines of romantic love and never questions their validity. Shakespeare's Troilus, on the other hand, is less simple and less innocent. He is not merely the conventional hero of a story of love's brittleness and folly; he is one who has himself seen half-way through the fictions of romantic love. Moreover, when we bear in mind the general spirit and intention of the play, it is reasonable to suppose that this scepticism of the Shakespearean Troilus was also the scepticism of his creator.

We can bring this transformation of Cressida and Troilus into sharper focus by concentrating on a common climactic point in both versions of the story – the first encounter of the two lovers.[1]

In Chaucer's poem, when Criseyde first approaches Troilus' 'sick-bed', Troilus is speechless with ecstasy and incredulity. His words, the moment he does find his tongue, are scanty enough, but they have the genuine romantic ring of abject though supplicatory abasement: 'Mercy, mercy, swete herte!' Gathering courage, he declares his devoted love and willingness to die for Criseyde. His protestations are followed by an interlude which sentimentalises but does not cheapen the scene, where Pandarus, weeping 'as he to water wolde', implores Criseyde to have pity on Troilus. Then comes the great lyrical moment when Troilus pours out his heart in a speech that is steeped in the cardinal sentiments of romantic love – his desire to be Criseyde's servant, his readiness to be content with a glance from her bright eyes, his promises

---

[1] In Chaucer, of course, this encounter really falls into two separate parts – the first meeting at the house of Deiphebus and the second in the chamber of Pandarus; but for the sake of comparison we may take these two passages together and set them beside Act III, Sc. ii. of *Troilus and Cressida*.

to be diligent in her service, secret and patient. This speech is such a fine specimen of the early romantic manner that it is worth quoting in full :

> 'What that I mene, O swete herte dere?'
> Quod Troilus. 'O goodly fresshe free!
> That with the stremes of your yen clere
> Ye wolden frendly somtime on me see;
> And thanne agreen that I may ben he,
> Withouten braunche of vice in any wise,
> In trouthe alwey to don you my servise
>
> 'As to my lady right and chief resort,
> With al my wit and al diligence;
> And I to han, right as you list, confort,
> Under your yerde, egal to myn offence,
> As deth, if that I breke your defence;
> And that you deigne me so muche honoure,
> Me to comanden aught in any houre;
>
> 'And I to ben your verray humble trewe,
> Secret, and in my peynes pacient,
> And evere mo desiren fresshly newe
> To serve and ben y-like diligent,
> And with good herte al hoolly your talent
> Receiven wel, how sore that me smerte, –
> Lo, this mene I, myn owne swete herte.'[1]

On these terms Criseyde accepts Troilus as her servant, and she accepts him like a true lady of romance – a little remotely, without haste, conscious all the time of her 'honour', and warning him not to be too presumptuous or hopeful.

The opening of the second interview, in the house of Pandarus, is taken up with Troilus' imaginary jealousy. Though Shakespeare ignores this particular episode, he has a roughly parallel passage in which Cressida explains her past attitude to Troilus, and it should therefore be noted for the sake of future comparison that this jealousy is entirely the invention of Pandarus: Criseyde's own conduct has been completely blameless, she does not attempt to utilise the situation as a practised coquette might have done, and she forgives Troilus swiftly and sincerely. In the ensuing stanzas, which form what is virtually a prothalamion, followed

[1] *Troilus and Criseyde*, Bk. III, 127-147.

by a typical medieval aubade,[1] we have a celebration of 'Benigne Love, thou holy bond of thinges', a renewal of Troilus' vows of service and utter submission, and his eager desire to be shown the way of virtue and chivalric conduct:

> So techeth me how that I may deserve
> Your thonk, so that I thorugh myn ignoraunce
> Ne do no thing that be you displesaunce.
>
> For certes, fresshe wommanliche wif,
> This dar I seye, that trouthe and diligence,
> That shal ye finden in me al my lif;
> N' I wol not, certein, breken your defence;[2]

Criseyde, for her part, expresses complete faith in her knight.

Coming fresh from such passages to Shakespeare's play, we cannot miss the sharp difference of intention and atmosphere. Not instantly, perhaps, do we perceive the change, for when we first hear Troilus, in the two speeches 'I stalk about her door' and 'I am giddy, expectation whirls me round', he is very much the lyrical lover of romance. But very soon the spirit of the scene is coarsened by the brisk commercial traveller's prosy chatter and lewdness of Pandarus, a character quite different from Chaucer's figure of the same name. When Cressida enters, Troilus is for a moment, like Chaucer's hero, speechless, but he recovers, and, after a single sincere, natural remark – 'O Cressida! how often have I wished me thus' – he joins with Cressida in a mechanical prose dialogue that is stilted and rhetorical in manner and sophisticated and slightly cynical in its matter, which includes a hit at one of the main conventions of romantic love-making:

Troilus: O Cressida, how often have I wished me thus!
Cressida: Wished, my lord! The gods grant, – O my lord!
Troilus: What should they grant? what makes this pretty abruption? What too curious dreg espies my sweet lady in the fountain of our love?
Cressida: More dregs than water, if my fears have eyes.
Troilus: Fears make devils of cherubins; they never see truly.
Cressida: Blind fear, that seeing reason leads, finds safer footing than blind reason stumbling without fear: to fear the worst oft cures the worse.

---

[1] It is interesting to note that there is one instance of this form in Shakespeare, in the morning farewell of Romeo and Juliet.
[2] *Troilus and Criseyde*, Bk. III, 1293-1299.

The 'Dark' Comedies 149

Troilus: O, let my lady apprehend no fear: in all Cupid's pageant there is presented no monster.
Cressida: Nor nothing monstrous neither?
Troilus: Nothing, but our undertakings; when we vow to weep seas, live in fire, eat rocks, tame tigers; thinking it harder for our mistress to devise imposition enough than for us to undergo any difficulty imposed. This is the monstruosity in love, lady, that the will is infinite and the execution confined; that the desire is boundless and the act a slave to limit.
Cressida: They say all lovers swear more performance than they are able and yet reserve an ability that they never perform, vowing more than the perfection of ten and discharging less than the tenth part of one. They that have the voice of lions and the act of hares, are they not monsters?[1]

This dialogue deserves quoting in almost its entirety because the more one reflects upon it the more remarkable it appears. Here is a major climax of the play – the first meeting of two lovers of romantic legend. Remembering the parallel passages in Chaucer's poem, knowing Shakespeare's perfect mastery of the romantic mode of love-making in his earlier comedies, we might well anticipate a poetry full of fire, intense excitement, abandon and exaggeration. Instead, we run into this prose – a dry, spiritless, formal conversation that is little more than a piece of rhetorical padding. Nor is there any inherent dramatic justification for this, unless – which is extremely unlikely – we are intended to believe that Troilus was rigidly and slavishly bound to Pandarus' injunction, 'You must be witty now'. For all Troilus' innate scepticism and Cressida's shallow insincerity, the natural and appropriate thing was for Troilus to declare his devotion in the high romantic style, at which he had shown himself an adept in his two main speeches at the beginning of the scene. As it is, we must suspect that this speech really betrays Shakespeare's boredom with the whole manner of romantic love-making.

Soon after Cressida's explanation of her previous attitude to Troilus, a 'confession' that, in its insincerity, pretence of innocence, calculation and provocative coquetry, contrasts sharply with Criseyde's discussion of Troilus' jealousy, there is another odd jarring passage that sounds more like Shakespeare himself than any words Troilus and Cressida would have been likely to

[1] *Troilus and Cressida* III. ii. 64-97.

utter in such circumstances. This time the incongruity is in the candour and plain-speaking of the lovers: after Cressida's deliberate ambiguities and pretence not to be able to explain herself in words ('I speak I know not what'), Troilus quite patently fails to play up to her, and, for a moment, shows a clear understanding of her with his blunt, 'Well know they what they speak that speak so wisely'.[1] Cressida's frank retort is no less out of part:

> Perchance, my lord, I show more craft than love;
> And fell so roundly to a large confession,
> To angle for your thoughts.[2]

Perhaps by some super-subtle trick of coquetry, an attempt to bewilder Troilus with a sense of her contradictions and complexity, such a Cressida might have followed up her deceptions with the sharp shock of truth; but that would have been a dangerous, delicate stratagem calling for abundant intelligence, a quality that Cressida nowhere reveals. It seems more reasonable to take these lines as another instance of the perfunctory, and at the same time destructive, temper in which Shakespeare wrote this scene so rich in possibilities for courtship of the romantic kind.

Another clash of discord follows with Troilus' confession of his innate scepticism of women and romantic love – 'O! that I thought it could be in a woman' – which is, in its turn, abruptly succeeded by two speeches in the traditional romantic style where both the lovers pledge their oaths of fidelity and constancy. But this vein is preserved for a few moments only: there is another disharmony, another expression of insidious anti-romantic sentiment, as Pandarus ushers the lovers off to the strains of his comfortably salacious chatter, and with a realistic ironic aside to the bawds and whores who were likely to be present in any average Elizabethan audience: 'I will show you a chamber with a bed; which bed, because it shall not speak of your pretty encounters, press it to death: away!

> And Cupid grant all tongue-tied maidens here
> Bed, chamber, Pandar to provide this gear!'[3]

How far from Chaucer too, and how revealing, is the spirit in which Shakespeare has invested the scene of the following

[1] 158-159.
[2] 160-162.
[3] 215-220.

morning. There is no need to draw this difference out into paraphrase and fine, perhaps tedious, detail, for there is a common incident to both stories that is saturated with the quintessence of each. Both Criseyde and Cressida have the thought (and the natural hope) that their lovers may turn straight back to them. In Chaucer the incident is treated with spontaneous directness and innocence:

> 'But herte myn, withoute more speche,
> Beth to me trewe, or elles were it routhe;
> For I am thyn, by God and by my trouthe!
>
> 'Beth glad for-thy, and live in sikernesse;
> Thus seide I nevere or now, ne shal to mo!
> And if to you it were a gret gladnesse
> To torn ayein sone after that ye go,
> As fayn wolde I as ye that it were so,
> As wisely God myn herte bring at reste!' –
> And him in armes took and ofte kiste.[1]

In Shakespeare there is the atmosphere of Restoration comedy:

> *Cressida:* My lord, come you again into my chamber;
>   You smile and mock me, as if I meant naughtily.
> *Troilus:* Ha, ha!
> *Cressida:* Come, you are deceived, I think of no such thing.
>   (*Knocking within.*)
>   How earnestly they knock! Pray you, come in:
>   I would not for half Troy have you seen here.[2]

Even the knocking contributes its suggestion of promiscuity.

However, the difference between Chaucer and Shakespeare (at the time when he was writing this play) is not confined to the words, actions, and characters of the two pairs of lovers. When we have made all allowance for the humour and irony of Chaucer's poem and for the typical medieval awareness, apparent in the conclusion, of the conflicting claims of religion and earthly love, *Troilus and Criseyde* remains an idealisation of love as a supreme human experience, 'the consummation of his [Chaucer's] labours as a poet of courtly love'.[3] This idealisation is deepened and extended by the spirit that envelops the events and characters

---

[1] *Troilus and Cresyde*, Bk. III, 1510-1519.
[2] *Troilus and Cressida*, IV. ii. 37-42.
[3] C. S. Lewis, *The Allegory of Love*, p. 176.

of the story: we feel it, for instance, in Chaucer's reluctance to treat the last part of the legend, and in the manner in which he skips over the tale of Criseyde's disloyalty. More than that, we feel it in his frequent apostrophes in praise of Love, in such passages as the opening stanza of Book III:

> O blisful light, of which the bemes clere
> Adorneth al the thridde hevene faire!
> O sonnes lief, O Jove's daughter dere,
> Plesaunce of love, O goodly debonaire,
> In gentil hertes ay redy to repaire!
> O verray cause of hele and of gladnesse,
> Y-heried be thy might and thy goodnesse![1]

In Shakespeare's treatment of the story, on the other hand, all idealisation of this kind has evaporated. If we are conscious of any atmosphere at all over and above the hard and explicit statement of the distressing love-story, it is the effluvia of Thersites' diseased imagination: 'Lechery, lechery; still, wars and lechery; nothing else holds fashion: a burning devil take them!'[2]

It is in this change of atmosphere that we can best set the figure of Pandarus. In *Troilus and Cressida* Pandarus serves two main functions: he is the means whereby the lovers are brought together, and, as we have indicated in our analysis of the scene of the lovers' first meeting, he is the voice of commentary that cheapens and coarsens their story. Moral strictures on his character would be out of place, for he is harmless, ineffectual and, at times, slightly amusing. But if Shakespeare never seriously intended that he should be brought to the bar of moral judgment, we must recognise him as one of the tribe to whom he has given his name, one of the 'brethren, and sisters, of the hold-door trade', in which capacity he directly addresses the audience several times.

Chaucer's Pandarus is a rich, complex creation of an entirely different order. He is, at times, the voice of prosaic common sense; he is a comic character, and he is the go-between, employing more craft and subtle diplomacy than the Shakespearean Pandarus, in bringing the two lovers to bed. But his prosaic common sense springs from the world of ordinary life, not from the stews; his humour lies more in his verbosity than in his salaciousness, which anyhow is more delicate and ironic than the bawdy of

---

[1] This happens to be a fairly close translation of Boccaccio's *Il Filostrato*.
[2] *Troilus and Cressida*, v. ii. 195-197.

Shakespeare's Pandarus; and, if he acts the formal part of the go-between, he is above all the serious man of sentiment and the servant of love in the medieval style, who permeates the atmosphere of the poem with the romantic conception of love as the consummation of human experience and the height of human bliss, even when it is touched with pathos and suffering. As C. S. Lewis puts it in his fine and discriminating analysis of Pandarus,[1] 'He is inside the magic circle of courtly love – a devout, even a pedantic and lachrymose, exponent of it. But he, like everyone else, except the lovers themselves for short moments in "the fury of their kindness", sees also the hard or banal lineaments of the work-day world showing through the enchanted haze'.

Faintly superimposed over the Troilus-Cressida story in Shakespeare's play and helping to connect it with the Graeco-Trojan War, there is the second famous love affair of Helen and Paris. Though this is not developed to any great extent, it is treated with the same astringent anti-romanticism as the tale of Troilus and Cressida. No one appears to think of Helen and Paris as two great romantic lovers. Some, like Hector and Troilus in their more rational moments, regard Helen as merely worthless when measured against the bloodshed she has caused; some, like Diomedes, abuse her as a cheap whore, 'So much contaminated carrion weight'; while to most she and her lover are just one more target for the hoary jest of 'horns' and cuckoldry. In the one scene in which Shakespeare presents the two lovers to us he does not quite indulge himself in the blatant anti-romantic temper of Rupert Brooke's sonnet –

> Oft she weeps, gummy-eyed and impotent;
>   Her dry shanks twitch at Paris' mumbled name.
> So Menelaus nagged; and Helen cried;
> And Paris slept on by Scamander side –

but the difference between the spirit of Shakespeare's scene and Brooke's sonnet is only one of degree. The setting is a smug domestic one; Paris has dwindled from a great lover to an uxorious husband, and Helen is a comfortable, matronly figure, slightly overblown.

Before we leave the play we must turn to one other salient aspect of Shakespeare's anti-romantic satire. We have already

[1] *The Allegory of Love*, p. 194.

noted[1] how *Troilus and Cressida* is the one play that Shakespeare has placed in a medieval chivalric setting. The warriors on both sides are represented as 'knights', the siege of Troy is transformed into a medieval type of warfare, with fair ladies like Helen and Hecuba watching the combats from a grandstand vantage, and much of the central part of the play is taken up by a challenge and joust of arms, the excuse for which is Hector's conventional chivalric boast:

> Hector, in view of Trojans and of Greeks,
> Shall make it good, or do his best to do it,
> He hath a lady, wiser, fairer, truer,
> Than ever Greek did compass in his arms.[2]

Of course there was nothing original in this translation of the classical siege of Troy into terms of medieval chivalry. It was a stock anachronism of the Troy books like Caxton's translation of Le Fèvre's *Recueil des Histoires de Troie*, which was probably Shakespeare's chief source for his historical material. What is significant is that Shakespeare accompanies his sceptical, anti-romantic treatment of the legend of Troilus and Cressida with a merciless, and at times crude, denigration of chivalry.

On the surface perhaps, both the challenge of Hector and its outcome is pure romance. The Greeks provide a champion to encounter Hector, the combat between Hector and Ajax is conducted according to the strict code of the lists, the truce is faithfully honoured by both sides, and afterwards there is feasting and entertainment among the assembled knights. But there is much more than this to the episode. For instance, barely has the challenge been delivered by Aeneas with all the amplitude and fanfaronade of conventional chivalric rhetoric when the ludicrous image is intruded of the senile Nestor thrusting his withered brawn into his vantbrace to maintain –

> . . . that my lady
> Was fairer than his grandam.[3]

Again, for the love-sick Achilles, pining (among other causes) for Polyxena, Hector's sister, the words of the challenge are so much 'trash', too childish for repetition. But these are small, and

[1] Chapter 4, p. 77.
[2] *Troilus and Cressida*, I. iii. 273-276.
[3] Ibid., I. iii. 298-299.

perhaps debatable, details. What cannot be missed is that all this artificial convention of challenge and joust is twisted to something much more sordid and crudely realistic – to the manœuvres of the shrewd politician Ulysses, who is scheming to knock some sense into the heads of the proud, factious, beef-witted 'knights' who are supposed to be fighting on the Greek side. Thersites' voice may not be the voice of Shakespeare – or it may be one of several voices of choric commentary, but what Thersites says about the Grecian knights is, beneath its extravagant scurrility, the truth of the play. Indeed, there is nothing in all Thersites' gibes vile enough to describe the last act of the 'knight' Achilles – his barbarous butchery of Hector when he has caught him unarmed and alone.

What did Shakespeare mean by this picture of the Greek knights? Perhaps, as some critics have suggested, it was simply an attempt to scoff at and belittle the *Iliad* translations of the 'rival' poet Chapman – if Chapman was that rival. But what is more likely is that Shakespeare was actuated by the same iconoclastic spirit that had determined his treatment of the Troilus and Cressida story. Following the example of Lydgate,[1] Henryson and Caxton in their detraction of the Greek heroes, he was out to show that all the paladins of antiquity and medieval romance, of Homer and Spenser (though, like a true Elizabethan, Shakespeare would not have bothered much with this distinction), were 'lustful brutes and stupid bullies'.[2] He might be exaggerating, but his play would be none the worse for that as a corrective to those who, like Spenser, still hankered fondly after the outmoded ideals of medieval chivalry.

The validity of such an interpretation is confirmed, if somewhat paradoxically, by his more restrained and balanced picture of the Trojan knights. These heroes – Hector, Troilus and Paris – have no Thersites to bedaub them with mud; nor do they deserve such treatment. But while of more attractive dispositions than their Greek opposites, they are scarcely less beef-witted, especially when they are sacrificing themselves and their city to an extravagant and distorting sense of 'honour'. The centre of Shakespeare's attack on the limitations of this fundamental concept of chivalry is the scene (irrelevant from a strictly dramatic point of view)

---

[1] *History, Siege and Destruction of Troy.*
[2] For the context of this quotation see Grierson's *Cross Currents in English Literature*, p. 143.

in which Priam and his sons debate the possibility of returning Helen to the Greeks. Honour, as it is here represented, is nothing more than a narrow, anti-social principle that leads a man to ignore the interests and welfare of a whole community for some purely selfish, or at best family, motive. It may also be twisted dishonestly, as when Paris assumes that the keeping of Helen is 'honourable' and will therefore wipe off 'the soil of her fair rape'. Above all, honour is fundamentally irrational, openly derisive of all considerations of reason and common sense:

> Nay, if we talk of reason,
> Let's shut our gates and sleep: manhood and honour
> Should have hare-hearts, would they but fat their thoughts
> With this cramm'd reason: reason and respect
> Make livers pale and lustihood deject.[1]

Even Hector, the most sensible voice in the debate, after arguing shrewdly and plausibly for the return of Helen, suddenly abandons his own better judgment and falls in blindly with the others – so hypnotic upon him is the compulsion of the word 'honour'.

§

A consideration of the attitudes towards romantic love revealed in *All's Well* and *Troilus and Cressida* will perhaps enable us to describe with a little more precision than some criticism of the past the disenchantment commonly attributed to these plays. The mood of disgust and disillusionment in *Measure for Measure*[2] also has an obvious reference to romantic love. In this play Shakespeare passes beyond scepticism to a cynical and complete disregard of the values and attitudes that had been cherished by romance. Nowhere in the oppressive sultry atmosphere of *Measure for Measure* is there a breath of those delicate zephyrs of love that fan through the earlier comedies. A young man, of the same stock as Valentine and Lysander, falls foul of the law 'upon the act of fornication'; another man jilts his betrothed when, through misfortune, she fails to provide the promised dowry; and the jilted lady recovers her rights by a trick in which she submits herself to the lust of the man who has deserted her. Instead of the slightly amusing amateur of the 'hold-door' trade

---

[1] *Troilus and Cressida*, II. ii. 46-50.
[2] Based on Whetstone's *Promos and Cassandra*, a dramatisation of a novella of Cinthio.

Pandarus, we have the obnoxious professional Pompey, while there is a new type of depraved character introduced in the sickly, foul-mouthed whoremonger Lucio. The background, always obtrusive, is a grey, fly-blown one of wenching, 'French crowns', and brothels.

However, this sour spirit of disillusionment and cynicism[1] is only one of the salient features of the 'dark' comedies. Another, no less striking, is the sense of strain, frustration, unresolved conflict in their artistry. We feel that, for once in his life, Shakespeare was uncertain of his medium, that he was struggling, not always with success, to refashion it so that it might correspond with radical changes in his vision.

This cleavage between Shakespeare's mind and art, which is a flaw running through all three of the plays under present review, stands out conspicuously in *Measure for Measure*, a work which, while it could only have been written by a great poet, certainly falls short of great poetry and great drama. There is, for instance, something peculiarly unsatisfying in the play's treatment of evil. At times Angelo's unbridled lust is impressive and convincing, a disruptive, elemental force that threatens to destroy Angelo himself and spread misery and suffering around him. It is made to sound so much like the real thing:

>   What is't I dream on?
> O cunning enemy, that, to catch a saint,
> With saints dost bait thy hook! Most dangerous
> Is that temptation that doth goad us on
> To sin in loving virtue: never could the strumpet,
> With all her double vigour, art and nature,
> Once stir my temper; but this virtuous maid
> Subdues me quite.[2]

Yet this passion, at once animal and sophisticated, that might have been one of the lawless, egotistical impulses that devastate the world of the tragedies, is trimmed and adulterated to the

---

[1] In his stimulating study of *Measure for Measure* and *Much Ado* (*From Shakespeare to Joyce*, pp. 235-268) E. E. Stoll vigorously emphasises the comedy of these two plays, especially their comic irony, minimises almost to vanishing point the element of disgust and disillusionment, and will have no truck with the idea that this element derives from Shakespeare's personal experience. But he achieves this minimisation by skipping all too lightly over the sordid Pompey scenes in *Measure for Measure*, while in dismissing the subjective factor he does not face up to the question why Shakespeare went to such stories at this period.

[2] *Measure for Measure*, II. ii. 179-186.

needs of an artificial, romantic plot – to the safe, all-knowing supervision of the disguised Duke (who having, when he surrendered his authority to Angelo, praised him as a model of virtue, later admits his knowledge of Angelo's perfidious treatment of Mariana); to the fantastic deception by which Mariana substitutes herself for Isabella; and to the conventional happy ending where Angelo is forgiven and tamely paired off with the woman he has so shamefully treated. We feel, and with something of a sense of having been cheated, that what has happened is after all just a game and not to be taken too seriously:

> By this Lord Angelo perceives he's safe:
> Methinks I see a quickening in his eye.
> Well, Angelo, your evil quits you well:
> Look that you love your wife.[1]

'Look that you love your wife' – what a preposterous ending to the history of a man like Angelo! And how the perfunctory, conversational tone of these lines clashes with the compact intensity of such a passage as the one quoted above.

But why, it may be objected, does the wickedness in such romantic plays as *The Two Gentlemen of Verona* and *Much Ado About Nothing* not affect us in the same way? Why are we never tempted for a single moment to take these plays seriously? Why do we swallow their wildly romantic stories and conventional endings without the slightest sense of a cheat?

The answer to such questions lies in the difference between the characters of Proteus and Don John on the one hand and Angelo on the other. Don John and Proteus are simply puppets, and the evil in each of them has no significance except as a motive in the plot. But Angelo – at least in the first part of *Measure for Measure* – is a convincing character in whom Shakespeare has represented a subtle, complicated working of lust; and Angelo is quickened into life precisely because Shakespeare was vitally interested in that form of wickedness. But barely has life been breathed into Angelo when he has to be distorted to the necessities of a romantic story. In Proteus and Don John there is no such sense of distortion or arrested life, since they are kept throughout in strict subordination to the needs of an incredible story.

Nor, so long as Shakespeare clung to the romantic type of plot, could this frustration that we discern in the treatment of Angelo

---

[1] *Measure for Measure*, v. i. 499-502.

be easily avoided, for, to be significant in art, evil and the suffering and misery it produces must be terrifyingly near to the stuff of real life. Even when, as in the Shakespearean tragedies, evil is largely transformed into poetic symbolism it must remain rooted in human nature and move in a credible world that is parallel, for all its simplification and heightened intensity, with the real world. The world created by romance, on the other hand, was a realm of unashamed, and often child-like, make-believe. Never had it accommodated more than one important human emotion, and even that had been manipulated to a highly artificial and idealised form.

Moreover this preoccupation with the problem of evil that we glimpse in the figure of Angelo is only one symptom of Shakespeare's changing outlook, which by the turn of the century was becoming more reflective, philosophic and visionary. Time and again in *Measure for Measure* (as in *All's Well* and *Troilus and Cressida*) we come across passages that reveal new impulses of interest and awareness striving for poetic expression. Lines like the following, for instance, might easily have come from one of the great tragedies:

> Merciful heaven,
> Thou rather with thy sharp and sulphurous bolt
> Splitt'st the unwedgeable and gnarled oak
> Than the soft myrtle; but man, proud man,
> Drest in a little brief authority,
> Most ignorant of what he's most assured,
> His glassy essence, like an angry ape,
> Plays such fantastic tricks before high heaven
> As make the angels weep.[1]

There are several more passages of this grave, impassioned, visionary kind in the arguments between Angelo and Escalus and between Angelo and Isabella on mercy and justice, as well as in the often-quoted lines of the Duke and Claudio on death.

Such passages are the 'splendid poetry' that every critic wishes to salvage from these dark, enigmatic and rarely acted comedies. Torn from their context they are indeed magnificently impressive. But if we listen to them in the run of the play in which they occur they produce a slight discord. When Macbeth breaks out into 'She should have died hereafter' or Cleopatra into 'Give me

[1] *Measure for Measure*, II. ii. 114-122.

my robe, put on my crown', we are under the spell of perfect art: the effect of the words is direct, complete, spontaneous because the words are the essence of the speaker and the speaker a convincing symbol of human experience and human nature. But when Isabella utters such a speech as the one quoted above we are teased by an irrepressible scepticism that not all Shakespeare's spell can charm away. Could such a shallow, cold-blooded creature as Isabella, aware only of an abstract and formal virtue, ever conceivably utter lines like those, so warm, pitiful and extensive in vision? Could the Duke whom we observe in the rest of the play have uttered such a speech as 'Be absolute for death', or was Shakespeare, for the moment, merely using him as a mask?

We are forced back to the conclusion we have already indicated. So long as Shakespeare's mind and sensibility were predominantly lyrical, aerated with wit and a sense of humour, romance was a happy medium in which to work. By its long tradition romance was framed for lyricism, especially of love, while it lent itself admirably, through dramatic adaptation, to wit and comedy of a certain kind. But for the sensibility, thought, and vision that were soon to be expressed in the great tragedies romance was, in its general run, an inadequate and unsuitable mode.[1] In spite of this, whether through conservatism, force of habit, the pressure of keeping his company constantly supplied with plays, or a combination of all these forces, Shakespeare attempted for a time to work inside the old romantic type of story, even when his dynamic poetic impulses were radically changing. Here is a discrepancy that offers us an invaluable clue to the elucidation of one of the mysteries of these three comedies – their failure[2] as works of art.

[1] Apart from *Hamlet*, which may have come to Shakespeare in an already dramatised form, and *Othello*, none of Shakespeare's tragedies derives to any great extent from a romantic source.

[2] In *From Shakespeare to Joyce* (pp. 235-268) E. E. Stoll attempts a defence of *Measure for Measure* and *All's Well*. But while he is sound – as so often – in attacking those who demand psychological verisimilitude and in stressing the overriding necessities of the plot and situations, the 'predominant dramatic tone', he is surely wide of the mark in describing these plays as 'alive, interesting, exciting, poetical too'. Judged by the test of stage popularity – a criterion which Stoll of all critics should accept – *Measure for Measure*, *All's Well*, and perhaps even *Troilus and Cressida*, are failures.

CHAPTER SEVEN

THE 'ROMANCES'

THERE IS one word that all writers use as a label for Shakespeare's last plays:[1] they are his 'romances'. But, more often than not, the word suffers the usual smudge of imprecision, as when Dowden writes: 'There is a romantic element about these plays. In all there is the same romantic incident of lost children recovered by those to whom they are dear – the daughters of Pericles and Leontes, the sons of Cymbeline and Alonso. In all there is the beautiful romantic background of sea and mountain.'[2] Of course, all this is vaguely true; but the second sentence particularises too narrowly, and the third blurs the image of the last plays by superimposing over it another image of Wordsworthian romanticism. Tillyard's remark, 'when we call Shakespeare's last plays romances, I suppose we mean that his material is remote and improbable and that he uses the happy ending',[3] is better, though there is a half-apologetic air of vagueness about it.

For every student of Shakespeare's last plays then, there is this important preliminary question to be answered: In what senses of the word are *Pericles, Cymbeline, The Winter's Tale* and *The Tempest* to be described as 'romances', and can this word be used with precision? This question directly raises a second: What changes, what threads of continuity can be traced between the 'romances' and the 'romantic' comedies?

For a start it should be noted that, whereas in the tragedies of his middle period Shakespeare had borrowed his stories from a variety of sources, in his last plays he returns continuously to the same material that he had used for the non-historical plays of his earliest years as a writer. With the exception of *The Tempest*, whose plot cannot be ascribed to any known source, all the so-called 'romances' derive directly from one branch or another of romantic literature. Like *As You Like It, The Winter's*

[1] I am including in this group *Pericles* and *The Two Noble Kinsmen*, following the opinion that gives the last three acts of *Pericles* and a substantial part of *The Two Noble Kinsmen* to Shakespeare. But even if it were proved conclusively that Shakespeare had no hand in *The Two Noble Kinsmen* and only a slight one in *Pericles*, these two plays would still be of importance for this study.
[2] *A Shakespeare Primer*, pp. 55-56.
[3] *Shakespeare's Last Plays*, p. 71.

Tale[1] is based on a contemporary pastoral romance, Greene's *Pandosto*; like *All's Well That Ends Well*, the main Posthumus-Imogen story of *Cymbeline* comes from Boccaccio; *The Two Noble Kinsmen* follows the line of *Troilus and Cressida* back to Chaucer, being a dramatisation of *The Knight's Tale*,[2] itself a free adaptation of Boccaccio's poem *Teseide*; and the story of *Pericles* is taken partly from Chaucer's contemporary Gower and partly from an Elizabethan novel by Twine adapted from Gower's *Confessio Amantis*.

Not, of course, that Shakespeare follows these originals slavishly: to the end of his days as a dramatist he remained a confirmed borrower, but he was always a prince, never a beggar, in his borrowings. He took what he pleased, he transmuted the duller metals into his own gold, and he spent lavishly. On the other hand, the alterations that he makes in his last plays are rarely away from the spirit of the romantic tradition, and in several instances he brought his story closer than its source to the conventions and temper of romance. For example, he softens the crude Latin-comedy bet of Posthumus in Boccaccio's story by making the wager grow from an earlier, invented incident in which Posthumus, with typical knightly panache, had vaunted the incomparable beauty and virtue of his mistress and challenged to combat anyone who denied her surpassing excellence. Again, Shakespeare's contrite Leontes, restored to and reconciled with Hermione, is a much more characteristic figure of romance than Greene's Pandosto, who, killing his wife by his accusations and cruel treatment, falling in love with his own daughter, and finally slaying himself, belongs more to the type of Elizabethan and Jacobean play that went in boldly for blood and depraved enormity.

Deriving from such sources, each of the last plays is obviously romantic in the sense that it is the dramatisation of a good story – good because it is filled with incident.[3] With slight alterations

---

[1] A slight point to be noticed about *The Winter's Tale* is that four of its character names, Leontes, Antigonus, Archidamus, and Mopsa, occur in *Arcadia*, while the name Florizel may come from *Amadis de Gaul*. Admittedly, neither of these tales had any notable or direct influence on *The Winter's Tale*; but the names are probably a significant pointer to Shakespeare's reading.

[2] *The Knight's Tale*, which may have given Shakespeare some hints for *A Midsummer Night's Dream*, had already been dramatised in Edwards' lost *Palamon and Arcite* (1566). Henslowe four times records a play of this title, but we do not know whether or not these entries refer to Edwards' work.

[3] Cf. A. Thorndike, *The Influence of Beaumont and Fletcher on Shakespeare*, p. 134: 'The material of the plots, never taken from history nor resembling real life, *is of a sort that we call romantic, of a sort that gives theatrical novelty and variety*.' [My italics.]

The 'Romances'

the title-page of the quarto *Pericles*, with its reference to 'the whole history, adventures and fortunes of the said Prince' and to 'the no less strange and worthy accidents' of Marina, would serve for any of the romances. *Cymbeline*, which sweeps into the two hours' traffic of the stage the story of a banished husband's wager on his wife's fidelity, a war between the Britons and the Romans, a king's recovery of his long-lost sons, and includes in these stories a princess who wanders disguised as a youth, who is buried and comes to life again, a poisoner queen, a headless corpse, attempted murders and an attempted ravishment, the appearance of spirits and the god Jupiter, an escape from execution, visions, and an oracle, is perhaps outstanding for its unflagging abundance of narrative excitement. But both *Pericles* and *The Winter's Tale* fall little short of *Cymbeline* in this respect, and even *The Tempest*, though its narrative is much slighter, is brisk-moving and full of incident when seen on the stage.

All this mass of incident, this vigour and excitement of narrative, is characteristically romantic in that it is quite unhampered by any considerations of verisimilitude. Like those of the comedies, the plots of the romances aim deliberately at the far-fetched, the astounding and the incredible. With realism jettisoned, extravagance becomes a virtue. *Cymbeline* is crammed to bursting with such fairy-tale stuff – a husband prepared to let a seducer put his wife's fidelity to the test, that seducer smuggling himself in a trunk into the lady's bedroom (Imogen, the lady, conveniently forgetting to ask why the store of plate has to be deposited in her bedroom of all places, or why it has to be stowed in a trunk large enough to conceal a man), Imogen fleeing to the one remote spot in Britain where her long-lost brothers live and being readily accepted, Briton as she is, as page to the Roman General Lucius, a battle in which two men and two youths put the Roman legions to ignominious rout, and Cymbeline after the battle failing to recognise his own daughter. These are the kind of incidents that Johnson was referring to when he castigated *Cymbeline* for 'the folly of the fiction, the absurdity of the conduct ... and the impossibility of the events in any system of life'.[1] But such strictures as these, based on the criterion of realism, are quite irrelevant to the romance type of story, and they would certainly have meant nothing to Shakespeare, who was content to satisfy the tastes of an audience that had been conditioned by centuries of romantic verse and

[1] *Johnson on Shakespeare*, ed. Walter Raleigh, p. 183.

prose to enjoy a story of fantastic make-believe. And the incredibilities of *Cymbeline* can be paralleled by a score of others from *Pericles*, *The Winter's Tale* and *The Tempest*, like the miraculous preservation of Thaisa, washed ashore in her coffin and restored to life by the magical arts of Cerimon, the escapes of Marina from the violence of a murderer, pirates, and brothel-keepers, and the pretended death of Hermione, which demands that her husband shall be tricked into the belief that she is dead and buried, that he shall remain in his deception for over sixteen years though she lives concealed in the same neighbourhood, and that – for a grand climax to this chain of marvels – he shall take his wife's living body for a statue. It is unnecessary to cite similar examples from *The Tempest* since the entire plot of this play is dependent on the activities of an all-powerful and privileged magician.

Besides this general romantic quality of the narrative of the last plays there is the recurrence of particular romance conventions. Once more we are entertained with all-deceptive disguises and mistaken identities: Imogen masquerading, like Julia, Rosalind, and Viola, as a youth, Imogen mistaking the body of Cloten for her husband, Posthumus dressing himself up as a common soldier, Polixenes present, as a stranger guest, at his son's Arcadian betrothal. There are also the familiar dreams and touches of the supernatural: the visions of Antigonus and Posthumus, the appearance of gods and goddesses, the oracle upon which the whole of *The Winter's Tale* turns. And, of course, there is *The Tempest* where, perhaps using Cerimon as his prototype, Shakespeare gave over his play for the first time to the enchantments of a wizard, with his staff, his familiar spirit, and his spells and enchantment.

Again, these plays are characterised by the quality of movement and of abrupt changes of scene that we find so frequently in the romance tale, as well as in Shakespeare's comedies. *Cymbeline*, with the wanderings of Imogen and its sudden transitions between Britain and Italy, between the Court and the remote parts of Wales, is perhaps outstanding in this respect, but there is also considerable movement in both *Pericles* and *The Winter's Tale*. As with so much that concerns these last plays, *The Tempest* is an exception, for here in his conduct of plot Shakespeare approaches almost as near to the classical Unity of Place as he does to the Unity of Time.

All this reversion in narrative to the manner of the comedies necessitated a parallel reversion in characterisation. In the plays of his middle period from *Julius Caesar* to *Anthony and Cleopatra*, and to a lesser extent in the later history plays, Shakespeare had achieved a new quality of psychological realism. This quality is not of course what is commonly understood to-day by that term – the realism in portraiture and analysis of the novelist, the realism that can to some extent be tested against the findings of the psychiatrist; it is poetic and dramatic realism. But, in spite of probable confusions and certainly the opposition of Professor Stoll, we must insist on the realism of Shakespeare's tragic characterisation, for with all the simplification, distortion, and intensification of the poetic and dramatic process that has created them, most of the characters of the plays of the middle period are projected out of essential human nature. Their motives, attitudes and developments are in the main – and certainly within the logic of the play that contains them – real, consistent and credible; they are shaped in the round; and they live on vividly in the imagination, though naturally our particular image of Hamlet or Lear, Lady Macbeth or Cleopatra, may not be that of the next man, or indeed – to touch on the tantalising and insoluble – the image that Shakespeare intended. This fundamental psychological truth of the plays of the middle period is what distinguishes them above all else from the rest of his work and from the bulk of Elizabethan and Jacobean drama; and it is the quality that justifies Coleridge's famous dictum, 'the interest in the plot is always in fact on account of the characters, not *vice versa*, as in almost all other writers; the plot is a mere canvas and no more'.[1] Morover, even when the characters lack the force and reality of Macbeth or Othello or Antony, they are in the general run vigorously animated.[2]

But, with all respect to such a giant Shakespearean as Coleridge,[3] his generalisation is basically untrue for the romances. We may grant that these plays are never so completely dominated by plot

---

[1] *Recapitulation and Summary of the Characteristics of Shakespeare's Drama* (*Lectures and Notes on Shakespeare*, ed. T. Ashe, p. 239).
[2] For my use of this term, see Ch. 4, p. 91.
[3] In the last pages of *Shakespeare's Comic Characters* (pp. 133-135) John Palmer sharply attacks Coleridge's statement, or, rather, argues that his antithesis is an unreal one. He maintains that, while Shakespeare's plots do serve to illustrate character, they also condition it, and that in some instances characters are ruthlessly manipulated to further the ends of the plot. It should be pointed out, however, that Palmer is here concerned with the comedies.

and situation as the works of Beaumont and Fletcher; that they contain strokes of acute psychological observation; that occasionally, as when Antonio prevails upon Sebastian to murder Alonso, the interplay of personality and motive is managed with all Shakespeare's old cunning and subtlety; that they present a number of brilliantly animated characters, notably of the minor type like Paulina, Autolycus, Cloten, Gonzalo, Trinculo and Stephano. There are always exceptions to every broad generalisation about Shakespeare. But when we have given due weight to all these qualifications, it remains true that in the romances Shakespeare reverted, as he was compelled to by the romantic nature of his stories, to the type of character that is more than half pasteboard. Unless we are actually in the theatre, when the art and personality of the actor may do much to satisfy us, how simple and unsubstantial, for instance, are most of the main characters of *The Tempest* – Alonso, Sebastian, Antonio, Ferdinand and Miranda – once we measure them against the figures of the tragedies.[1] Even Prospero, who certainly impresses himself on the imagination, is chiefly the poetry that Shakespeare has put into his mouth. And what is true for *The Tempest*, the greatest of the romances, is true for the others. In *The Winter's Tale*, for example, what are Leontes and Hermoine, Polixenes, Florizel and Perdita but names, the names of puppets – speaking some magnificent verse, of course – who dance to the compulsive strings of an extravagant, highly coloured story?

For it is not merely in the superficiality and sketchiness of the portraiture, the tendency to divide his characters into rigid categories of black and white, that Shakespeare reverts to the style of the comedies. The motivation, too, is often weak and thoroughly unplausible. Compare, for instance, the jealousy of Othello and Leontes. We can believe easily and unreservedly in Othello's jealousy, for – one or two theatrical conventions apart – it is real; real because it is of slow, cumulative growth, because it has to contend with opposing forces in Othello, because it is supported by so many appearances and by so many devilish subtleties of persuasion. But who can believe the monstrous and instantaneous jealousy of Leontes? It is like some gigantic, incredible Genie suddenly released from a tiny bottle.

[1] Cf. A. Thorndike, op. cit., p. 137: 'The characters [of the romances] show, above all, a surprising loss of individuality. They are less consistent, less subtly drawn, less plausibly human; they are more the creatures of stage situations'.

Nor is this preposterous jealousy of Leontes by any means an exceptional instance of unconvincing motivation. It can be paralleled by many similar examples like the sudden reform of Lysimachus in the brothel scene of *Pericles* and the strange acquiescence of Marina later in accepting this reformed whoremonger as her husband, like the eagerness of the supposedly devoted Posthumus in allowing his wife to be assailed by a declared seducer, the readiness of Leontes to marry only a wife of Paulina's choice and by the unrelenting behaviour of Hermione, a generous and tender-hearted woman, in pretending to be dead for sixteen long years in order to punish a thoroughly chastened and repentant husband. Admittedly, motivation of this kind is not absent from the tragedies. *Lear* starts off with an obvious twitch of the puppet-strings. But once we have accepted, or closed our eyes to this preliminary intrusion of the fairy-tale,[1] the rest of the play, like the largest part of the tragedies, is convincingly and realistically motivated. With the romances, on the other hand, we return to the type of motivation that is predominant in the comedies. As the price that we pay for our far-fetched romantic stories we must accept behaviour and motives that are quite incredible and sometimes, as with Posthumus and Hermione, inconsistent with the disposition of the particular character concerned.

Some readers no doubt would wish to make an exception in favour of some of the women characters like Imogen,[2] Perdita and Miranda. Certainly these are sweet and winsome creatures, expecially when played by an attractive actress. But though they occasionally flash with life, and though – as when Perdita of the flower-speeches says

---

[1] However, this fantastic element is dissolved to some extent by the suggestion that Lear has already divided the kingdom, before the play opens, on more natural grounds of affection, etc.

[2] Quiller Couch's defence of *Cymbeline* against Johnson (see *Shakespeare's Workmanship*, Ch. xiii) consists largely of a panegyric of Imogen. But to my mind E. M. W. Tillyard is much nearer the mark when he describes her (op. cit., p. 31) as mainly a 'conventional figure', 'at times a human being, at times a Griselda of the medieval imagination'. A Thorndike (op. cit., p. 139) is in agreement with Tillyard when he writes: 'In comparison with these heroines [Rosalind, Beatrice], an analysis of Imogen's character fails to supply really individual traits; one is thrown back on a general statement of her perfectibility'. 'The tributes of Iachimo, Posthumus, Pisano, Guiderius and Arviragus do more to create our ideas of Imogen's beauty of character than anything she says or does' (p. 140). Thorndike's dry comment on all three of the main heroines is worth repeating: 'these three heroines ... who seem to many to possess the lasting suggestiveness of noble ideal conceptions of human nature, could have appeared on the stage only as ordinary heroines' (p. 141).

> ... this dream of mine, —
> Being now awake, I'll queen it no inch further,
> But milk my ewes and weep —[1]

they are ballasted by that down-to-earth common sense that is never long absent from Shakespeare's general picture of feminine nature, they are slight and shadowy figures playing their necessary part in the story. Even Imogen, the most impressively drawn of the heroines, is involved in such fantastic situations that it is often difficult to take her seriously. For instance, in her interview with Iachimo she provides the one plausible element in this extravagant scene by refusing to believe Iachimo's lies. But scarcely has this strength of her mind and convictions been made real and plausible before she is transformed into a puppet by the promptness with which she accepts Iachimo's pretence that he had fabricated his fairy-tales about Posthumus merely to test her.

What can be said in truth about these women is that they are idealised figures who belong to the main romantic tradition, though as a slight corrective to the more sugary sort of appreciation, we should notice that two of the villains of these plays are women — Dionyza (the name of a born evil-doer if ever there was one) and the Queen in *Cymbeline*.

The setting of these last plays, too, is unmistakably romantic. Since the time of Shakespeare's comedies, writers like Jonson and Middleton had widened and diversified the social context of drama, particularly of comedy, to include a broad and colourful cross-section of bourgeois life. Where, at most, there had been odd scenes given over to servants, clowns and 'low-life' characters of the humorous type, there were now many plays that reflected throughout the everyday world of the mass of the people. But these innovations had no marked effect upon Shakespeare, who in his last plays, as in the comedies,[2] kept consistently to the courtly environment of romance. Indeed, when we have allowed for the brothel scenes in *Pericles* and for *The Tempest*, where he returns to his old comedy-formula of using humble characters for a distinct sub-plot, it is hardly an exaggeration to say that the romances are even more courtly and aristocratic in their setting than the comedies.

---

[1] *The Winter's Tale*, IV. iv. 458-460.

[2] The social setting of the tragedies has nothing to do with the romance tradition. Tragedy, according to the most widely accepted ideas, had of necessity to concern itself with the great and exalted.

Pastoralism also – that late, renaissance backcloth and costume for so much romantic sentiment – is plainly evident, notably in the second half of *The Winter's Tale* and in that scene of *The Tempest* where we are entertained with the pageant of Ceres and Juno and the dance of the nymphs and harvesters.

As in backcloth, dress, speech, manners – their bright, obvious exterior – so in their more tenuous, ultimately undefinable spirit these plays are closely akin to the comedies and, with them, to romance. In the tragedies Shakespeare, prompted by some impulse that we can only dimly guess at, had dared to gaze boldly into that frightening, mind-shattering world of anarchy and devastation which is always a potential reality about mankind, and which, in an age like Shakespeare's, when the old medieval order was crashing, up-torn from its deepest roots, and the modern bourgeois world thrusting out its first violent, crude growth, must have seemed unusually imminent. The ethos of this vision is not uniformly dark, nor is the total impression one of unrelieved despair, depression, or cynicism; goodness in a multitude of forms is still prominent, and men and women, for all their blindness, folly and wickedness, are significant, sympathetic, even noble and rich in half-realised qualities of mind, imagination, energy and love. But with these solacing, inspiriting features, and perhaps – comparing the effect of Shakespeare with Swift – *because* of them, the vision that Shakespeare communicates is one of the most terrible in all literature: monstrous evil and wickedness are prolific and largely triumphant, goodness is frustrated, tormented, and often defeated, and the moving forces commonly appear blind, purposeless and derisive, degrading man to the level of brute anarchy:

> It will come,
> Humanity must perforce prey on itself,
> Like monsters of the deep.[1]

But in the last plays, recovering the spirit of the comedies, Shakespeare informs his drama with what Quiller-Couch calls 'the mellowly romantic atmosphere':[2] all is ordered by a positive, controlled, and altogether benign temper and shaped to a pattern of ideal poetic justice. The virtuous are vindicated and rewarded in the invariably happy ending, and the wicked, never allowed

[1] *King Lear*, IV. ii. 48-50.
[2] *Shakespeare's Workmanship* (1931), p. 176.

a wide or devastating scope, are forced to confession, penitence, and a just punishment. But this justice, poetic not legal, is always, as we feel most intensely in *The Tempest*, sweetened and assuaged with mercy, forgiveness and reconciliation. Even the gods, no longer killing for their sport, are directly on the side of justice and moral order: on the one hand, Jupiter watches over the destiny of the repentant Posthumus and preserves him from execution, on the other, the vile, incestuous King of Antioch and his daughter are blasted by the gods.

§

At this point it is worth glancing at *The Two Noble Kinsmen* (an unduly neglected play apart from the puzzle of its authorship), for while this romance essentially belongs to the same dramatic type as the four plays we have been considering, it also stands distinctly apart from them. Only in a slight measure can this difference be ascribed to the probable participation of Fletcher, who indeed frequently appears to be doing his best to ape a Shakespearean manner. What really marks *The Two Noble Kinsmen* off from the rest of the romances is that its substance and spirit derive more completely than any of them from the oldest layer of the romantic tradition. Its setting (nominally in ancient Greece) is prominently and consistently medieval,[1] and its story – if we exclude the incidental episodes of the gaoler's daughter – is unique among the plays in which Shakespeare had a hand for its dependence upon and fidelity to the chivalric code.

The first act, which is given to Shakespeare by most scholars who have investigated the authorship of the play, deals entirely with a typical exploit of chivalry. While on his way with Hippolyta to their marriage ceremony, Duke Theseus, an approved knight whose 'fear'd sword . . . does good turns to the world',[2] is accosted by three ladies, queens in distress. Their plaint is that King Creon of Thebes has refused to allow the burial of their husbands who have been slain in battle – a blatantly unchivalric piece of conduct that Chaucer aptly and simply brands as 'vileynye'. The ladies beg Theseus to help them: they ask that their husbands shall be given a proper burial and the miscreant Creon punished. Like a true knight – though he requires more eloquent entreaty than

---

[1] There are, of course, the medieval scenes of jousting, feasting, and the winning of a fair lady in *Pericles*. But this part of the play is not Shakespeare's work.
[2] I. i. 51-52.

The 'Romances'

in Chaucer's tale to stir him to immediate action – Theseus fights down the temptations of the flesh and postpones his wedding to lead an expedition against Creon. His mission is completely successful: Creon is defeated, and the first act closes to the strains of a dirge as the three queens escort their husbands' bodies to burial.

In between the four scenes that present this story there is interposed the dialogue between Palamon and Arcite (Scene ii). Dramatically this scene of course fulfils the necessary function of introducing the two chief protagonists of the play, but it is also something of a variation on the chivalric theme of the rest of the act, with the reiterated word 'honour'[1] striking the keynote. To preserve their 'honours' both Palamon and Arcite are contemplating flight from Thebes. The city, as they see it, is stewing with corruption; their uncle, King Creon, is a selfish and wicked tyrant; and – especially galling to two young aspiring knights – the fighting men, 'sweating in an honourable toil', are denied their rightful reward and recognition.[2] Palamon even hints of a creed in which fighting is a necessary purge for the selfish decadence of peace. However, if honour is prompting Palamon and Arcite to leave their native city, honour also constrains them to stay when they hear that Theseus is marching to attack Thebes. Creon may be the black tyrant they have painted him, his cause may be thoroughly bad; but like feudal knights they owe a 'service' to Thebes. So, too, when we next see them in Theseus' prison, their sentiments are entirely of a chivalric kind: what they most regret in their captivity is that there will be no hunting for them, no children to bring up as warriors in emulation of the heroic deeds of their fathers, no more jousts where

> The hardy youths strive for the games of honour,
> Hung with the painted favours of their ladies.[3]

And what comforts them is their vows of everlasting friendship and the reflection that in the sanctuary of prison they are removed from all those temptations that beset those who 'desire the ways

---

[1] If Shakespeare did have a substantial hand in *The Two Noble Kinsmen*, this treatment of honour and the general attitude towards chivalry show that the mood of *Troilus and Cressida* was not a lasting one.

[2] All this may well be an oblique comment on Jacobean England. There is even the possibility that the neglected 'martialist, who did propound to his bold ends honour *and golden ingots*' (I. ii. 17-18) was a reference to Raleigh.

[3] *The Two Noble Kinsmen*, II. ii. 13-14. (Thorndike gives this scene to Fletcher.)

of honour'. It is while they are discoursing in this strain that Emilia comes into the garden below their cell gathering roses, and in an instant her bright eyes shrivel up all their papery philosophisings and oaths of friendship. Like true romantic lovers they both fall in love with her at first sight[1] – Palamon a few seconds before Arcite, and so the rivalry that is to be the subject of the rest of the play is born. Once more we are engaged in an old and favourite conflict of romance – love against friendship.

There is no need to describe in detail the well-known story of the rivalry which, apart from the conclusion, follows Chaucer's narrative closely. The single-hearted, fanatical dedication of the two young knights to their mistress, even when all achievement of their love seems hopeless; their courtesy[2] to one another, as when each helps to arm the other in their first fight, or when Arcite offers Palamon the use of his own sword; every turn and situation of the plot, like Arcite's refusal to take advantage of Palamon when he is unarmed, weak from hunger and in shackles,[3] like their combat in the wood to settle their dispute, their refusal to accept the ignominious offer of life with banishment from Emilia, and their eager acquiescence in Theseus' plan of a tourney in which the victorious knight shall receive Emilia's hand and the loser a shameful death – all the spirit and motion of the play are obviously generated from the old chivalric code; and unless we can temporarily accept the conventions of chivalry, the plot is absurdly impossible in the extreme. The background to these events, too, retains the typically romance setting of Chaucer's tale – the castle, the rose garden, the woods, the May morning, and the field of tournament.

Yet while it is unnecessary to stress the obvious chivalric nature of the play, there are one or two points that may be overlooked. For instance, it should be noted that there is, surprisingly enough,

---

[1] In asserting his right to love Emilia, Arcite utilises an interesting distinction between love and love in its most exalted romantic form. Twice in the first moments of dazzle-blind ecstasy Palamon had cried, 'She is a Goddess'. Arcite turns that extravagance against Palamon with:

> I will not, as you do, to worship her
> As she is heavenly and a blessed Goddess:
> I love her as a woman, to enjoy her:
> So both may love.
> (II. ii. 199-202)

[2] But there is a jarring note – Fletcher's probably – when Palamon and Arcite bait each other with sarcastic references to their former loves (III. iii.).
[3] Compare Achilles' butchery of Hector in *Troilus and Cressida*.

little trace of the solitary, dejected and lugubrious vein of romantic love that is to be found in *The Knight's Tale*, notably in the description of Arcite:

> His slepe, his mete, his drynke, is hym biraft,
> That lene he wexe and drye as is a shaft;
> His eyen holwe, and grisly to biholde,
> His hewe falow, and pale as asshen colde,
> And solitarie he was and ever allone,
> And waillynge al the nyght, makynge his mone.[1]

Again, while the Emelye of Chaucer is a typical lady of the lists, visibly present to encourage her lovers, the Emilia of Shakespeare and Fletcher is a far more sensitive creature whom not even Theseus and Hippolyta can prevail upon to witness the 'deeds of honour' to be performed in her name. On the other hand, if in some respects the play lacks some of the knightly and romantic elements of the poem, in others it embodies more of the essence of chivalry. For instance, the service of Theseus to the three distressed queens in *The Two Noble Kinsmen* and his victory over the temptation of immediate physical pleasure is heightened by the fact that at the very moment when the queens intercede with him he is on his way to marriage with Hippolyta; in *The Knight's Tale* Theseus and Hippolyta are already married. Again, in *The Knight's Tale* Theseus' treatment of the wounded Palamon and Arcite is harsh, and curtly disposed of by Chaucer:

> Out of the taas the pilours han hem torn
> And han hem caried softe unto the tente
> Of Theseus, and ful soone he hem sente
> To Atthenes, to dwellen in prisoun
> Perpetuelly, he nolde no raunsoun.[2]

In *The Two Noble Kinsmen*, too, Theseus dooms the two cousins to perpetual imprisonment, but there is no reference to the grim 'pilours', while Theseus, generous in his praises of Palamon and Arcite, orders that no cost or energy should be spared to heal their wounds.[3]

However, from the point of view of romantic conceptions, the major difference between *The Knight's Tale* and *The Two Noble Kinsmen* emerges from the figure of the heroine. In Chaucer's

---
[1] *The Knight's Tale* (Globe edition), 1361-1366.
[2] Ibid., 1020-1024.
[3] *The Two Noble Kinsmen*, I. iv. 30 ff.

tale Emelye is shadowily insignificant. Obviously, for the sake of the tale, there had to be a maiden, sister to Hippolyta, as the object of Palamon's and Arcite's rivalry. Chaucer's Emelye is that; but she is little more. Indeed, on one of the rare occasions when he does display any interest in his heroine he appears to regard her as a trivial minx, with an eye to her main chance, for when Arcite, flushed with victory, rides by and glances up at her, Chaucer dismisses her response with a cynical and singularly unromantic aside:

> And she agayn hym caste a freendlich eye
> (For wommen, as to speken in comune,
> Thei folwen al the favour of Fortune).[1]

The Emilia of *The Two Noble Kinsmen* is an altogether different figure; she is a noble and, in many ways, admirable character, far more worthy than Emelye of the devotion and sacrifices of her two knights; and she is a much more prominent figure in the story, particularly in her honest, but baffled, attempt to decide between the merits of her two lovers. We cannot, of course, generalise from a single Chaucerian heroine, but, comparing the poem with the play, we cannot help feeling the force of two centuries of literary evolution. What has made Emilia so different from her earlier incarnation is largely the growth and the change in the doctrines of romantic love.

§

We are now in a position to offer some preliminary answer to the questions posed at the beginning of this chapter. To the first, it may be replied that the term 'romances' can be applied to *Pericles, Cymbeline, The Winter's Tale* and *The Tempest* in the restricted and historical sense of the word. Secondly, because there is this common romantic element, we may trace a broad line of continuity between the comedies and the romances. If anyone should still doubt this continuity, he might be advised to undertake a crude piece of dramatic surgery which, fortunately, need only be performed in the imagination. Let him amputate from *As You Like It*, or, better still for the experiment, from *Much Ado*, a large part of the comic matter; let him then expand the serious parts of these plays to fill most of the five acts. In our hands, no doubt, the outcome of this dissection would be a lifeless

---

[1] *The Knight's Tale*, 2680-2682.

monstrosity. But if the operation had been performed by Shakespeare himself, would not the result be a play with the substance and much of the spirit of the romances?

On the other hand, exaggerated as the view is that regards the romances as a sharp and original point of departure in the evolution of Shakespeare's dramatic art,[1] it must be at once admitted that there are distinctive and significant changes between the comedies and the romances. All considerations of the alleged Beaumont and Fletcher influence apart, Shakespeare was not the kind of writer to repeat himself; nor, after the lapse of time and the experience of the tragedies, is it likely that he would have found it easy to copy his earlier triumphs, even if this had been his deliberate intention.

One obvious difference between the comedies and romances, though this does not make *Cymbeline* or *The Winter's Tale* less 'romantic' than say *A Midsummer Night's Dream*, is that the last plays tend to be longer[2] and certainly much more discursive than the comedies: 'long-drawn romances turned into dramas' Quiller Couch calls them.[3] This difference arises from two causes. In the first place, the romances, apart from *The Tempest*, cover a much longer period of time than any of the comedies. The events of *Cymbeline* occupy many months and those of *Pericles* and *The Winter's Tale* over sixteen years. *Pericles* and *The Winter's Tale* especially, though it is the heroines who are pictured from babyhood to adult years, remind us of Sidney's famous gibe against the ramshackle plays of his time:

> Now, of time they are much more liberal, for ordinary it is that two young Princes fall in love. After many traverses, she is got with child, delivered of a fair boy; he is lost, groweth a man, falls in love, and is ready to get another child; and all this in two hours' space: which how absurd it is in sense even sense may imagine.[4]

---

[1] See, for instance, M. R. Ridley's *Shakespeare's Plays* (p. 204) where the writer asserts that the romances 'are quite different in kind and in temper from any that had preceded them'. H. B. Charlton (*Shakespearian Comedy*, p. 267) strongly supports the opposite view: 'These romances have obvious affinities with Shakespeare's earlier comedies; *they are* comedies even more than tragi-comedies'.

[2] *Cymbeline* (3,276 lines) and *The Winter's Tale* (2,960) are substantially longer than most of the plays in the main group of comedies, whose average length is slightly under 2,500 lines. *Pericles* (2,375) is of average length, while *The Tempest* (2,016) is, apart from *The Comedy of Errors*, the shortest of all Shakespeare's comedies and romances.

[3] *Shakespeare's Workmanship*, p. 195.

[4] *Apologie for Poetrie* (*Elizabethan Critical Essays*, ed. Gregory Smith, Vol. I, p. 197).

This change is not fortuitous, for, as Quiller Couch clearly shows, the reconciliation theme, which is so important in these last plays, usually requires time for its working out. In the second place, there is rather less concatenation of scenes in the romances than in the comedies and certainly far less than in those plays of Beaumont and Fletcher that are sometimes regarded as Shakespeare's model. The romances come closest of all Shakespeare's work to Aristotle's definition of 'epeisodic' drama – plays 'in which the episodes or acts succeed one another without probable or necessary sequence'.[1]

But if this looseness of structure distinguishes the romances from the tragi-comedies of Beaumont and Fletcher, *Cymbeline* from *Philaster*, it may nevertheless have arisen from the fact that Shakespeare was aiming at the same theatrical effect as these two dramatists – the presentment of a number of sensational situations, and that his attention was focused more on these effects than the organisation of his plot. Certainly there is a sharp line of distinction between the comedies and romances in this matter. In the romances Shakespeare is much more sparing of uneventful, expositionary scenes than he had been in the comedies. Very rare, too, are those static scenes of wit-play and conversation, so frequently found in the comedies; the dialogue is limited, fairly strictly, to the needs of a continuously moving action. Above all, there is much more in the romances of the theatrical and sensational type of scene, much more playing on suspense and surprise. Episodes like the Statue scene in *The Winter's Tale* or the scene in *Cymbeline*[2] that includes a fight between Guiderius and Cloten and the return of Guiderius with Cloten's head, the entry of Arviragus with the apparently dead Imogen in his arms, the burial of Imogen and her startled awakening beside a headless corpse which she believes to be her husband, represent something new in Shakespeare's art. Admittedly, these two scenes are perhaps outstanding in their kind, but they are certainly not exceptional. In *The Tempest*, for instance, which is probably the least dramatic play of this group, we find five clear instances of a similar type of scene – the shipwreck,[3] the intended murder of Alonso, which is prevented by Ariel, the episode of the illusionary

---

[1] Following Quiller Couch's translation in *Shakespeare's Workmanship*, p. 198.
[2] IV. ii.
[3] In this respect it is interesting to compare the opening of *The Tempest* with the opening of *Twelfth Night*, where Shakespeare omitted to dramatise the shipwreck in his source-story.

banquet with its thunder and lightning and Ariel disguised as a harpy, Prospero's display of 'some vanity' of his art, and the sudden appearance of Ferdinand and Miranda playing chess.[1]

One important consequence of this emphasis on the surprising and sensational, for which – to distinguish the romances from the comedies – we might borrow Professor Ellis Fermor's term *'theatrical* romance',[2] is that the characterisation is thinner, the motivation more deficient, and the emotion more strained and false in the romances than in the comedies. The shadowiness of so many of the lovers and leading personages is common to both groups of plays. But if we make a comparison at the level of the animated characters it is obvious that the romances contain fewer of these than the comedies and none of the excellence of Malvolio, Jaques, Bottom, Beatrice and Benedick. This difference between the two groups of plays is even more striking if we examine the motivation. There is no character of equal importance in the comedies who is quite so unconvincing as Leontes, of whom Quiller Couch says bluntly but fairly, 'Shakespeare *had* time, or could have found time, to make [his] jealousy far more credible than it is. I maintain that he bungled it'.[3] And, as if our suspension of disbelief had not been sufficiently exploited, we are supposed to believe that this stupid and myopic creature would at once perceive the full truth of the situation as soon as the message of the oracle had been received and he had learnt of his son's death.[4] Posthumus is just as absurdly motivated, for besides the impossibility that such a devoted, even uxorious husband, would allow Iachimo to attempt his wife's seduction, we simply cannot believe that a husband so assured of his wife's virtue would decide to murder her on the strength of Iachimo's word, especially when even the indifferent Philario is far from convinced. Posthumus, of course, swallows Iachimo's report for the same simple reason that he made his preposterous wager in the first place: the needs of the story compel him to; and that is why Iachimo himself, having displayed a not incredible cunning and subtlety in his efforts to blacken Posthumus' character, crudely exposes himself by his absurd conclusion that Imogen should revenge herself on her

---

[1] A slighter point of difference between the plots of the comedies and romances, but one not to be ignored, is that the romances contain much less adventure and rather more intrigue than the comedies.
[2] *The Jacobean Drama*, p. 218.
[3] *Shakespeare's Workmanship*, p. 235.
[4] *The Winter's Tale*, III. ii. 154 ff.

debauched husband by going to bed with himself. Nor is it merely that the motivation in the romances is often perfunctory; sometimes it is lacking altogether. Once we have left Posthumus vowing Imogen's murder we do not meet him again till he returns to Britain with the Roman army. By then he is apparently utterly abashed and penitent: he wishes only to be killed in the imminent battle. But why? What has led him to change his mind about Imogen? We are not told. And why does Thaisa so readily give up all hope of ever seeing Pericles again? Once more there is no answer except the needs of the story.

This 'theatrical romance' as we have called it implies something else besides superficial motivation and scenes that are good 'situations' because they are surprising, sensational, or full of suspense. In order that these situations may be dramatically effective they must contain strong emotion. But this emotion is itself necessarily theatrical; it is spurious (and frequently remote) because it is untrue to real life, because there is no sufficient cause for it, because it is inconsistent with what we already know of a particular character, or because it arises from some unreality like a far-fetched misunderstanding. There is a good deal of emotion of this sort in the last part of *Much Ado*, but it is not till the romances that it becomes common and prominent. A good example of this theatrical emotion is Posthumus' furious outburst against women:

> Could I find out
> The woman's part in me! For there's no motion
> That tend to vice in man, but I affirm
> It is the woman's part: be it lying, note it,
> The woman's; flattering, hers; deceiving, hers;
> Lust and rank thoughts, hers, hers; revenges, hers;
> Ambitions, covetings, change of prides, disdain,
> Nice longing, slanders, mutability,
> All faults that may be named, nay, that hell knows,
> Why, hers, in part or all; but rather all.[1]

Declaimed by a good actor, these lines should stir us – a little: 'theatrical' emotion (for the term is not necessarily derogatory) implies that much at least. But we can never be absorbed, never touched to the heart by Posthumus' tirade because we cannot forget that it is based on an absurdity. There is remoteness; what we are listening to is, after all, only a play. This, too, is our

[1] *Cymbeline*, II. v. 19-28.

reaction to the grief of Guiderius and Arviragus over the supposedly dead Imogen, to the regret and penitence of Leontes in the Statue scene, to the sorrow of Alonso mourning for his dead son, to the pretended anger of Prospero against Ferdinand. ('This is unwonted Which now came from him',[1] says Miranda; and we readily believe her.) The plays of Beaumont and Fletcher affect us in the same way. But when we hear one of the great speeches of Othello or Troilus –

> Instance, O instance! strong as Pluto's gates;
> Cressid is mine, tied with the bonds of heaven:
> Instance, O instance! strong as heaven itself;
> The bonds of heaven are slipp'd, dissolv'd, and loos'd;
> And with another knot, five-finger-tied,
> And fractions of her faith, orts of her love,
> The fragments, scraps, the bits and greasy relics
> Of her o'er-eaten faith, are bound to Diomed –[2]

we are gripped and carried away. The emotion is authentic, not theatrical, for it is true to human nature and rooted in reality.

Another characteristic feature of the romances is their concern with evil, and evil that is, within limits, destructive.[3] Central to the plot of *Pericles*, there is Dionyza's intended murder of Marina; Posthumus has similar intentions towards Imogen, while the Queen plots to poison her husband and Pisano; Leontes' wicked jealousy, besides torturing his Queen, estranging Polixenes, and driving Camillo into banishment, is the indirect cause of the death of his son and of Antigonus. Even in *The Tempest*, where evil might have been treated entirely in retrospect, it remains a present reality: Sebastian and Antonio plot to kill Alonso, and Caliban enlists the help of Stephano and Trinculo to slit the throat of Prospero and rape Miranda. (Admittedly, Stephano and Trinculo are two unconvincing murderers, and such is the serenity of the island that we tend to forget their villainy, the reminder of which is as much a shock to us as it is to Prospero – 'I had forgot that foul conspiracy'.)

---

[1] *The Tempest*, I. ii. 497-498.
[2] *Troilus and Cressida*, v. ii. 153-160.
[3] E. M. W. Tillyard (op. cit., p. 25) stresses this destruction, which for him has a deep metaphysical significance: 'In the last three plays the old order is destroyed as thoroughly as in the main group of tragedies, and it is this destruction that altogether separates them from the realm of comedy in general and from Shakespeare's own earlier comedies in particular'. The metaphysical implications of this are discussed later in this chapter.

These elements in the plots of the romances produce a distressing note that is absent from the comedies, where evil is rare and destructive evil rarer still. Nevertheless this characteristic of the romances can be overstressed,[1] for actually the wickedness that is depicted in these plays is confined and diluted in several important ways. The theatrical emotion to which we have just drawn attention is one rarifying agent, just as it is in Beaumont and Fletcher; it creates an abiding sense of remoteness and unreality. Again, as in *Measure for Measure* and *Much Ado*, the pattern of the plots is such that wickedness is always under control, is merely allowed enough rope to hang itself. From the outset of the play we know that no further harm can come to Prospero and Miranda. Certainly Prospero is an all-powerful magician, but much of this same confident assurance is with us when we follow any of the other romances. Even if we were to read or see them for the first time (unimaginable state of unsophisticated innocence) we should be pretty certain that all must come right; and sometimes, as when Dr. Cornelius takes care to provide Cymbeline's Queen with harmless drugs, Shakespeare takes pains to see that we have no doubts about the outcome.

There is another, more subtle, way in which Shakespeare tends to dissipate what is potentially distressing in the romances. This concerns the words and the poetry, for while Shakespeare does not divert painful feeling into the elaborate decorativeness and prettiness of Beaumont and Fletcher, the tendency towards this kind of writing is unmistakably present. A capital instance of this diversion occurs in the soliloquy where Iachimo slips off the bracelet from the arm of Imogen while she is sleeping, notably in the lovely lines:

> 'Tis her breathing that
> Perfumes the chamber thus: the flame o' the taper
> Bows towards her, and would underpeep her lids,
> To see the enclosed lights, now canopied
> Under these windows, white and azure laced
> With blue of heaven's own tinct.[2]

Dramatically these lines are faulty: they are out of keeping with the reality of the scene and with the character of Iachimo. But they achieve another effect, with the addition of lyric beauty:

---

[1] As by Tillyard. See later in the chapter.
[2] *Cymbeline*, II. ii. 18-23.

they obliterate reality, so that we hardly feel at all the vileness of Iachimo or the potential distress of the scene. In the same way the pain of Imogen's believed death is softened by the prettiness of Arviragus' description:

> Thus smiling, as some fly had tickled slumber,
> Not as death's dart, being laughed at; his right cheek
> Reposing on a cushion;[1]

and also by the sweet fancies of the brothers' duet:

> Gui.: If he be gone, he'll make his grave a bed;
> With female fairies will his tomb be haunted,
> And worms will not come to thee.
> Arv.: With fairest flowers,
> Whilst summer lasts, and I live here, Fidele,
> I'll sweeten thy sad grave: thou shalt not lack
> The flower that's like thy face, pale primrose, nor
> The azured harebell, like thy veins, no, nor
> The leaf of eglantine, whom not to slander
> Out-sweetened not thy breath.[2]

When Guiderius, suddenly displeased with his brother's verbal embroidery, interrupts him bluntly with

> Prithee, have done;
> And do not play in wench-like words with that
> Which is serious.[3]

he is measuring Beaumont and Fletcher by Shakespeare's tragedy.

Possibly this dissipation of emotion through verbal decorativeness is most noticeable in *Cymbeline* and may be evidence of this play's special debt to Beaumont and Fletcher. But it is also to be discerned in the other romances, particularly in the Statue scene of *The Winter's Tale*. On the other hand, it is never more than a tendency. Not only did Shakespeare eschew the sustained passages of sentiment and prettiness that are so common in Beaumont and Fletcher, but he still retained from the tragedies and 'dark' comedies his power of objectifying stress and emotion in direct, compact, sinewy speech. Such is Posthumus' speech on his return to Britain, the only fault of which is that it is unmotivated:

---
[1] *Cymbeline*, IV. ii. 210-212.
[2] Ibid., IV. ii. 215-224.
[3] Ibid., IV. ii. 229-231.

> Gods! if you
> Should have ta'en vengeance on my faults, I never
> Had lived to put on this: so had you saved
> The noble Imogen to repent, and struck
> Me, wretch more worth your vengeance. But, alack,
> You snatch some hence for little faults; that's love,
> To have them fall no more: you some permit
> To second ills with ills, each elder worse,
> And make them dread it, to the doers' thrift.
> But Imogen is your own: do your best wills,
> And make me blest to obey![1]

Yet, while this element of pain and wickedness, however much confined and diluted, distinguishes the romances from the comedies, these plays are no less clearly separated from the tragedies. We have already indicated two of the major differences: there is the distinction between reality and theatricality in the matter of situation and emotion, and there is also the unbridled immensity of evil and suffering in the tragedies. These differences are so palpable that nothing further need be said here. But there is a third fundamental point of contrast: the romances are unique for their emphasis on reconciliation, especially through the young, and – perhaps not always so vividly appreciated – for their emphasis on penitence and forgiveness.

Again there is no cause here to analyse this theme, which is not of course to be confused with what are usually mere formal happy endings in the comedies. For one blessed moment the critics are in agreement. But perhaps we may repeat, if only as a tribute to his excellent writing on the romances, Quiller Couch's description – one in his liveliest manner – of the quintessence of these plays:

> Desdemona sacrificed, dead by her pillow: Cordelia limp in Lear's arms.... That cannot be the end of it all! 'Nay,' you hear Shakespeare say, 'if I were God now....' 'But,' says he, 'I am Shakespeare and feel myself a god, being able to create some few things. Then this shall *not* be the end. There may or may not be another world in which wrongs are redressed. But there *is* a continuance of this world in newer generations that we surmise – how wistfully! You promise heavens free from strife, but this warm, kind world is all I know; and in it ... Desdemona's fate and Cordelia's shall *not* be the last word, and the sins of the fathers shall *not* be visited on the

[1] *Cymbeline*, v. i. 7-17.

children.' And so we have Marina, Perdita, Miranda created for us: creatures of loveliness made to love and conceive children, renewing the promise of the world.[1]

§

There are still several other salient differences between the romances and comedies, chiefly concerning their common romantic ground, that must be considered.

In the first place, while the romances are still very much stories of love (though it might be maintained that the strength of this ingredient is slightly reduced[2]), their love-interest is markedly different from that of the comedies. Young lovers are far less prominent, and there is comparatively little love-making. Two of the plays, *Cymbeline* and *The Winter's Tale*, are primarily dramas of married life. And even where young lovers like Perdita and Florizel are allowed to have their fling they rarely speak, seriously or in raillery, to that sacred book of romantic love that had been such a large and absorbing interest in the comedies.

At first sight *The Tempest* might appear once again to present a large exception to these general conclusions. The love-story of Ferdinand and Miranda might seem to be as fully and directly in the romance tradition as any love-story of the comedies, for we are again transported to the world of a youth and a maid, to the 'swift business' of love at first sight, vows of purity and chastity, ordeals and trials that the hero must endure uncomplainingly to merit the hand of his lady, to scenes of courtship whose music is composed on the old notes of 'service', 'honour', 'mistress', and so on, and to snatches of the traditional lyric love-address, as when Ferdinand bursts into:

> Admired Miranda!
> Indeed the top of admiration! worth
> What's dearest to the world! Full many a lady
> I have eyed with best regard, and many a time
> The harmony of their tongues hath into bondage
> Brought my too diligent ear; for several virtues
> Have I liked several women; never any
> With so full soul, but some defect in her

---

[1] *Shakespeare's Workmanship*, p. 273.
[2] Notably in *Pericles*, where, apart from the hero's brief and knightly winning of Thaisa, there is no love-story to speak of.

> Did quarrel with the noblest grace she owed
> And put it to the foil: but you, O you,
> So perfect and so peerless, are created
> Of every creature's best![1]

Yet the more we immerse ourselves in this story of Miranda and Ferdinand, which is, after all, only a small part of the play, the more conscious we become of change from such a love-story as that of *A Midsummer Night's Dream*. Perhaps, after Spenser, we must accept the stress that is thrown by Act I, Scene iv, on marriage as a natural and necessary consummation of love in the light of an extension or transformation of the creed of romantic love. All we need notice in passing is that this emphasis is far more pronounced than in any of the comedies. Nor, probably, should we attach too much significance to the abrupt dismissal of Venus and her son,[2] so long the romantic symbols of lawless, passionate, and often sensual love. What is less easy to dismiss is the feeling that Ferdinand is a more prosaic and longer-headed young man than any of the heroes of the comedies. Certainly it is not his fault that for his trial of love he is compelled to play the token, artificial role of a 'patient log man', reminding us somehow of the principal boy in a pantomime; nor can he or Miranda help the fact that the course of their love is so smooth and certain. But undoubtedly the first circumstance (and possibly the second) does divest Ferdinand of some of the glamour of the typical romance hero, whose usual lot it is to struggle and suffer in adversity. Even more suggestive of his worldly and balanced common sense is the first part of his promise not to assail Miranda's virginity before they have been married:

> As I hope
> For quiet days, fair issue, and long life,
> With such love as 'tis now, the murkiest den,
> The most opportune place, the strongest suggestion
> Our worser genius can, shall never melt
> Mine honour into lust.[3]

To found our entire interpretation of Ferdinand on a few unguarded words like these would be absurd; nevertheless this hope for a long and tranquil life with children who will be a joy

---

[1] *The Tempest*, III. i. 37-48.
[2] Ibid., IV. i. 85 ff. Compare especially the speech of Iris with the more traditional sentiments of *A Midsummer Night's Dream*, I. i. 169 ff.
[3] Ibid., IV. i. 23-28.

to him, this anticipation of a mature man who realises that, however important sexual love may be, it is only one of several substantial satisfactions in married life, is not the attitude of the typical romance lover, for whom the lyrical love of courtship is a complete and enclosed world of bliss, rarely admitting a view of domestic felicities, and for whom the present moment of ecstasy is an eternity of time.

Further, the entire love-story of Miranda and Ferdinand diminishes, as no love-story of the comedies does, into one small sweet phrase against the larger and graver harmonies of Prospero's vision of mortality and transience, the magical words of which continue to echo through the last part of the play long after Prospero has uttered them:

> The cloud-capped towers, the gorgeous palaces,
> The solemn temples, the great globe itself,
> Yea, all which it inherit, shall dissolve
> And, like this insubstantial pageant faded,
> Leave not a rack behind. We are such stuff
> As dreams are made on, and our little life
> Is rounded with a sleep.[1]

This diminution and transformation of the love-interest suggests another possible distinction between the comedies and the romances. In his essay on Philip Massinger, T. S. Eliot has a penetrating passage in which he puts his finger on what is perhaps the outstanding characteristic of Jacobean romantic drama: 'the debility of romantic drama does not depend upon extravagant setting, or preposterous events, or inconceivable coincidences. ... It consists in an internal incoherence of feelings, a concatenation of emotions which signifies nothing.'[2] This acute piece of diagnosis, which runs close to Coleridge's remark that 'the plays of Beaumont and Fletcher are mere aggregations without unity',[3] is not applied by Eliot to Shakespeare's romances, and few would think of condemning the Shakespearean romances as hotchpotches of emotion signifying nothing.[4] But this particular para-

---

[1] *The Tempest*, IV. i. 152-158.
[2] *Elizabethan Essays* (Faber Library edition, pp. 167-168.)
[3] *Lectures and Notes on Shakespeare*, ed. T. Ashe, p. 400.
[4] A. Thorndike however – perhaps to support his thesis – emphasises the lack of emotional unity in Shakespeare's romances: 'Shakespeare was no longer dealing with stories exemplifying one central emotion, he now took plots dealing with every variety of emotion. . . There is an evident choice of intense, exaggerated emotions; there is no sign of unity.' (Op. cit., p. 134).

graph of Eliot is not without some bearing on Shakespeare's last plays, since – always excepting *The Tempest* – these dramas do undoubtedly lack the firm unity and organisation of his best work, which would include at least four of the comedies. If we have ignored this criticism of Eliot's in our demonstration of the romantic characteristics of the last plays, that is because a lack of emotional coherence is not a feature of the romantic tradition, though no doubt a number of isolated works in that tradition could be condemned on this score. But Eliot's analysis, so far as we can with justice apply it to Shakespeare's romances, does suggest an interesting speculation. All Shakespeare's comedies have an intense and vigorous individuality: no other dramatist has produced such a wide and rich variety of comic plays. At the same time, as we have shown, they are all bound together, separately and collectively, by one dominant tone – the sentiments, boldly reflected or humorously criticised, of romantic love. In his last plays, while he has revived so much of the manner and material of romance, Shakespeare was no longer seriously interested in those sentiments. Is that a reason, even the primary reason, why these plays are lacking in emotional unity, why they tend, at times dangerously, to the 'aggregation' of Beaumont and Fletcher?

Indirectly, we have already touched on the second fundamental difference between the romances and the comedies: that is the marked decrease of the comic element. Once again we must place a strong mark of exception against *The Tempest*, where the comical scheme and mishaps of the drunken Stephano and Trinculo, abetted by Caliban, form a distinct sub-plot much on the model of the comedies. There is also, of course, Cloten and Autolycus, the latter an original and brilliant addition to Shakespeare's comic gallery. But, apart from these characters and their adventures, there is almost an entire absence of humour – at least of deliberate humour: nothing in *Pericles*, just a trace in *Cymbeline* and *The Two Noble Kinsmen*. Nor is it merely that the humour of the mechanicals has disappeared. The old irrepressible wit of the lovers and courtly folk has vanished too, though Sebastian and Antonio, with Gonzalo and his utopian dreams as a tempting bait, do make at least one crude attempt at a comeback.[1]

We may, if we please, regard this diminution of the comic

[1] *The Tempest*, II. i. 143 ff.

element as a fortuitous and isolated development. We may
egard it as a natural effect of the years of tragedy and – if we
subscribe to such highly speculative theories – of Shakespeare's
own chastening experience. Yet, when we remember how much
of the humour of the comedies, of clowns and courtiers alike,
depended on the doctrines and sentiments of romantic love, how,
indeed, Shakespeare's 'comedies' evolved into comedies in our
modern sense of the word largely through their creator's increasing, though always humorous, criticism of the romantic attitude,
we have strong grounds for believing that the simultaneous
disappearance of humour and of romantic love were intimately
connected.

Finally the romances must, of course, be separated from the
comedies on grounds of poetic style. A thorough investigation of
the difference – of the new blank verse of the romances for
instance, with its note of 'stillness and sweetness',[1] its loose and
sinewy approximations to conversational speech – would take
us some distance away from the field of this study. But there is
one difference that should be noted since it has some bearing on
points that have already been discussed. Of the comedies we may
say that where the verse is not purely dramatic (that is to say,
directly dependent on the business of the scene) it tends towards
the lyrical. Wherever Shakespeare is not strictly a comic
dramatist he is usually the Shakespeare of the *Sonnets*, *Venus and
Adonis*, *The Rape of Lucrece*. The comedies are full of such lyric
snatches as:

> If ever you have look'd on better days,
> If ever been where bells have knoll'd to church,
> If ever sat at any good man's feast,
> If ever from your eyelids wiped a tear
> And know what 'tis to pity and be pitied,
> Let gentleness my strong enforcement be;[2]

or – to give a different sort of example – the Duke's comment on
Feste's song:

> Mark it, Cesario, it is old and plain;
> The spinsters and the knitters in the sun
> And the free maids that weave their thread with bones
> Do use to chant it.[3]

[1] E. M. W. Tillyard, *Shakespeare's Last Plays*, p. 9.
[2] *As You Like It*, II. vii. 113-118.
[3] *Twelfth Night*, II. iv. 44-47.

In the romances, on the other hand, the verse, when it is deflected, more often inclines towards the meditative and contemplative. Such a deflection is Imogen's speech:

> Had I been thief-stol'n,
> As my two brothers, happy! but most miserable
> Is the desire that's glorious: blest be those,
> How mean soe'er, that have their honest wills,
> Which seasons comfort;[1]

or the poignant lines of Polixenes:

> We were, fair queen,
> Two lads that thought there was no more behind
> But such a day to-morrow as to-day,
> And to be boy eternal.[2]

This difference of inclinations is not in any sense absolute; reflective passages abound in the comedies, and, quite apart from the decorative pieces in the Beaumont and Fletcher style, there are many lyrical movements in the romances. But, measured as a whole, these two different deflections of the verse do separate the comedies and the romances in yet another important respect.

§

There is one further question of importance that remains to be considered. Why in his last years as a dramatist did Shakespeare return to romance?

One answer to this question is contained, by implication at least, in Lytton Strachey's contention that Shakespeare's last plays represent the work of a writer 'bored with people, bored with real life, bored with drama, bored, in fact, with everything except poetry and poetical dreams.'[3] Bored – or terrified – by reality, Shakespeare wished to escape into a world of day-dream, make-believe and artifice, which, for a writer of his time, meant the world of romance. Perhaps Spenser escaped in the same way and for the same reason.

This answer is quite unsatisfactory. As works of art the romances, even in their poetry, are certainly inferior to the tragedies, and perhaps to the pick of the comedies. But they are not the products of boredom, nor do they manifest a lack of vitality. To take up

---

[1] *Cymbeline*, I. vi. 5-9.
[2] *The Winter's Tale*, I. ii. 62-65.
[3] 'Shakespeare's Final Period', *Books and Characters* (1922), p. 60.

but one point in Strachey's contention, it is completely untrue to say that Shakespeare in his last plays was 'bored with drama'. As we have shown, he was intensely interested in a new type of theatrical effect, and though it is permissible to argue that this development marks a degeneration in his work, it is absurd to call a writer indifferent or exhausted when he is launching out into fresh and persistent experiments. Further, as Tillyard points out – and his reminder applies with equal force to Spenser – romance was not to Shakespeare's contemporaries what it was to later writers of the Romantic Revival; it was not necessarily escapist.[1]

A much more plausible answer is the one that stresses the influence of Beaumont and Fletcher upon Shakespeare in his last years. Partly to utilise the new and more elaborate type of indoor stage at Blackfriars, and partly to meet the taste of the Jacobean court for sentiment and spectacle, these two dramatists in their tragi-comedies, were treating romance in a new way: they were writing 'theatrical romances', and the theory is that Shakespeare, impressed by the success of these younger dramatists, followed their example.

There may be something in this view,[2] which was forcibly presented by Ashley Thorndike at the beginning of the present century in his study *The Influence of Beaumont and Fletcher on Shakespeare's Last Plays*. But until the dates of *Cymbeline* and *Philaster* can be exactly settled there always remains the possibility that the initial impulse towards this new type of romantic drama came from Shakespeare himself and not Beaumont and Fletcher. In any event Thorndike makes too much of the similarities between Shakespeare and his younger rivals.[3] There are many obvious correspondences, it is true, and we have already noted many of these – the general tragi-comedy formula that blends the painful and distressing with the humorous, the striving after surprising and startling situations, the theatrical emotions, and

---

[1] 'When ... Shakespeare began using romantic material at the end of his career instead of Holinshead and Plutarch, it was not necessarily because he wanted to "escape" or to be less serious. The "feigned" history he chose to draw on was taken quite as seriously by his contemporaries as the true history he abandoned.' (*Shakespeare's Last Plays*, p. 12.)

[2] Tillyard (op. cit., p. 6) states the present position sensibly and moderately: 'The question of Beaumont and Fletcher's influence on Shakespeare has, in fact, been warehoused rather than disposed of for good.'

[3] Tillyard also appears to lean slightly in this direction: 'An unprejudiced reader can hardly avoid admitting the probability that Shakespeare was very much aware of Beaumont and Fletcher indeed'. (Op. cit., p. 6.)

the fondness for pretty and decorative effects. But when we have given these similarities their proper weight, we cannot fail to perceive the essential difference between Shakespeare's plays and those of Beaumont and Fletcher. Turning from any one of the romances, even from *Cymbeline*, to *Philaster* or *A King and No King*, we feel that we are entering a different world; and the change that we feel cannot be limited to the richer texture of Shakespeare's verse, important as this difference is. The Beaumont and Fletcher plays are much more completely dominated by love and sex than Shakespeare's romances;[1] there is more exploitation of pathos,[2] more preoccupation with guilt, and, above all, far more sensation, especially sensation of the piquant kind, as when Aspatia has to prepare Evadne for the marriage-bed with the man who was to be her husband, or Arbaces believes himself to be in love with his own sister. Incredible as Shakespeare's motivation frequently is, his characters are less conditioned by the plot than those of Beaumont and Fletcher, and it would be hard to find anything in the romances so utterly unconvincing as the repentence of Evadne or the scene[3] in which Melantius worms the truth out of Amintor about his relations with Evadne, is about to assault him as a liar, and then is prepared to believe him on the strength of their friendship. Further, though Shakespeare secures much more emotional unity than Beaumont and Fletcher, he does not achieve their tight-packed cohesion of structure, where the time covered by the action is comparatively short and one scene leads directly into another. Added together, all these differences amount to a very considerable sum, and while they do not destroy the case of those who believe that the Beaumont and Fletcher influence is an important one, they should be a check on any tendency to overrate this influence.

Not necessarily excluding this second explanation of Shakespeare's return to romance, there is also the view that regards the final plays as a natural and organic development out of the tragedies.

---

[1] Thorndike (op. cit., p. 133) maintains that Shakespeare's romances, like the plays of Beaumont and Fletcher, have their basis in 'a story of pure and sentimental love'. Elsewhere he stresses as a kinship between Shakespeare and Beaumont and Fletcher the special 'prominence given to a sentimental love-story'. But, if we consider all Shakespeare's romances together, the love-stories are less prominent than Thorndike alleges; nor can they be generally described as pure and sentimental.

[2] Nothing in Shakespeare corresponds with the scene in *The Maid's Tragedy* (II. ii.), which is entirely devoted to exploitation of the pity of Aspatia's situation.

[3] *The Maid's Tragedy*, III. ii.

The 'Romances'

One of the most recent expositions of this view, and in many ways the best, is E. M. W. Tillyard's book, *Shakespeare's Last Plays*. In this study Tillyard conducts his argument along two main lines. In the first place, he maintains that the romances are integral with the tragedies because they represent the 'final regenerative phase' that had started with *Antony and Cleopatra* and *Coriolanus*:[1] 'The first part of my argument is, that one of Shakespeare's main concerns in his last plays, whether deliberately taken up or fortuitously drifted into, was to develop the final phase of the tragic pattern, to add, as it were, his *Eumenides* to the already completed *Agamemnon* and *Cheophoroe*, a process repeated by Milton when he supplemented *Paradise Lost* with *Samson Agonistes*.'[2]

Up to this point Tillyard's thesis is not a novel one; the special slant he gives it is to insist, with the backing of Miss M. Bodkin's *Archetypal Patterns in Poetry*, that the supplement of reconciliation and regeneration is a logical and necessary part of tragedy. This leads him to lay particular emphasis on the themes of regeneration and reconciliation and to see all the romances as plays that are modelled to a very definite pattern: 'We find in each the same general scheme of prosperity, destruction and re-creation. The main character is a King. At the beginning he is in prosperity. He then does an evil or misguided deed. Great suffering follows, but during this suffering or at its height the seeds of something new to issue from it are germinating, usually in secret. In the end this new element assimilates and transforms the old evil. The King overcomes his evil instincts, joins himself to the new order by an act of forgiveness or repentance; and the play issues into a fairer prosperity than had at first existed.'[3]

There is, of course, much truth in this argument and analysis. But it is open to two strong objections, a general and a particular one. Its general deficiency is that it is much more a theory of what the tragic vision ought to be than a theory of what that vision actually is. There is some support for it, though perhaps not so much as Tillyard assumes, from Greek drama. There is little support from Elizabethan tragedy.

This general objection leads straight – and more profitably – to the particular weaknesses in his argument, for his attempt to

---

[1] Tillyard quotes (p. 21) with approval from A. C. Bradley: '*Coriolanus* makes the transition to the latest works, in which the powers of repentance and forgiveness charm to rest the tempest raised by error and guilt'.

[2] Op. cit., p. 20.

[3] Op. cit., p. 26.

ground his theory in the romances entails some strained, and at times extravagant, interpretation.

Consider, for instance, his analysis of *Cymbeline*. We may dismiss, as a detail, the fact that the main character is *not* a King. But in order to keep his pattern of the King in a state of prosperity who commits an evil or misguided act, Tillyard has to indulge, rather excessively in the Bradleyan vice of 'anterior'[1] speculation. We are asked to believe that Cymbeline's error in his prosperity was to suspect the innocent and trust the vicious: he banished Belarius and married a bad woman. But in the play that Shakespeare has given us we are little concerned with these previous acts as sins or errors; their moral significance simply does not enter the play; their importance is merely narrative. The Queen is a bad woman who is scheming and intriguing; the banishment of Belarius has occurred only to start off a familiar, and apparently ever-popular, romance story – the recovery of long-lost children. Nor can we seriously feel Cymbeline's suffering for sin (so Tillyard appears to regard the King's feelings about the loss of Imogen) as in any sense a consequence of this alleged, and certainly far remote, 'evil or misguided deed'.

The third part of Tillyard's master-pattern, the re-creation and the assimilation of the old by the new, is also very dim to perceive in *Cymbeline*. We do not feel that the King overcomes his evil instincts (if he ever had any), and he certainly does not impress us as a figure of regeneration. He suffers from some twinges of guilt, admittedly; but chiefly we see him as a small and overwhelmed figure – overwhelmed by his tremendous good fortune and puzzled by the complicated pattern of events through which it has all come about.[2]

But it would be unfair to confine our objection to one particular play, especially as Tillyard himself admits that his master-pattern is imperfectly represented by *Cymbeline*.[3] For this reason it is

---

[1] I hope this term is self-explanatory: it describes the critical game of constructing a world outside the given material of the play – 'How many children had Lady Macbeth?'

[2] There is also in Tillyard's analysis of this play a somewhat blatant example of assuming what he has to prove: 'Bearing in mind the very close connection of the last three plays, and arguing back a little from the last two to *Cymbeline*, we cannot doubt that the above account truly represents part of the play's intention'. (Op. cit., p. 27.)

[3] 'By making an intellectual abstract of the plot we may convince ourselves that Cymbeline is regenerate at the end of the play; but from reading the play we can only say that he fails to stir our imagination and that his regeneration is a thing quite dead.' (Op. cit., p. 28.)

necessary to note two general distortions that are to be found in his treatment of all the romances.

First, his insistence on the supplementary nature of the romances leads him not only to exaggerate their regenerative element but also to assume some very questionable definitions of tragedy. For instance, he regards Act II, Scene i, of *The Tempest* as a re-enactment of the earlier tragedy in so far as Antonio attempts to repeat his previous crime of deposing a ruler. But is this episode where two villains plot to murder the sleeping king really 'tragic' – particularly in the Shakespearean sense of the word? Is even the earlier parallel situation to which it points and which is presented to us retrospectively through Prospero's account to Miranda, essentially tragic? Certainly the Bradleyan formula of Shakespearean tragedy, that of a 'great' character destroying himself through some sin or weakness, requires correction and amplification, since, as notably in *Lear*, the sin or the folly of the hero may be significant primarily for the forces of evil that it unleashes in others. But – and we are treading dangerously near to the never-never land of 'anterior' speculation – was Prospero 'great' in any sense? Was his bookishness and retirement from affairs of state even a tragic weakness, comparable with Hamlet's? Was not the situation dominated, as it should not be in tragedy, by the evil designs of Antonio?

The same assumption of blurred definitions occurs in Tillyard's discussion of the first half of *The Winter's Tale*, which he considers to render worthily 'the destructive portion of the tragic pattern'. But does the first part of *The Winter's Tale* do anything of the kind? Is not poetic realism an essential part of Shakespeare's tragedy, and is not this picture of Leontes' jealousy incredible and highly artificial?[1] Much more appropriate, surely, for Shakespeare's treatment of Leontes would be Professor Ellis Fermor's description of the work of Beaumont and Fletcher – that it 'endows with remoteness all emotions, so that the strongest passions fail to engulf us, however fiercely the characters seem to be shaken by them.'[2]

The second, and even more prominent, distortion to all Tillyard's surveys of the romances is that he reads into them an

---

[1] To be quite fair to Tillyard it should be made clear that he regards the study of Leontes as a convincing one: Leontes' jealousy, he writes, is 'terrifying in its intensity'. (Op. cit., p. 41.)

[2] *The Jacobean Drama*, p. 201.

altogether excessive, and even at times fantastic, depth of symbolism. Is there even a hint in Shakespeare prompting us, as Tillyard would have it, to interpret the panic of Cymbeline's army and his capture as an image of 'the rottenness of what he and his then state of mind stand for',[1] or to interpret Cymbeline's rescue by his sons as a rescue of the new life that has been obscurely germinating? In *The Winter's Tale*, Act IV is regarded not only as an exercise in pastoralism, vivified by realistic touches of the English countryside, but also as a symbol of the new life 'into which the old horrors are to be transmuted'.[2] Perdita, now the hunt for symbols is on, becomes 'the play's main symbol of the powers of creation' and of 'original virtue',[3] while the references to Apollo have a peculiar importance attached to them as 'fertility symbolism'.[4] So in Tillyard's analysis of *The Tempest* he talks of 'fertility symbolism embodied in Miranda',[5] and in his last chapter his symbol-divination takes a freshly inventive turn when he boldly described *The Winter's Tale* in pure religious and Dantesque terms: 'The motives of hell and purgatory in Leontes are obvious enough, while the statue scene is conducted in a rarefied atmosphere of contemplation that suggests the motive of paradise.'[6]

The difficulty with this sort of interpretation is that it is difficult to *prove* that it is mistaken; and if the centuries of Shakespearean criticism have taught us one thing it is that we can read almost anything into his plays, as we can into the Bible. We are all Protestants when it comes to reading Shakespeare, and we insist on reading him with the sturdy independence of the inner light, perhaps because, like religion, he is so important. Possibly there is a certain amount of symbolism in Shakespeare, in the tragedies as well as the romances; but this must, surely, be slight and incidental, since Shakespeare was first and foremost a dramatist (and a dramatist of the theatre, not of the study). He was not primarily a lyric or reflective poet, and he was certainly not a prophet like Blake. Moreover, the impression left by his work as a whole is that his fundamental impulse was always towards the concrete – in human experience as in language. Perhaps this is the truest and ultimately the profoundest thing we

[1] Tillyard, op. cit., p. 27.
[2] Op. cit., p. 43.
[3] Op. cit, p. 44.
[4] Op. cit., p. 46.
[5] Op. cit., p. 57.
[6] Op. cit., p. 84.

The 'Romances'

can say about his genius. If it is, we should be most sparing and tentative in our reading of symbolism into any of his plays.

To sum up the objections to Tillyard's first main argument: his contention that the romances have an organic and even necessary connection with the tragedies compels him to trace in them a common pattern of prosperity, suffering and destruction, and a final, more excellent state of renewal and prosperity. But while this pattern represents to some extent a true picture of these last plays, it is a much more general and perhaps superficial approximation than Tillyard allows. Moreover, it leads him to make far too much of the themes of reconciliation, repentance (and perhaps regeneration), and it produces considerable distortion, particularly in his excessive reading of symbolism into these plays. What is true of his analysis when stripped of the shaky generalisations of tragedy based on Miss Bodkin's book, and of its shakier symbol-reading, is that the romances are distinguished from the comedies because they contain more suffering and destruction and from the tragedies because they embody a final phase of prosperity and reconciliation.

§

Even if Tillyard's first main argument were completely valid, by itself it would leave something of a gap. Why, we should naturally ask, did Shakespeare revert so completely to romance to express this tragic supplement of reconciliation and regeneration? But Tillyard has endeavoured to bridge the gap. He maintains that Shakespeare's attachment to the theme of regeneration, coupled with a new turn for contemplation, stimulated him to a more acute awareness of the 'different planes of reality' and that romance was at that time the most suitable medium for the communication of such an awareness. Shakespeare's aim, he writes, was 'to express something that can be vaguely called metaphysical, some sense of the complexity of existence, of the different plans on which human life can be lived'.[1] 'The general effect of the rapidly changing incidents, the extraordinary accidents, the mixture of improbability with moral wisdom, would express a sense of wonder, of the strange mix-up of things, that would easily provide a co-relative to a newly-

[1] Op. cit., p. 60.

sharpened sense of the many planes on which life could be lived.'[1]

Theoretically at least, we can admit that romance may be an admirable medium for representing the real and the ideal, observation and imagination. But the preliminary link in this second main argument of Tillyard's is by no means firm. No doubt much may be said for contemplation[2] producing a sense of the complexity of existence and driving a writer in search of a form that will reflect the different planes of experience. But does a preoccupation with regeneration and reconciliation (and, after all, Tillyard throws the main weight of his argument on this preoccupation) necessarily entail a sense of the different planes of reality? It is not easy to follow the logic of this inference.

But once more the deficiency of Tillyard's theory is most apparent when we attempt to square it with the reality of Shakespeare's plays.

In the first place, there is Tillyard's attitude to the characters, whose combination of realism and symbolism he maintains to be one of the means whereby Shakespeare expresses his new sense of the different planes of reality. We have already objected to this excessive symbol-reading that represents Miranda as a fertility-image. But another objection may be added here, namely that symbolism in the strict sense of the word is not a common characteristic of the figures of the average romantic story, prominent though it may be in the *Faerie Queene*. There is an abundance of unreality, of course, but this feature, which is not synonymous with symbolism, usually arises either because the characters are personifications of abstract qualities or, most frequently, because they are

---

[1] Op. cit., p. 72. S. L. Bethell in his recent study, *The Winter's Tale*, follows a very similar line to Tillyard, except that his analysis of this play is in explicit Christian terms. But even if Bethell's thesis of Shakespeare's 'profoundly Christian interpretation' of life is valid (and I, for one, would not admit this), he appears to me to offer no convincing reasons why this outlook led Shakespeare, and led him at this particular period, back to romance for his artistic form. In fact, in one unguarded moment, Mr. Bethell talks about the '*unromantic* otherworldliness of orthodox medieval religion' (p. 112), which, according to him, is one of the two principal components of the play. Also his remark that 'romance and the pleasures of the world were holiday indulgences, delightful and refreshing at the time but with a bitter after-taste' (p. 111) implies that Shakespeare must have radically re-shaped romance to his purposes. Yet Mr. Bethell nowhere attempts to maintain this implication. Part of this confusion, I suspect, arises from a somewhat vague use of the word 'romance' and its derivatives.

[2] There is an incidental objection to Tillyard's argument here: certainly there is more contemplation in the romances than in the comedies; but there is much contemplation in the tragedies.

puppets who enact some far-fetched, impossible story. The obvious and common-sense explanation of the mixture of realism and unreality in the characters of the romances is that Shakespeare – not because he was a genius, but because he was a dramatist – was always alert to infuse a breath of life into his puppets, if he possibly could.

Secondly, Tillyard's search for his 'different planes of reality' leads him into some strange positions. For instance, he will have nothing to do with Granville Barker's contention that *Cymbeline* is an exercise in virtuosity; he insists that Shakespeare's attempt to dramatise three different stories springs primarily from his desire (of which he may have been dimly conscious at this stage) to express different planes of reality. But, apart from the important objection[1] that these three stories fail to suggest varying planes of reality, is the plot construction of *Cymbeline* really different in kind from that of *The Merchant of Venice*, with its grim thriller of a Jew's villainy (paralleled by the Iachimo-Posthumus story), its pretty fairy-tale of the caskets (paralleled by the tale of Imogen and Cymbeline's reunion with his long-lost sons), its story of the elopement and the theatrical farce of the ring episode? Would Tillyard read any metaphysical theories of 'planes of reality' into this complicated narrative or into half a dozen other plays outside the romances into which Shakespeare has ingeniously woven several diverse stories?

The brief analysis of the planes of reality in *The Winter's Tale* and *The Tempest* is no more convincing. In *The Winter's Tale*, Tillyard contrasts the paranoic world of Leontes with the everyday world of the courtiers and Hermione. But are not contrasts of this sort to be often observed outside the romances – in *Macbeth*, for instance, where the hero's diseased, extravagant world of paranoia is contrasted with the everyday domesticities of Lady Macduff and with the vision, expressed through several characters, of a state of health in the political and social order? Thrown over *The Tempest*, Tillyard's net captures some even sorrier specimens – 'delicate transitions', 'large bold contrasts' and 'small subtle contrasts'.[2] We can agree with him, in opposition to the Lytton Strachey view, that there is an artistry about *The Tempest*

---

[1] Tillyard himself admits this: 'Shakespeare's attempt in *Cymbeline* to convey his feeling of different planes of reality ends in the queer phantasmagoric effect of a welter of unreality rather than in a vision of those different planes standing out in sharp and thrilling contrast'. (Op. cit., p. 76.)

[2] Op. cit., p. 78.

that reveals Shakespeare at the height of his powers; but these contrasts and transitions – is there one of Shakespeare's major plays where they are not to be found in abundance? Here is theory dying through chronic under-nourishment.[1]

But if Tillyard's more elaborate arguments fail to convince us as an explanation of Shakespeare's return to romance, he does offer us, in passing, one simple answer that probably gives us as much of the truth as any. Quoting Sir Edmund Chambers,[2] he draws attention to the vast stock of romantic literature behind writers of Shakespeare's time and to the continuous pressure and influence that this literature exerted upon them.

On the basis of this observation we may perhaps frame an answer to our question thus: Right from the days of Lyly and Greene, and earlier, dramatisations of romance had been highly popular with the audiences of the time. The young Shakespeare, helped by the example of Lyly and Greene, was quite happy to cater for this taste and made romance the main ingredient of his own comedies, assimilating a good deal both of its substance and spirit, its type of story and its attitude to love.[3] By the time of the 'dark' comedies he had certainly become highly sceptical of the romantic attitude to love, and perhaps, for a while at least, rejected it. He may also have grown a little bored with the romantic sort of plot. But the chief reason he broke away from romantic comedy was that it was inadequate, as the 'dark' comedies must have told him, to express the thought, emotion, and vision which then possessed him. Romance may not be all holiday, all entertainment, all artifice; but even when treated gravely, as it was by Sidney and Spenser, it puts life and reality at a remove. When the fiery compulsion of his tragic mood was spent, Shakespeare returned to the romantic type of drama, partly because the romantic tradition was always exercising a powerful influence on writers, partly because the romantic play was, along with the chronicle, his first love, and probably – for it does Shakespeare's reputation no harm to stress such material

---

[1] My subject has forced me to concentrate on my disagreements with Tillyard. But – not to leave a wrong impression of my opinion of his book – I would hasten to add that there is much in it that I admire.

[2] *Shakespeare: A Survey*, p. 288.

[3] I find it surprising that Tillyard should write (op. cit., p. 12): 'when Shakespeare *began* using romantic material at the end of his career instead of Holinshed and Plutarch, &c.' This cannot be an oversight, for later, when discussing Shakespeare's treatment of Imogen, he describes Shakespeare as being 'new to the technique of romance'. (p. 34.)

considerations – because Beaumont and Fletcher were showing that new variations, which were both fascinating and popular, could be constructed out of the old romantic material. But there were departures and innovations in the plays of Beaumont and Fletcher, while the Shakespeare of 1608, whether he owed anything to his young heirs-apparent or not, had stared too long into the dark pit of things to be the Shakespeare of 1598. Hence his romances are not identical with the romantic comedies, though the two groups of plays have many features in common.

ADDITIONAL NOTES TO CHAPTER TWO

(*a*) This chapter leaves unsolved at least one large problem, the full consideration of which would be more appropriate in a monograph on Lyly than in this present study. Assuming our general conclusions to be valid, through what channels did the romance tradition reach Lyly?

One likely link, one would suspect, would be Italian drama. Bond, in his chapter 'A Note on Italian Influence in Lyly's Plays' (Vol. II, pp. 473-485), suggests that Lyly may have been present when the Italian troupe performed before Elizabeth at Windsor in 1577-78, and admits that Lyly may have been acquainted with one or two plays like Ariosto's *Suppositi* (possibly in the original and probably in Gascoigne's version) and Tasso's *Aminta*. Also, while he can trace no detailed connection between Lyly's work and Italian pastoral drama, Bond is of the opinion that Lyly must have been familiar with Italian plays of this type. But, apart from these suppositions, his conclusion in the main is that there is little discernible evidence of an Italian influence in Lyly's comedies.

I cannot pretend to any independent investigation of this question. But while Bond's conclusions may be correct, the truth may still be that Lyly was influenced by Italian drama, which, as we saw at the end of the last chapter, was certainly known in England. What many scholars are inclined to overlook is that an artist can be powerfully influenced without revealing in his work any explicit instances of borrowing. This fact may complicate the task of neatly cataloguing a writer's 'influences', but it must never be ignored.

(Bond also mentions several other Italians, besides the dramatists, whose work Lyly may have read – Boccaccio, Petrarch, Tasso and Sannazarro, and lesser figures like Domenichi, Capella and Castiglione.)

What might seem another probable link is French and English Petrarchian poetry. But, setting aside the difficulty of ascribing with confidence to Lyly the poems Bond has assembled in his edition, I cannot find much evidence of the Petrarchian manner in these poems, which, on the contrary, have a strong misogynist flavour. On the other hand, there is good reason for believing

Additional Notes to Chapter Two

that Lyly had read some of Chaucer and of the *Faerie Queene*, so that he probably derived some of the romantic traditions through native sources.

(*b*) If we follow the contentions of C. S. Lewis, it might be argued that Lyly's treatment of love in a cynical, misogynist spirit keeps him in the romance tradition rather than sets him against it: 'The truth is that "cynicism" and "idealism" about women are twin fruits on the same branch – are the positive and negative poles of a single thing – and that they may be found anywhere in the literature of romantic love, and mixed in any proportions.'[1] Mr. Lewis finds this negative element in Jean de Meun, Chaucer (Pandarus in *Troilus and Criseyde*), Malory, Hawes, and even in the sonnet-sequences. 'The history of courtly love from the beginning to end may be described as an "amorous-odious sonnet", a "scholar's love or hatred".'[2]

One hesitates to dispute the opinions of a critic so deeply and sensitively acquainted with medieval literature; and there is certainly no ignoring this negative element in the romantic tradition. But I should prefer to interpret it in another way – as a tendency bound always, by a natural reaction, to be present, and stimulated by outside influences like Ovid; as an incidental, if conspicuous, reaction to the tradition, and not an essential part of it. To represent the romantic attitude itself as essentially ambivalent seems to me an error. Surely, romantic love was a revolution in sensibility precisely because, as Mr. Lewis himself admits elsewhere, its essence was a courtly, adoring, idealising attitude towards women? 'Romance . . . reverence for women . . . the idealising imagination exercised about sex.'[3]

Further, the negative element in Lyly is not incidental; it is hardly less prominent than the positive romantic element. I find it impossible to subsume these two attitudes in Lyly in a single concept of 'romantic love'; and to me there is all the difference in the world between Lyly's comedies and Spenser's *Amoretti*, which, though it contains a negative element, is of one romantic piece throughout.

(*c*) One important minor subject of romance that Mr. Lewis examines in *The Allegory of Love* is the conflict and debate between

[1] *The Allegory of Love*, p. 145.
[2] Ibid., p. 145.
[3] Ibid., p. 10.

Diana and Venus. These two goddesses and their forces roughly personify the antithesis between chastity and sexual passion, though in his analysis of such works as the *Romance of the Rose*, the *Flower and the Leaf*, Lydgate's *Reason and Sensuality* and the *Faerie Queene* (Bk. IV, Canto VI, verses 11-25), Lewis is at pains to show that this antithesis is not absolute. Thus Diana often recognises love, and Venus is frequently softened and presented in an admirable way: Venus 'is passion, lawless and natural, who sometimes works hand in hand with courtly love, but has no need of his assistance, and often works without him'.[1]

Now it is possible that we may trace the figures of Venus, Cupid and Diana, prominent in Lyly's comedies, and the debate and dissension between them, back to this part of the romance tradition, where an immediate link may well have been Googe's *Cupido Conquered* (1563), a late example of the love allegory and of what Lewis calls, the 'psychomachy' between Diana, Venus and Cupid. In *Sapho and Phao* there is conflict between Venus, with her strong sexual desire for Phao, and Cupid who favoured Sapho, a courtly heroine of romantic sentiments. (Here it should be noted that in the main romantic tradition Cupid, though the son of Venus, was associated with courtly love and refined sentiment.) In *Gallathea* Venus, this time assisting her son, is in strife with Diana, who is definitely the champion and 'goddess of chastity'. Venus is represented in her worst light in *The Woman in the Moon*, where Cupid plays an insignificant role. In this play it is the influence of Venus that transforms Pandora into a wanton:

> I'll have her witty, quick, and amorous,
> Delight in revels and in banqueting,
> Wanton discourses, music and merry songs;

(III. ii. 2-4)

and

> Away with chastity and modest thoughts....
> All those are strumpets that are over-chaste,
> Defying such as keep their company.
> 'Tis not the touching of a woman's hand,
> Kissing her lips, hanging about her neck,
> A speaking look, no, nor a yielding word
> That men expect; believe me, Sol, 'tis more,
> And were Mars here he would protest as much.

(III. ii. 16-25)

[1] *The Allegory of Love*, p. 133.

Cupid recovers stature and power in *Love's Metamorphosis*, where he is more adult, more the God of Love of the romantic tradition.

Apart from *Gallathea*, Diana, the antithesis to Venus, is less prominent in Lyly's comedy. But what she symbolises – chastity and virginity that may give a tardy consent to faithful and elevated love – is represented elsewhere in the goddesses Cynthia and Ceres, and in the princess Sophronia.

BIBLIOGRAPHY FOR MAIN REFERENCES

TEXTS

Chaucer, *Works*, Globe Edition.
Spenser, *Poems*, Globe Edition.
Sidney, *Works*, ed. A. Feuillerat.
Lyly, *Works*, ed. R. W. Bond.
Greene, *Plays and Poems*, ed. J. Churton Collins.
   Plays, ed. T. H. Dickinson, Mermaid Series.
Shakespeare, *Works*, Globe Edition.
   Apocrypha, ed. C. F. T. Brooke.
Beaumont and Fletcher, *Plays*, ed. J. St. Loe Strachey, Mermaid Series.

CRITICISM

S. L. Bethell, *The Winter's Tale*.
F. S. Boas, *Shakspere and his Predecessors*.
H. B. Charlton, *Shakespearian Comedy*.
S. T. Coleridge, *Lectures and Notes on Shakespeare*, ed. T. Ashe.
A. Quiller-Couch, *Shakespeare's Workmanship*.
B. Croce, *Ariosto, Shakespeare, and Corneille*.
M. C. D'Arcy, *The Mind and Heart of Love*.
De Rougemont, *Passion and Society*.
E. De Selincourt, Oxford *Spenser (Introduction)*.
U. Ellis Fermor, *Jacobean Drama*.
H. J. C. Grierson, *Cross Currents in English Literature of the XVIIth Century*.
   Metaphysical Poetry (Introduction).
C. H. Herford, *Shakespeare's Treatment of Love and Marriage*.
W. P. Ker, *Mediaeval Literature*.
   Epic and Romance.
C. S. Lewis, *The Allegory of Love*.
J. Palmer, *Shakespeare's Comic Characters*.
J. Spens, *Spenser's Faerie Queen*.
E. E. Stoll, *From Shakespeare to Joyce*.
Lytton Strachey, *Books and Characters*, 'Shakespeare's Final Period'.
A. Thorndike, *The Influence of Beaumont and Fletcher on Shakespeare*.
E. M. W. Tillyard, *The Poetry of Sir Thomas Wyatt (Introduction)*.
   Shakespeare's Last Plays.
Elizabethan Critical Essays, ed. Gregory Smith.
Cambridge History of Literature, Vols. I, IV and V.

INDEX

Amadis de Gaule, 12, 35, 162n
Amoretti, 14n, 15, 16, 16n, 17, 17n, 18, 19, 21, 22, 201
'Animated' Characters, 88, 88n
Apollonius of Tyre, 71n
Apologie for Poetrie, 21; comedy of 'delight', **33-4**; 36, 175
Arcadia, 12, **23-32**, 34, 61, 63, 76, 79, 80, 82, 86, 86n, 96, 162n
Ariosto, 12, 38; Orlando Furioso, 54, 76, 123; Suppositi, 71, 73, 200
Aristophanes, 77
Aristotle, 86, 176
Astrophel and Stella, 17, 21n, 25n, 31n
Attwater, A. L., 140n
Austen, Jane, 88

Bandello, 12, 76, 123
Beaumont, Francis, 32
Beaumont and Fletcher, 166, 176, 179, 180, 181, 185, **189-90**, 199
Belleforest, 76
Bembo, 14
Bethell, S. L., 196n
Blake, William, 194
Boccaccio, 12, 136, 137, 138, 152n, 162, 200
Bodkin, M., Archetypal Patterns in Poetry, 191, 195
Boiardo, 12
Boisteau, 76
Bond, R. W., 35, 37, 37n, 41n, 47n, 200-1
Bradbrooke, M. C., The School of Night, 92n
Bradley, A. C., 87, 191n, 192, 193
Brooke, Arthur, Romeus and Juliet, 76, 76n
Brooke, Rupert, 153

Capella, 200
Capellanus, Andreas, De Arte Honeste Amandi, 13, 14, 18n, 114
Castiglione, The Courtier, 14, 200

Cavalcanti, 14
Caxton, Recuyell of the Historyes of Troye, 140n, 154, 155
Chambers, E. K., 123n, 136n, 198
Chapman, George, 155
Charles I, 140
Charlton, H. B., 13n, 30n, 35, 68n, 69n, 70, 73, 89, 101, 103-4, 114n, 136n, 140n, 175n
Chaucer, 18, 18n, 39n, 201; Troilus and Criseyde, 14, 30, 30n, **140-53** passim, 162, 201; Knight's Tale, 162, **170-4**
Chretien of Troyes, 98
Cinthio, 12, 54, 76
Coleridge, 137n, 165, 185
Colin Clout's Come Home Again, 12n, 16n, 17n
Collins, Churton, 54n, 64, 65
Commedia dell' Arte, 35
Croce, B., 35, 84

Daniel, 12n
Dante, 14, 15, 16, 20, 194
D'Arcy, M. C., 13n, 15n
De Rougemont, 13, 15, 16n
'Derring-do', 18, 40, 77
Desportes, 12
Dickinson, T. H., 66
Digges, Leonard, 123
Domenichi, 200
Donat, Robert, Production of Much Ado, 132-5 passim
Donne, 11, 17, 87, 126
Don Quixote, 19n
Dowden, E., 115n, 118-20, 161
Dryden, All for Love, 117n
Du Bellay, 12

Earl Mar's Daughter, 11
Edwards, Richard, Damon and Pithias, 24n, 53n; Palamon and Arcite, 24n, 162n
Eliot, T. S., 185-6

205

Index

Ellis-Fermor, U., 177, 193
Epithalamion (Spenser), 17, 21

Faerie Queene, The, 13n, 14, 15, 18, 76, 196, 201, 202
Fair Em, 55n
Fairy Lore and Shakespeare, 109n
Famous History of Friar Bacon, The, 55n, 62
Famous History of George a Green, The, 55n
Ficino, 14
Fletcher, John, 170, 171, 172n, 173
Flower and the Leaf, The, 202

Gammer Gurton's Needle, 37
Gascoigne, *Supposes*, 35, 53n
Gervinus, 118-119
Giovanni, Ser, 76
Gnosticism, 13n, 15, 15n, 16n, 17n
Googe, *Cupido Conquered*, 202
Gosson, 35, 35n
Gower, *Confessio Amantis*, 71n, 162
Granville-Barker, 197
Gray, Thomas, *Elegy*, 90n
Greene, Robert: sources of plays, **54-5**; dramatisation of love adventures, **56-7**; absence of romantic love sentiment, **57-9**; romantic narrative, **60-2**; motivation and characterisation, **62-3**; women characters, **64-5**; 'low-life' characters, **65**; setting, **65-6**; spirit and atmosphere, **66**; summary, **66**
  Poems, 59n, 60, 64; *Visions*, 60n
  Also mentioned: 77, 86, 89, 135, 162, 198
Grierson, H. B., 13n, 17n, 22-3, 155
Guevara, 49
Guinicelli, 14
Guy of Warwick, 11, 12

Harington, John, trans. of *Orlando Furioso*, 54n
Harrison, G. B., 62
Hawes, 201
Hecatommithi, 54

Henryson, *The Testament of Cresseid*, 140n, 143n, 155
Henslowe, Philip, 162n
Herford, C. H., 78-9, 86n
Huon of Burdeaux, 76
Hurd, 26n
Hymn in Honour of Beauty, An, 17, 17n, 48
Hymn in Honour of Love, An, 14n, 16, 16n, 18n, 19n, 20

Ingannati, Gl', 76, 76n
Inganni, Gl', 76n
Isaacs, J., 68
Italian Renaissance Drama, 11n, 32, 35, 200

Jameson, Mrs., 88
Johnson, Samuel, 137, 163
Jolly Pinder of Wakefield, The, 55n
Jonson, Ben, 11, 67, 77, 84, 87, 89, 124, 139, 168

Ker, W. P., 30n
Kingis Quair, The, 17
Knight of the Burning Pestle, The, 32
Knight's Tale, The, 162, **170-4** *passim*
Kyd, Thomas, 54

Latin Comedy, 11, 38, 68, 69, 71-2, 73
Lee, Sidney, 12n
Le Fèvre, *Recueil des Histoires de Troie*, 154
Lewis, C. S., *The Allegory of Love*, 12, 13n, 14n, 15, 15n, 17n, 18, 18n, 141, 151, 153, 201, 202
Lodge, Thomas, 12n, 54, 76
Lydgate, *History, Siege and Destruction of Troy*, 155; *Reason and Sensuality*, 202
Lyly, John: *Euphues*, 24n, 42n, 44n, 47, 47n, 48, 48n, 49, 50n
  Plays: classical elements, sources, and treatment, **36-37**; unities, **37**; classical allusions, **38**; courtly setting, **38**; romantic characters, **38-40**; romantic elements in the plots, **40**; pastoralism, **41**; spirit, **41**; love

theme, **41-2**; reflection of romantic love, **42-6**; unromantic attitude to love, **46-51**; summary, **53**; influence of Italian drama and romantic tradition generally, **200-1**; ambivalence of Lyly's attitude to love, **201**; Diana-Venus debate, **201-3**
  Also mentioned, 66, 91, 94, 104, 135, 198

Malory, 201
Manichaeanism, 13*n*
Marlowe, 11, 54, 55, 56, 61, 62
Meun, Jean de, 201
Middleton, Thomas, 168
Milton, John, 98-9, 191
Miracle and Morality Plays, Influence of, 11
Molière, 87
Montemayor, 12, 76
Morte d'Arthur, 12
Munro, J., 76*n*, 86*n*

Neo-platonism, 14, 14*n*, 17, 21, 48*n*, 98
North, Thomas, *The Dial of Princes*, 49

Ovid, 36, 60, 201

Painter, *The Palace of Pleasure*, 35, 136
Palmer, John, 107*n*, 133*n*, 165*n*
Palmerin, 12
Pandosto, 162
Pastoralism, 31, 31*n*, 32, 33, 38, 41, 90, 128, 130-1, 169, 194
Petrarch and Petrarchianism, 12, 14, 15, 15*n*, 16, 17, 21, 32, 46, 74, 98, 107, 117, 122, 126, 200
Plautus, 11, 70; *Menaechmi*, 68, 71; *Amphitruo*, 68
Prothalamion (Spenser), 17

Quiller-Couch, A., 82*n*, 167*n*, 169, 175, 176, 177, 182-3

Raleigh, Sir Walter, 171*n*
Ralph Roister-Doister, 37
Restoration Comedy, 75, 129, 151
Riche, Barnabe, *Apolonius and Silla*, 76
Ridley, M. R., 175*n*

Romance: various forms of, **12**; as a type of narrative exemplified by *Arcadia*, **23-32**; story of love, **23-6**; adventure and the marvellous, **26-8**; coincidences, **28**; disguise and mistaken identity, **28**; 'poetic' justice, **28-9**; motivation and characterisation, **29-31**; setting, **31-2**
Romance of the Rose, 202
Romance, 'theatrical', 177, 178, 189
Romantic Attitude to Love, **12-23**; love as a moral force, **13-14**; feudal aspect, **13n**; relation to religion, **15-16**; spiritualisation, **16-17**; marriage, **17-18**; humility, **18**; courtesy, **18**; secrecy, **18n**; cult of dejection, **19-20**; poetic inspiration, **20-1**; image of the Lady, **21-2**; reflected in *Arcadia*, **25-6**
Ronsard, 12

Saintsbury, George, 140
Salernitano, 76*n*
Sannazarro, 200
Seneca, 11
Shakespeare: sources of the 'romantic' comedies, and treatment, **76**; type of romantic love story in the comedies, **77-85**; motivation and characterisation, **85-9**; social and scenic setting, **89-91**; reflection of romantic love, **91-100**; detachment from romance and criticism of it, **101-35**; shift of centre of gravity in the comedies, **122-4**; Henry V's rejection of romantic love-making, **124-5**; attitude to pastoralism, **130-1**; production problem of *Much Ado*, **132-5**; comparison of *Troilus and Cressida* with *Troilus and Criseyde*, **140-56**; strain of working with romance in *Measure for Measure*, **156-60**; some characteristics of the 'Romances', **161-70**; Romances and romantic comedies contrasted, **175-88**; explanations of the return to romance, **188-99**
  Principal references to plays: *Comedy of Errors*, **67-71**; *Taming of*

the Shrew, 71-5; *Merry Wives of Windsor*, 75; *Two Gentlemen of Verona*, 101-5; *Love's Labour's Lost*, 105-9; *Midsummer Night's Dream*, 109-14; *Romeo and Juliet*, 114-22; *Much Ado, As You Like It, Twelfth Night*, 122-32; *Much Ado*, 132-5; *All's Well*, 136-40; *Troilus and Cressida*, 140-56; *Measure for Measure*, 156-60; *Pericles, Cymbeline, Winter's Tale, Tempest*, 161-99 *passim*; *Two Noble Kinsmen*, 170-4
Sonnets, 99, 107-8
Also mentioned: 23, 30, 37, 38, 39, 48, 50, 53, 56, 58, 65, 66

Shaw, G. B., 77, 84
Shepheard's Calendar, The, 19, 19n, 22n
Sheridan, R. B., 84
Sidney, Philip: (see *Apologie for Poetrie, Arcadia, Astrophel and Stella*)
Also: 12, 32, 33, 37, 87, 198
Sir Bevis, 11, 12
Spens, J., 24n
Spenser, Edmund: (see *Amoretti, Colin Clout's Come Home Again, Epithalamion, Faerie Queene, Hymn in Honour of Beauty, Hymn in Honour of Love, Prothalamion, Shepheard's Calendar*)
Treatment of romantic love, **12-23**

Also: 24n, 32, 33, 48, 87, 92, 99, 123, 155, 184, 189, 198, 201
Stoll, E. E., 78n, 86-87, 87n, 88, 88n, 157n, 160n, 165
Strachey, Lytton, 188-9, 198
Swift, Jonathan, 169
Swinburne, 140n

Tale of Gamelyn, The, 12, 76
Taming of A Shrew, The, 74
Tancred and Gismunda, 35
Tasso, 12, 201
Tawney, R. H., 33, 33n
Terence, 11, 54, 70
Thorndike, A., 162n, 166n, 167n, 185n, 189-90, 190n
Tillyard, E. M. W., 15n, 19n, 23, 23n, 35, 86n, 161, 167n, 179n, 187, 189, 189n, **191-8**
Tottel, *Miscellany*, 15
Tristan and Isolt, 76n
Twine, Laurence, 162

Wechssler, 13n
Whetstone, *Promos and Cassandra*, 35, 156n
Whibly, C., 33n
Wilde, O., 84
Wilson, J. Dover, 80, 125
Wyatt, Sir Thomas, 12, 15n

EASTERN COLLEGE
LIBRARY
ST. DAVIDS, PA. 19087